Quality Assurance
in
Higher Education

Quality Assurance in Higher Education

Proceedings of an International Conference Hong Kong, 1991

Edited by

Alma Craft

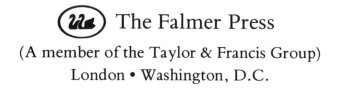 The Falmer Press

(A member of the Taylor & Francis Group)
London • Washington, D.C.

UK The Falmer Press, 4 John Street, London WC1N 2ET
USA The Falmer Press, Taylor & Francis Inc., 1900 Frost Road, Suite 101, Bristol, PA 19007

First published 1992

A catalogue record for this book is available from the British Library

Library of Congress Cataloging-in-Publication Data are available on request

ISBN 0 75070 070 X Cased

Jacket design by Caroline Archer

Typeset in 10/12pt Bembo by
Graphicraft Typesetters Ltd, Hong Kong

Printed in Great Britain by Burgess Science Press, Basingstoke on paper which has a specified pH value on final paper manufacture of not less than 7.5 and is therefore 'acid free'.

Contents

Contents

Foreword

In July 1991 the Hong Kong Council for Academic Accreditation (HKCAA) hosted an invitation conference on Quality Assurance in Higher Education. Over 100 senior representatives from accreditation bodies and from higher education attended and spent three days in discussion of quality assurance issues. Delegates came from Australia, Belgium, Canada, China, France, Germany, Hong Kong, India, Indonesia, Ireland, Kenya, Korea, the Netherlands, New Zealand, Nigeria, Puerto Rico, Philippines, Singapore, South Africa, Sweden, Taiwan, the United Kingdom, and the United States of America. Edited versions of the formal presentations appear in this publication; together they offer a review of international developments in quality assurance in higher education.

The conference was opened by His Excellency Sir David Wilson, GCMG, the Governor of Hong Kong, who spoke of the major expansion of tertiary education provision in Hong Kong, which involves doubling the number of first year first degree places between 1990 and 1994. He stressed the importance of maintaining and wherever possible raising academic standards, and the role of the HKCAA in meeting this challenge.

Conference participants were welcomed by Dr David Bethel, Chairman of the HKCAA, and Dr Raymond Ho, Chairman of the Conference Organising Committee, and also by the Honorable John Chan, the Hong Kong Secretary for Education and Manpower. All stressed the value of international links. In the context of world-wide changes in higher education and increasing student mobility, they emphasized the need to extend knowledge and understanding of different quality assurance systems.

With this in mind, an International Network for Quality Assurance Agencies in Higher Education (INQAAHE) was launched during the conference. The publication of these conference proceedings is intended to disseminate current ideas and information on quality assurance in higher education, and to facilitate further exchange of views.

Foreword

The HKCAA gratefully acknowledges the support of the B Y Lam Foundation and the Hong Kong Government in making funds available for the conference and the initial administration of the Network.

Editor's Introduction

For a long time, degree level education was the preserve and privilege of a handful of university institutions, with an élite faculty staff teaching a relatively narrow range of subjects to a small group of very able students. While higher education systems remained small, institutions were allowed considerable freedom to run their own affairs. Academic staff were expected to aim for and achieve excellence, and comparability of quality between institutions and over time was assumed.

Since World War II, the higher education systems in many countries have changed radically. More universities have been founded and new kinds of tertiary institutions established (polytechnics, liberal arts colleges, colleges of higher education). Institutions have become larger through expansion or merger, and the percentage and absolute number of students has increased very substantially. The composition of the student body has altered significantly as gender, class, race and age participation has broadened. Degree programmes have widened to include new subject areas such as business studies, nursing, education, computing. To meet the needs of this expanding tertiary sector of education, the 'community of scholars' has grown rapidly in size and scope, and overall costs have escalated.

Such changes are extending educational opportunity and providing the knowledge and skills required by society. But the extent of changes in scale, coverage, personnel and cost has inevitably led to concern and debate about ways of ensuring the quality as well as the quantity of graduates. The public (often represented by government) is no longer willing to place total confidence in the 'ivory tower' image of tertiary institutions, but expects independent evidence that higher education is providing good quality and value for money.

There has been a variety of responses to the growing demands for public accountability, including the establishment of agencies specifically concerned with quality assurance in higher education, some of which have the power to accredit (i.e. guarantee the quality of) institutions or programmes. The international conference on which this book is based provided an opportunity for senior representatives from such agencies to share their ideas and experience. The following chapters are edited versions of the papers presented at the conference, and they explore some of the issues.

The book opens with an overview by Dr Malcolm Frazer, Chief Executive of the Council for National Academic Awards, an accreditation and degree awarding agency which has pioneered quality assurance strategies in the UK's non-university sector. Its policies and practices involving detailed course-by-course validation by peers as well as regular institutional reviews, have been effective and influential. Drawing on his international experience Dr Frazer reviews the Why? What? and How? of quality assurance in higher education, but his paper also raises a central difficulty: what does quality in higher education actually mean? He concludes that a precise definition is illusory, and proposes instead that a *profile* of qualities can offer a much more informative and useful description of institutions and courses. This question of definition is taken up by other contributors. Dr Vroeijenstijn (Chapter 8), for example, agrees that quality cannot be defined precisely, concluding that 'quality is like love ... everybody recognizes it. But when we try to give a definition of it, we are standing with empty hands.'

Part 2 presents examples of international developments in quality assurance. Where formal agencies have been established, they may have very considerable powers and even control over the approval and funding of degree programmes. Allan Sensicle (Chapter 5) writes about the work of the Hong Kong Council for Academic Accreditation, established in 1990 to undertake institutional reviews and detailed course appraisals in the non-university institutions of Hong Kong. Its recommendations to government are a key factor in course approval. Ashoka Chandra (Chapter 6) describes the proposal to introduce mandatory accreditation for Indian higher technical education, alongside the strengthening of voluntary accreditation for the university sector. In France the Comité National d'Evaluation, directed by André Staropoli (Chapter 3), is responsible to the President for the evaluation of higher education. Although it has no formal sanctions, it has significant moral authority, since government (and industrial) funding are likely to take account of the Comité's assessments. Nigeria and Kenya have introduced strict accreditation controls, South Africa is proposing to do so, and China operates a centralized system for course approvals (see Appendix).

These governmental or semi-governmental bodies generally make their judgments and recommendations on the advice of expert academic peers. Other quality assurance bodies use similar peer review processes, but are 'owned' by the institutions themselves and independent of government. In the United States, for example, mass higher education developed earlier than in most other countries, and the post-secondary institutions collaborated to develop a voluntary system of accreditation where groups of peers attest to the competence of an institution to meet its stated mission. Marjorie Peace Lenn (Chapter 11) describes this process of institutional accreditation, and

Leslie Benmark (Chapter 12) explains the complementary role of professional (engineering) accreditation in the US.

The Netherlands is currently moving away from state regulation towards self-regulation by the institutions. Ton Vroeijenstijn (in Chapter 8) outlines how the Association of Dutch Universities organizes visiting committees of peers to provide external quality assessment of a range of academic disciplines across the universities. Jan Kalkwijk reports on the Ministry of Education's 'meta-evaluation' of the Association's work (Chapter 7), and the differing perspectives and expectations of these two levels of evaluation are revealed.

Universities in Australia and the UK have also collaborated to set up their own systems of external quality assurance. Both countries are experiencing major changes in their higher education systems. In Australia universities and other tertiary institutions have merged to form a 'unified national system' with large self-accrediting universities, and Professor Kwong Lee Dow describes how the Academic Standards Panels of the Australian Vice-Chancellors' Committee monitor standards in degree courses in each discipline across the country. In the UK, where the 'binary' system of universities and polytechnics is being dismantled, an Academic Audit Unit has been established by the Committee of Vice-Chancellors and Principals. Peter Williams (Chapter 10) describes the work of the Unit in seeking to provide independent assurance that the university sector has adequate and effective internal mechanisms for monitoring the quality of teaching and learning. Neither the UK nor the Australian approach embodies sanctions. Each is intended to influence quality through critical appraisal by peers.

Marianne Bauer from the Swedish National Board of Universities and Colleges (Chapter 9) also argues that the institutions themselves should be responsible for ensuring that there is adequate quality assurance in higher education, and that the emphasis should be on formative evaluation rather than on accountability and control. Drawing on her involvement in an OECD study of the use of performance indicators, she comments that evaluation systems in higher education vary with the political culture and institutional system in which they function; this makes comparison of quality and performance within and between countries problematic, and yet it is increasingly demanded.

As yet, the German higher education system has no nation-wide quality assurance agency, and Edgar Frackmann (Chapter 4) examines some of the parallels (and differences) between higher education and industry in developing quality assurance and quality control strategies. Although it is felt that responsibility for quality should remain with the institutions, the implicit, 'clan-like' quality assurance of traditional German universities is under pressure. Public discussions and initiatives are insisting that internal quality assurance mechanisms should be made more visible and explicit.

The importance of international collaboration is underlined by Fritz

Dalichow who reports (in Chapter 13) on the European Commission's ERASMUS academic exchange programme, and on the success of the first year of the European Community Course Credit Transfer System (ECTS). Both schemes are encouraging increased international mobility of students (and staff), and depend for their operation on the mutual recognition by institutions of the quality of courses and qualifications offered elsewhere.

Part 3 of the book focuses on quality assurance in Hong Kong tertiary institutions. In the non-university institutions, as already indicated, degree programmes are validated by the Hong Kong Council for Academic Accreditation. Diana Mak and Austin Reid present a detailed case study of the Hong Kong Polytechnic, which reflects on the relationship between internal and external validation. They comment that many academics may see validation as a personal threat, and suggest that there may be particular cultural difficulties for Chinese staff in accepting the Western notion of critical peer review. They strongly endorse the movement in Hong Kong (and elsewhere) towards an interactive model where validator and validated work in partnership through rigorous and open academic dialogue.

The developing Open Learning Institute of Hong Kong is also subject to accreditation by the Hong Kong Council for Academic Accreditation. In Chapter 15 Raj Dhanarajan and Andrea Hope illustrate how the role of external advisors and assessors is integrated with the Institute's systematic internal procedures for ensuring the quality of courses, teaching materials and tutorial support.

The universities in Hong Kong are not subject to external validation. But Professor Leung and Dr Shen (Chapter 16) describe the external examiner system used in Hong Kong University (and most other Hong Kong institutions) to monitor exit standards and maintain comparability with course coverage and quality of outcomes elsewhere. Subject specialists from other (mainly overseas) universities assess the quality of student achievement in projects, coursework and examination papers, and confirm or moderate the internal examiners' judgments as appropriate.

Throughout these accounts and analyses of quality assurance in higher education systems around the world, the tension between autonomy and accountability, and between formal accreditation and self-assessment is a constant refrain. Most contributors agree that explicit external procedures can prevent complacency and can legitimize internal systems in the eyes of the public. Some express their reservations about the validity and value of performance indicators. Others doubt the wisdom of using industrial analogies and metaphors in explaining and developing quality-related concepts and practices.

During the international conference at which these papers were presented, participants suggested that peer review by subject-specific panels alone — without reviewing the institutional context — may fail to take account of the broader purposes of higher education; and, correspondingly, institutional review alone may not be able to assess the quality of teaching and learning in particular subjects. A *composite* approach encompassing regular institutional audit as well as subject area reviews was favoured.

The need to disseminate information about quality assurance arrangements and to share experience and expertise is clear. As David Bethel's conclusion emphasizes, respect for other systems must be built on knowledge and understanding of how they function. Dialogue and debate about policies and practices can stimulate fresh ideas and new approaches. In this spirit, the Hong Kong Council for Academic Accreditation hopes that the publication of these papers will contribute to improving and enhancing the quality of higher education everywhere.

Part 1

Context

1 Quality Assurance in Higher Education

Malcolm Frazer

This chapter reviews current approaches to quality assurance in higher education. The author explores why there is concern for quality, what is meant by quality and how quality can be assured; he draws on the arrangements for dealing with quality in higher education in a variety of countries, and refers to some key publications. He offers some definitions and explanations of some of the terminology used in the literature. The final section considers the potential contribution of an international network of the various types of national agencies concerned with quality in higher education.

Introduction

The 1990s may become known as 'the decade of quality', in the same way that efficiency was a major theme during the 1980s. In industry, in commerce, in government circles and now in higher education the word 'quality' is on everyone's lips: 'quality control', 'quality circles', 'total quality management', 'quality assurance', and so on. The maintenance and enhancement of quality, and attempts to define and measure quality, are now major issues for higher education in many countries.

Explanations of Some Key Terms

University

For convenience, 'university' is used throughout this paper to include all types of institution (colleges, polytechnics, technical and vocational institutes, universities, etc.) providing higher education. Many countries (e.g. Germany, Hong Kong, Netherlands, New Zealand, Republic of South Africa, United Kingdom) have a non-university sector of higher education. Institutions in these sectors will nevertheless be described here as universities. It is worth noting that often the better developed approaches to quality assurance are to be found in the non-university sectors.

Quality Control

Clearly every enterprise needs to have a system to check whether the raw materials it uses, the product it makes, or the service it provides reach minimum pre-defined (threshold) standards, so that the sub-standard can be rejected. Often this can only be done on a sampling basis. Typically there is a group of controllers or inspectors, who are independent from the main workforce, and who have powers to reject sub-standard products or services. Years ago industry learnt that this form of quality control was not enough. Most employees felt that the quality of the product or service was not their responsibility, that it did not matter if a sub-standard product was passed to the controllers, and that improving quality was not their concern. Industry therefore introduced the concept of quality assurance. This does not mean that quality control (i.e. passing or rejecting at pre-defined standards) is not needed. Quality control is necessary but not sufficient for any enterprise to be successful. The word 'enterprise' in this paragraph is to be interpreted as widely as possible. It includes manufacturing industry, service industry (e.g. banking) and public utilities (e.g. hospitals and universities). It is worth re-reading this paragraph and substituting the word 'university' for the word 'enterprise'. Many questions come to mind. Are the raw materials of the university its students, its teachers and researchers or its curriculum? Is the service the university provides its teaching, its pastoral care of students or the learning facilities such as libraries, and computer facilities? Is the product of the university its graduates and the competences they have acquired (examination results or employment destinations) or the new knowledge generated by research? Clearly all these aspects of a university's activities contribute to its overall quality; but they are interrelated. No university could, or should, employ groups of controllers or inspectors to examine each of these aspects in isolation. The overall quality of a university must be the concern of everyone who works there. This leads us to quality assurance.

Quality Assurance

As defined here, and by many in industry, quality assurance has four components. These are that:

1   everyone in the enterprise has a responsibility for *maintaining* the quality of the product or service (i.e. the sub-standard rarely reaches the quality controllers because it has been rejected at source);

2   everyone in the enterprise has a responsibility for *enhancing* the quality of the product or service;

3   everyone in the enterprise understands, uses and feels *ownership* of the systems which are in place for maintaining and enhancing quality; and

4   management (and sometimes the customer or client) regularly checks the validity and viability of the systems for checking quality.

If the word 'university' replaces 'enterprise' throughout this paragraph, then a university which takes quality assurance seriously emerges as a self-critical community of students, teachers, support staff and senior managers each contributing to and striving for continued improvement. This chapter is mainly about quality assurance in higher education. This phrase has been overused and possibly even misused, and so in addition to describing the why, what and how of quality assurance, an attempt is made in this section to differentiate it from other aspects of quality in higher education. Readers may also wish to refer to a recent overview of quality assurance and accountability in higher education (Loder, 1990).

Quality Audit

A scrutiny by a group external to the university to check that the quality assurance and quality control processes are appropriate and working properly has been described as 'quality audit'. The concept of quality audit has been developed in the United Kingdom, where in 1990 the Committee of Vice-Chancellors and Principals established a small Academic Audit Unit using experienced academics on temporary secondment from universities (see Chapter 10). Recent proposals from the UK Government (Department of Education and Science, 1991) include the establishment of a Quality Audit Unit with a somewhat similar role. Quality audit is neither concerned with a university's mission or objectives (inputs) nor with how successfully these objectives have been attained (outputs), but solely with the processes by which the university checks on the relations between its inputs and outputs. Sometimes quality audit is confused with accreditation.

Accreditation

This term has different meanings in various parts of the world. In the North American sense it can apply either to institutions or to programmes (subject or professional areas).

Accreditation assures the educational community, the general public, and other agencies or organizations that an institution or programme

(a) has clearly defined and educationally appropriate objectives, (b) maintains conditions under which their achievement can reasonably be expected, (c) is in fact accomplishing them substantially, and (d) can be expected to continue to do so. (Chernay, 1990)

It is noteworthy that in this definition of accreditation there is no requirement to judge whether the objectives (mission, aims) of an institution or programme are to meet any specified, or threshold standard. (For a description of the accreditation system in the United States seen through British eyes, see Adelman and Silver, 1990.) In many other countries, accreditation would imply that at least a threshold standard was intended and being achieved. For example, in the United Kingdom professional bodies accredit courses of study (programmes) meaning that graduates will be granted professional recognition.

The Council for National Academic Awards (CNAA) in the United Kingdom uses accreditation in a different sense. CNAA is an awarding body and has therefore a responsibility to ensure that its graduates have achieved at least a threshold standard. In the past it has validated (see below) each course or programme, but recognizing that real and enduring quality is best assured by the institutions themselves, CNAA has delegated authority, subject to certain safeguards, to validate and approve programmes to about forty institutions with a proven track record of quality assurance. In this sense accreditation means 'self-validation' which is different from quality audit (restricted to verifying processes) on the one hand and from 'accreditation' in the United States sense as described above on the other. (For a full description of the CNAA approach to accreditation, see Harris, 1990.)

Validation

The process of approving a new programme, or allowing an existing programme to continue, is described as validation. It is a check that pre-defined, minimum standards will be (new programme), or are (existing programme) reached. Most higher education institutions take responsibility for approving their own programmes and do not involve external agencies or even external individual peer reviewers. Exceptions are the 'non-university' institutions in some countries (e.g. Hong Kong, Republic of South Africa, United Kingdom).

Peer Review

The involvement of people as active university teachers, as researchers or as practising professionals to offer advice and to make judgments and/or decisions about proposals for new programmes, the continuation or modification of existing programmes, the quality of research programmes or the quality of institutions is described as peer review.

Quality Measurement

For most products or services it is clearly possible to define, nationally or internationally, a minimum acceptable or threshold standard (e.g. percentage of vitamin C in orange juice, fuel consumption of a car, the number of trains arriving within x minutes of the scheduled time). If there is a single parameter defining the standard, then quality control is simple. Furthermore, if there are a number of similar products or services, applying the measurement enables them to be compared and even put in rank order. For example, orange juice from a number of manufacturers could be put in rank order based on the percentage of vitamin C, with some perhaps falling below the threshold. However, there would be little point in comparing, and then placing in rank order samples of orange juice and mineral water because mineral water is not purchased for its vitamin C. Furthermore, vitamin C content is not the only quality parameter for orange juice. Others might be the percentage of sugar, of other sweeteners, of 'orange flavouring', etc., to say nothing of more subjective factors such as taste. Quality in higher education is like quality in orange juice — it is multifaceted. Thus it is better to consider a 'quality profile' than to give a single measure for quality. The profile could be in the form of a bar chart of measurements on several pre-determined characteristics (see Figure 1). There can be no one measure of quality of a university (or department, programme, individual teacher), and it is essential to appreciate that it is meaningless to add the scores of different and unrelated characteristics of a profile. Furthermore, it is important not to confuse quality and cost or efficiency (see below). Quality profiles and 'best buys' are how consumer associations present the results of their investigations.

There are confusions about quality measurement in higher education. It is sometimes assumed that quality measurement involves people *external* to the university assigning objective, *quantitative* scores or performance indicators which are then *norm-referenced* (i.e. the measures are relative to other universities leading to comparisons by placing them in a rank order or in bands, e.g. excellent, good, normal, poor, bad). Each of the words in italics will be taken in turn.

Quality measurement does not have to be made by *externals*. It is very desirable, as part of a university's quality assurance activities, that members of the university make measurements of particular characteristics of quality (e.g. number of students obtaining course-related employment within six months of graduating). If a national performance indicator is available for this

Figure 1.   A Quality Profile for Characteristics 1–6

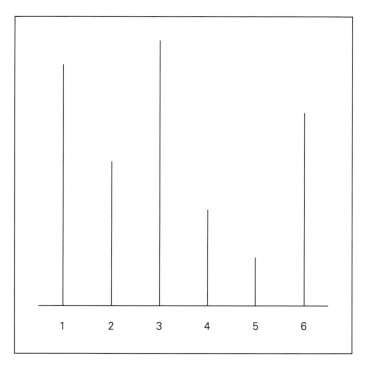

characteristic, then the university can internally see where it stands in comparison to other universities.

Quality measurement does not have to involve an *objective, quantitative* score. To return to the example of orange juice and the characteristic of taste: an orange juice manufacturer will assemble a panel of experts and consumers, train them and then under carefully controlled and 'fair' conditions ask them to make judgments about the taste of different samples. The responses of the panel might be converted to scores but nevertheless they remain judgments. In respect of universities the panel might consist of academic peers, students and employers.

Quality measurement does not have to be *norm-referenced*. For any characteristic of quality it would be possible to define criteria (standards) to be met. The university (or department, programme, individual teacher) then either meets the criteria (i.e. passes) or does not meet the criteria (fails) for the particular characteristic (see Figure 2).

Level, Standards and Quality

Sometimes these three concepts are confused. A doctorate programme is at a higher level than one leading to a baccalaureate. This does not mean that

Figure 2.   A Quality Profile of One Particular Characteristic for Universities A–F

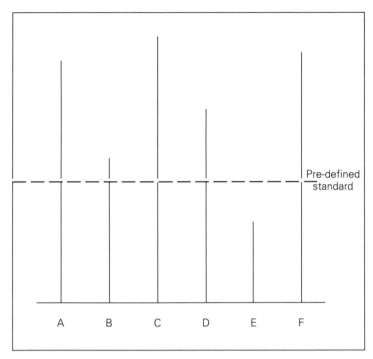

Pre-defined standard

A   B   C   D   E   F

University E fails to meet the pre-defined criteria and so is sub-standard for this characteristic.

doctoral programmes are of higher quality than baccalaureate programmes. For a programme at any particular level it is possible to define standards. Statements of standards alone do not define quality. Standards can be described, either in general terms or as specific statements of the knowledge, understanding, skills and attitude to be demonstrated by successful graduates. Is a high quality course one in which the standards are low but most graduates reach them, or conversely one in which the standards are high but few graduates reach them? Clearly, there is no simple answer. There would need to be comparisons with the intentions and outcomes of programmes leading to similar qualifications nationally and internationally. What is clear is that quality in higher education is a pervasive, but elusive concept, is multi-faceted, requires judgments by people with experience, and cannot simply be equated with excellence. Whereas standards refer to the intentions of a programme and the achievements of graduates who follow it, quality is much broader and includes standards as well as the processes of teaching and learning, the activities of departments and institutions and the congruence between the goals of a programme and the competences of its graduates. (For a comprehensive review of the meanings assigned to 'quality in higher education', see de Weert, 1990.)

Effectiveness

This is a measure of the match between stated goals and their achievement. It is always possible to achieve 'easy', low standard goals. In other words, quality in higher education cannot only be a question of achievements ('outputs') but must also involve judgments about the goals (part of 'inputs').

Efficiency

This is a measure of the resources used (costs) to achieve stated goals. It is unfortunate that governments frequently confuse quality in higher education with efficiency. Low standard goals might well be achieved at low cost.

Why Is There a Concern for Quality?

Accountability

Sometimes the question: 'why do we need quality assurance in higher education?' is answered by the word 'accountability'. That answer immediately provokes a second question: 'accountable to whom?' There are several answers to this question because higher education (from whole universities to individual teachers) is accountable to at least three different groups, depicted in the triangle in Figure 3.

Accountability to Society

In many countries there is a popular demand, and an economic necessity, for more higher education with consequential ever increasing costs, and in most countries society pays for much of this through taxes. Government acts for society in distributing funds to higher education either directly to the universities or indirectly through student grants or subsidized loans. Governments have a responsibility to society to ensure that what they 'buy' from higher education is acceptable and provides value for money. Several governments have established, or caused to be established, agencies concerned with quality and efficiency in higher education. However, accountability to society is not only a matter of return on investment. Universities exist to safeguard and transmit a cultural heritage. Society needs assurance that universities are not failing in this duty.

    Some universities or departments are of higher quality than others. How should the available funds be allocated? Should higher levels of funding go to departments of higher quality (a reward or 'carrot' to encourage all

Figure 3. *Accountability in Higher Education*

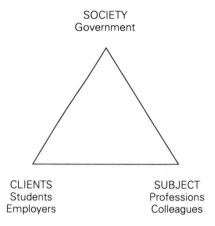

SOCIETY
Government

CLIENTS   SUBJECT
Students   Professions
Employers   Colleagues

departments to do better); or to departments with lower quality in order to raise them, at least to an acceptable threshold standard? There is no evidence that the former works, and to use this carrot one has to be certain of the objectivity of identifying departments of higher quality. As the funds to be distributed are finite, the danger is that departments assessed as having lower quality are deprived of funds, possibly driving quality even lower.

Accountability to Clients and to the Subject

The clients of higher education are the students and the employers of graduates. They desire to have the best possible education available and then to receive certification that particular levels of knowledge and professional competence have been achieved. The third corner of the triangle is the subject. The knowledge, skills and attitudes which comprise each subject must not be distorted, suppressed or misused. Teachers are accountable to their professional colleagues that the integrity of their discipline is upheld and that students develop positive attitudes towards the subject and its use in society.

Clarifying the Purpose

Before undertaking any evaluation of quality in higher education it is essential to be clear about the purpose. Each of the various agencies concerned with the quality of higher education can be positioned within the triangle according to its main purpose. For example, a funding body would be near the apex, whereas validating and accrediting bodies would be closer to the base. Purposes of evaluating quality include: (1) contributing to decisions on planning or funding; (2) validating; (3) granting professional recognition to programmes; (4) accrediting; and (5) making awards of degrees. Whichever of these it is, the overriding purpose is always to maintain and enhance quality. Confusion can arise because of lack of clarity about the object of the evaluation. Is it about research or teaching? The evaluation of the quality of research is outside the scope of this chapter and so most of what follows concerns the teaching function. The evaluation may focus on the whole university; a department; a programme or course; or an individual teacher. The relation between teaching and learning is much the same as between selling and buying. Nothing is sold until it is bought; nothing is taught until it is learnt. In other words, the essential purpose of universities, departments, programmes, and teachers is to promote learning. All this is summarized in Figure 4. There are twenty-five cells in the table, where each cell represents a possible purpose for an evaluation. By far the most important cell is marked ***, i.e. the purpose of evaluation is the maintenance and enhancement of the quality of learning.

What Is Meant by Quality?

Each cell in Figure 4 can be expanded so that characteristics of quality and the criteria for each characteristic are displayed. This is shown in outline form in Figure 5, where each of the twenty cells in the table could be the subject of a paper on its own. The two cells marked with an asterisk will be briefly developed; methods are discussed in the next section.

Some characteristics of a *teacher* in higher education are listed in descending order of importance in Figure 6. Figure 7 concerns the characteristics of *learning* and shows a list of knowledge, skills and attitudes that teachers hope their students will achieve.

How Can Quality Be Assured?

Self-evaluation

Real and enduring quality can only come by actions of the universities themselves. The basis for these actions must be self-evaluation. Inspection and quality control imposed solely from outside would not work. Self-evaluation — seeing oneself — is never easy, but without three aids it is virtually impossible. The first aid is a 'mirror', that is external assistance. The work of quality assurance agencies (accrediting and validating bodies, audit units, inspectors, etc.) is largely to help those engaged in higher education (whether it be an individual teacher or the university) to be self-critical and reflective. The second aid is training (staff development) for the task of self-evaluation. Third, there is a need for national and international information, such as qualitative and quantitative performance indicators as well as descriptions of

Figure 4. The Purposes of Evaluation of Quality in Higher Education

Pupose / Focus	Planning or funding	Validating	Accrediting	Awarding	MAINTAINING ENHANCING
University					
Department					
Programme					
Teacher					
LEARNING					***

Figure 5. Outline Display of Characteristics of Quality and Their Evaluation

Focus of evaluation	Characteristics of quality	Criteria for each characteristic	Purpose of evaluation	Method of evaluation
University				
Department –teaching –research				
Programme				
Teacher	*			
LEARNING	*			

best practice and innovation in teaching, learning and assessment both general and subject-specific. Much has been written about the use of performance indicators (Johnes and Taylor, 1990; Ramsden, 1991; Yorke, 1991). Sometimes comparative reviews are made covering all the universities in a country for a specific subject area. One example of such a sectoral review is the Australian report on physics (Australian Vice-Chancellors' Committee, 1990). These three aids have a cost; however, expenditure on them should not be seen as an optional luxury but as essential with a high priority. Two reviews, written from the perspectives of different countries — France (Staropoli, 1987) and Netherlands (Vroeijenstijn, 1989) — emphasize the importance of universities taking responsibility for their own quality.

External agencies can provide external help for self-evaluation through the important ingredient of peer review (Acherman, 1990). Peers should not only come from higher education; those actively engaged in industry, commerce and the professions must also be involved. Quality assurance agencies also act as mediators by bringing together the clients (students and employers) and the university, to ensure that student feedback and views of employers of graduates make their full contribution to maintaining and enhancing quality. Part of staff development programmes should be directed towards learning how to seek views of students and demonstrating that student feedback is valuable in improving programmes and teaching. Students also need training on how best they can contribute to the quality

Figure 6. *Characteristics of a Teacher*

Up-to-date professional knowledge, skills and competence in the subject. This is the sine qua non for every teacher.

Affective characteristics such as: love of the subject, a desire to share that love with others, a willingness to go on learning, a desire to help others learn and develop, and a willingness to self-evaluate performance as a teacher and to seek feedback from students and criticism from others, and finally a willingness to work in a team.

An understanding of how people learn, and of any special learning difficulties associated with specific knowledge and skills to be taught and with the particular students, a realization that the most important task in promoting learning is to motivate the students.

Personal characteristics such as: a sense of humour, patience, confidence, capacity for hard work.

Competence with teaching techniques including audiovisual and other methods, competence with assessment methods.

Figure 7. *Characteristics of Learning*

Love and respect for scholarship.

Love and respect for the subject and a desire to see the subject used to help society.

Desire to know more about the subject.

Competence in the subject consistent with the course aims.

Knowing how to learn.

Knowing the limits of their knowledge and skills.

Realization that learning is a lifelong process.

Problem-solving or opportunity-taking (i.e. problem recognition, definition and formulation of solutions, or approaches to solutions).

Knowing how to find out (i.e. how to use libraries and other databases).

Formulating an argument.

Integrating knowledge from different fields.

Communication skills (writing and reading; speaking and listening).

Critical analysis.

Working in a team.

assurance processes. External peers and internal evaluators all need workshops, conferences, publications, access to databases, etc. to provide the information on which to make judgments, and quality assurance agencies can offer this supportive role.

Aspects of Quality

Quality assurance should be comprehensive and examine inputs, processes and outputs (Barnett, 1987; Church, 1988). *Inputs* include factors relating to the students (qualifications, experience and aspirations), factors relating to the teaching staff (professional experience, qualifications, staff development on teaching, etc.), factors relating to the administrative and technical staff, and factors relating to the physical facilities (workshops, laboratories, classrooms and in particular the library). Another important aspect to be considered under the heading of 'inputs' is the intentions and planning of the courses. For every course, the team of teachers should have prepared a document setting out the context of the course, its aims and objectives, its structure, its content and teaching methods, and criteria for assessment. Such a document should be widely available, should be based on a self-critical planning process involving consultation with peers and clients.

Processes of teaching and learning are essential areas for self-evaluation. An effective course team will be constantly monitoring how the course is proceeding, the difficulties and successes of the students, and logistical and pedagogic problems. Both formal and informal methods should be used. Cultural and resource problems often prevent observation of teaching; further efforts should be made to introduce this at all levels, but it is essential for new entrants to the teaching profession to have support, including observation of their teaching, from more experienced colleagues. Other ways of monitoring the process include student feedback and regular self-critical planning and review meetings by the staff. The student feedback should not only be in the form of fixed response questions but should include regular interviews and discussions on an individual and group basis. Students should also be represented at meetings of the programme team, department, etc.

Outputs include examination results — comparison with national data; employers' views of graduates; graduate destinations; graduates' views after experiencing employment for some time (one year and five years — an alumni organization can be of considerable help in this respect); and reports from external examiners, from inspectors and professional bodies. The idea of external examiners is restricted to the United Kingdom and countries with similar higher education systems, and a recent study of the external examiner system has been published (Economic and Social Research Council, 1989). A useful source of information about institutional effectiveness and outcomes is also available (Nichols, 1989).

Externality

External assistance with self-evaluation cannot be achieved by documents alone. There should always be a visit by peers as part of the quality assurance process. The first stage must be a document reporting the self-evaluation. There can then follow one or more visits. These visits should not only consist of round table meetings for discussions about the documents between the evaluators and the course team, but should include opportunities, formal and informal, to meet teachers, students, employers, and support staff. These meetings are more successful if they are held where the teaching and learning is done, close to laboratories, workshops and libraries. The external peers should certainly visit these facilities and they should feel free to act rather as financial auditors do when carrying out an audit. That is, they can ask to see papers (minutes of a course team meeting, reports of examiners, examination questions and statistics, etc.).

The Stages of Evaluation

There are three stages to any evaluation: the submission of self-evaluation documents, one or more visits by external evaluators, and the preparation of a report. *Before* starting it is very important that the purpose of the evaluation should be clear to all those involved. Who commissioned the evaluation? Who is to receive the report? Who will be responsible for taking action based on the report, and who will oversee this action? It is also important before starting to agree on the procedures and methods for the evaluation, the costs and the timetable.

During the visit it is important that the evaluators are open and non-confrontational. Agreement and understanding of the purpose by all concerned should achieve this. Small meetings in various settings also help to achieve the openness which is required. If the interaction between evaluators and evaluated is confrontational, then it is unlikely that the evaluation will succeed. The evaluated will 'close up' and possibly withhold information, and certainly they will not easily accept and act on the findings.

After the visit it is important for there to be rapid feedback. It is common to give informal oral feedback immediately. There should also be review meetings as soon as possible after the evaluation is over so that both the evaluators and the evaluated can reflect on the process and learn from it. The evaluated should always be given an opportunity to check a preliminary report for factual accuracy.

Ultimate Sanction

It is for the university to deal with teachers, programmes or departments of unacceptable quality. If improvements are impossible, then ultimately there must be dismissal or closure. If the university fails to take action about quality below a threshold of acceptability, then there must be sanctions from outside. The nature of the sanctions will depend on the system operating in the particular country, but it may involve removal of accreditation by an accrediting agency, removal of approval or recognition of the university by the government, withdrawal of funding or closure.

National Agencies and the Need for an International Network

In a number of countries there are well established agencies concerned with quality in higher education. An attempt to classify them, with examples, is presented in Figure 8. Higher education is becoming more international and there is now a much greater mobility of teachers, researchers and students. It is therefore important that the objectives and functions of these different agencies should be widely understood. A loose international federation, or network, of higher education quality agencies should be established.* One of the first tasks of the network should be to produce an international database of agencies. For each country, the agency (agencies) might be classified under headings such as: name, address, year of formation, ownership, brief statement of the main purposes(s) and functions, brief statement of main methods used.

Figure 8. Examples of Agencies Concerned with Quality

1 UNIVERSITY OWNED AGENCIES	
United Kingdom	e.g. Committee of Vice-Chancellors and Principals; Academic Audit Unit
2 GOVERNMENTAL AGENCIES	
Inspecting/Evaluating e.g. France	Comité National d'Evaluation
Funding e.g. Germany	Deutsche Forschungsgemunschaft
Accrediting e.g. Hong Kong	Council for Academic Accreditation
Awarding e.g. New Zealand	New Zealand Qualifications Authority
3 NON-GOVERNMENTAL AGENCIES	
Accrediting institutions e.g. United States	Middle States Association of Colleges and Schools
Accrediting programmes (subject or professional areas) e.g. United Kingdom	Engineering Institutes

The production of the database would be only one function of the network. Others might include exchange of personnel; exchange of methods

---

* During the conference on which this book is based an International Network for Quality Assurance Agencies in Higher Education (INQAAHE) was launched. Details of the network are available from the Hong Kong Council for Academic Accreditation (HKCAA), 14 Floor, Ruttonjee House, 11 Duddell Street, Central, Hong Kong. Fax: 845 9910.

for, and best practice in, quality assurance; bilateral or multilateral cooperation concerning the quality of courses, programmes or institutions operating across national boundaries; and, perhaps more ambitiously, developing an international information service on quality assurance in higher education. It could also be helpful to produce a glossary of terms used in this field. At this stage involvement in the equivalences of qualifications is probably too difficult and would distract the network from other tasks. However, it is possible that the network might be able to help promote international credit transfer schemes.

An initial difficulty may lie in deciding which agencies are entitled to join. In some countries it is difficult to identify any agency other than the government itself, in others there is a single agency, but in many there are several, sometimes there are umbrella organizations 'accrediting the accreditors' (e.g. the Council on Postsecondary Accreditation in the United States).

The establishment of this network could and should assist individual agencies in reviewing and clarifying their purposes (the Why? and What? questions in this chapter), and in improving their methods (the How? question). However, the formation of a network should not detract from the essential theme of this chapter that quality assurance is ultimately the responsibility of the institutions themselves; real and enduring quality can only come from actions by the universities as a result of self-evaluation and peer review.

References

ACHERMAN, H.A. (1990) 'Quality Assessment by Peer Review: A New Area for University Cooperation', *Higher Education Management*, 2, 2, pp. 179–192.

ADELMAN, C. and SILVER, H. (1990) *Accreditation the American Experience*, London, Council for National Academic Awards.

AUSTRALIAN VICE-CHANCELLORS' COMMITTEE (1990) *Report on Physics* (by the Academic Standards Panel for Physics).

BARNETT, R.A. (1987) 'The Maintenance of Quality in the Public Sector of UK Higher Education', *Higher Education*, 16, pp. 279–301.

CHERNAY, G. (1990) *Accreditation and the Role of the Council on Postsecondary Accreditation (COPA)*, Washington, D.C., COPA.

CHURCH, C.H. (1988) 'The Qualities of Validation', *Studies in Higher Education*, 13, 1, pp. 27–44.

DE WEERT, E. (1990) 'A macro-analysis of Quality Assessment in Higher Education', *Higher Education*, 19, pp. 57–72.

DEPARTMENT OF EDUCATION AND SCIENCE (1991) *Higher Education: A National Framework*, London, HMSO.

ECONOMIC AND SOCIAL RESEARCH COUNCIL (1989) *The Role of External Examiners*, Swindon, ESRC.

HARRIS, R.W. (1990) 'The CNAA Accreditation and Quality Assurance', *Higher Education Review*, 23, 3, pp. 34–53.

JOHNES, J. and TAYLOR, J. (1990) *Performance Indicators in Higher Education*, Buckingham, The Society for Research into Higher Education and Open University Press.

LODER, C.P.J. (1990) *Quality Assurance and Accountability in Higher Education*, London, Kogan Page.

NICHOLS, J.O. (1989) '*Institutional Effectiveness and Outcomes Assessment Implementation on Campus: A Practitioner's Handbook*', New York, Agathon Press.

RAMSDEN, P. (1991) 'A Performance Indicator of Teaching Quality in Higher Education: The Course Experience Questionnaire', *Studies in Higher Education*, 16, 2, pp. 129–150.

STAROPOLI, A. (1987) 'The Comité National d'Evaluation: Preliminary Results of a French Experiment', *European Journal of Education*, 22, 2, pp. 123–131.

VROEIJENSTIJN, T.I. (1989) 'Autonomy and Assurance of Quality: Two Sides of One Coin', Conference paper available from the author at VSNU Posthus 19270, 3501 DG Utrecht, Netherlands.

YORKE, M. (1991) *Performance Indicators: Observations on Their Use in the Assurance of Course Quality*, London, Council for National Academic Awards.

Part 2

International Developments

2 Academic Standards Panels in Australia

Kwong Lee Dow *

Arising from concerns about apparent variations in standards and criteria for the award of degrees, the Academic Standards Program of the Australian Vice-Chancellors' Committee was established in 1987. Panels of academics were formed in physics, history, psychology, economics, computer science, English and biochemistry, to monitor standards in honours courses across the universities. Now, in the framework of a unified national system of Australian universities, the task of some panels has been extended on a trial basis to cover all undergraduate programmes in each discipline. Drawing on his personal involvement with the programme, the author evaluates these developments, assesses the strengths and limitations of this approach to public accountability, and anticipates possible future developments.

Academic standards panels have been functioning in the universities of Australia for four years. The initial panels formed in physics and history have completed their visits across the universities, and panels in psychology, computer science and economics will shortly conclude their visiting programmes. The most recent panels to be established are in the fields of English and biochemistry.

The first point to make is that these panels draw their legitimacy and authority from the institutions themselves. They are not creatures of government or government agency. The sponsoring body is the Australian Vice-Chancellors' Committee (AVCC), a body which, as the name implies, is a collective of chief executives of each of the universities of Australia.

The second point is that while the academic standards panels provide one significant means of monitoring standards, other complementary methods of evaluating standards are under investigation. The evaluation of quality of teaching, for example, by the use of appropriate performance indicators is under active consideration in Australia. Indeed, it is almost exactly a year

---

* In preparing this paper, the author acknowledges the reports of Mrs Bernice Anderson of the Secretariat of the Australian Vice-Chancellors' Committee.

since a parliamentary body, the Senate Standing Committee on Employment Education and Training, reported on *Priorities for Reform in Higher Education* (1990). The quality of teaching was identified as a priority, and the Committee commented that: 'Despite attempts in a number of reports over a period of more than three decades to focus attention on this problem, change has been very slow in coming'; it went on to recommend 'that the promotion of good teaching within higher education institutions be designated a national priority area and that, in the context of the development of profiles, institutions be requested to provide information on policies and programs which they have adopted to achieve this aim.' To further this aim, the Australian Vice-Chancellors' Committee and the Senate Standing Committee co-operated to hold a symposium on teaching quality in higher education to identify and publicize institutional practices which enhance the quality of teaching and learning in Australian universities. In other words, the academic standards programme of the AVCC is one important, major means of monitoring standards and quality, but it is only one means. At the institutional level other means are in place, or are under active development.

Background

The Academic Standards Program was established in response to a report on academic standards of a committee (chaired by the author) of the AVCC which met between 1985 and 1987 with terms of reference to:

examine the standards and criteria for the award of honours degrees;

examine the feasibility and benefit of introducing a system of external examining for honours degrees;

consider means of ensuring comparability of standards in courses both within and between universities;

develop a code of good practice and the dissemination of effective procedures for maintaining and monitoring academic quality and standards.

A specific concern at the time was the criterion of first class honours as a basis for the provision of Australian Postgraduate Research Awards. The selection committee for these awards had drawn explicit attention to the differing standards which seemed to exist in the award of first class honours between different faculties in the same university, and between the same faculties in different universities. Our report argued this way:

The class of an honours degree award should signify something similar if awarded in the same subject field by any of the Australian universities, and if awarded across different subject fields within a university or between universities. This is especially the case for the award of first class honours. The assumption is central to the award of a high proportion of the Australian Postgraduate Research Awards and to other awards which help finance postgraduate study. It is probably an assumption of many who employ university graduates, including universities themselves. Generally speaking, it is in the interests of the universities to ensure that, so far as is possible, this assumption accords with reality.

As we examined the data and talked with academic staff, it became clear that greater differences exist between subject areas in any one university than within any one subject area across the Australian universities. We decided therefore that it was more important to obtain consistency within particular disciplines across Australian universities than to seek consistency between the different subject fields. That is, the more important priority would be to get consistent gradings in physics courses across the country, rather than to convince physicists and historians that there should be consistency in the gradings between their disciplines.

We gave extensive consideration to the alternative of introducing a national system of external examining of honours degrees. While Australia is an inheritor of British practices in higher education, and the external examiner system is understood in Australia, we have never instituted a comprehensive practice of using external examiners in undergraduate courses. This probably can be traced to the distances between the few universities established in colonial times and perhaps, curiously enough, to the fact that extensive informal contacts existed between the professors in those universities. While some newer universities have used external examiners, the practice is not, and never has been, very widespread.

We defined the elements and the extent of an external examiner system: all departments in humanities, science and business faculties offering a four-year honours course would be visited annually by a departmentally appointed external examiner who would participate in the final gradings and classification of work submitted by honours students. Having canvassed this possibility and estimated its cost, we concluded that the benefits, though real, would be limited in the extent to which they could offer nationally consistent standards in a discipline. Also the costs (especially travel) would be high in a country with our distances, and we concluded that sharing information through peer review could be achieved more effectively through the establishment of small expert panels who would visit all relevant institutions and advise, subsequent to the examination process, on the standards of scripts, theses and projects.

As initially conceived then, an academic standards panel in a discipline would:

comprise some five to seven persons, respected in their discipline and drawn from universities across Australia;

over a three-year period, visit each university which had a department in the field of the panel, for discussion, review and reporting of matters relating to curriculum, assessment and gradings in honours courses;

review annually the statistics of honours gradings across all relevant departments, and draw attention to any major discrepancies or other relevant matters;

review student work after assessments had been completed. They would not, as do external examiners, participate directly in the actual assessment of students, but could conduct a post-hoc review as a check on comparability of gradings. Selected theses, reports and examination papers and scripts would be available either at the time of a visit or by other arrangement.

The AVCC accepted this major recommendation, and seven panels have been established, with the cooperation of all then existing Australian universities. Over the past four years a large body of persons, as panel members, have developed a good knowledge of the standards and standing of departments in their disciplines, and they are able to advise and influence the academic community.

It is the view of the AVCC Standing Committee on Education and Training which oversees the programme that this process offers more interaction and coordination than would the appointment of external examiners independently by individual universities. Many in the Australian academic world who are closely familiar with the external examining system in the United Kingdom still sometimes wonder about this decision. But despite some newer universities initially making independent use of external examiners, the UK pattern was never entrenched in Australia; given that fact in the mid-1980s, the preferred option has been to develop an alternative culture of expert panels who would visit all relevant university departments, even though less frequently, and on rather different terms.

The Panels at Work

At the time of writing this paper, there is available:

the completed final report of one panel (physics) which is now a public document. Twenty-one universities were visited, and the panel has drawn a number of conclusions about the state of honours programmes in the discipline across Australia, the effectiveness of the visiting programme and processes involved, and recommendations for future action (AVCC, 1990).

annual reports from each of the other panels prepared for the AVCC and its Standing Committee on Education and Training. These provide a guide to the panel's activities, its impressions and conclusions.

a large number of separate reports of visits by particular panels to individual institutions. Each panel produces a report on each visit, which is made available to the department concerned for comment before being finalized. This report, subsequently forwarded to the department from the vice-chancellor, serves as feedback to the department as a record of the visit.

reports of discussions held annually between panel chairs, the chair of the AVCC Standing Committee on Education and Training and the chair of the initiating committee for the programme.

From this documentation, four impressions might be mentioned:

1   As the physics panel has said publicly, and others have said less formally, the programme is an innovative approach to the issue of maintaining and monitoring standards, and its benefits have far exceeded those originally envisaged. The physics panel

> state without equivocation that its visiting program has been instrumental in achieving greater comparability of standards in honours physics across the Australian university system.... Departments engage in dialogue amongst themselves about issues previously ignored. Great value derives also from the spread of expertise brought to the department by the panel, whose members represent the combined experience of several other departments, each grappling with similar objectives and problems.... At a time when mobility of staff between institutions is somewhat restricted, the importance of the visiting program in breaking down the intellectual isolation of individual departments cannot be underestimated.

2   All panels report that they have been well received by departments and that the degree of cooperation has been excellent. While in some departments there is a measure of disagreement among staff about the conduct and content of the honours programme, this reflects a genuine concern with quality and standards rather than serious division within the department.

3   All panels are forming comprehensive views about the state of their discipline at this time in Australia. Two panels, for example, refer to the proliferation of specialist areas in their discipline and are urging restoration of some elements of a core curriculum requiring staff to

be able to specify what an honours graduate in that field can be expected to do.

One panel put it this way:

> While much of the content of the honours program need not be core material the panel did notice a tendency to 'self indulgence' in a number of universities, that is determining the content by what staff wished to teach rather than in accord with a considered view of what should be the content of such a program in the discipline.

4   The panels are able to monitor, in a way not earlier feasible, the extent of variation in the weighting of various components in the honours year. In each subject, panels report significant variations between the relative weight of coursework assessed by examination and supervised research assessed as a thesis or research essay or report. Panels are making recommendations on the extent to which such variation is legitimate and the extent to which there should be commonality. In programmes with a substantial research component, panels are drawing attention to the importance of supervision processes and to the need for 'examiners to have a good knowledge of the input from the supervisor before they mark the thesis'.

Future Directions for the Academic Standards Program

In recommending the establishment of the programme in 1987, the original report to the AVCC observed: 'While the initial priority may be with honours courses, these panels could equally assist in the maintenance of pass degree standards, and their comparability across universities, and where appropriate could similarly advise on Masters degrees by coursework.' Until this year, the AVCC has consistently directed the academic standards panels to confine their remit to honours programmes. The AVCC Standing Committee on Education and Training is of the opinion that, because of the restructuring of Australia's higher education, with the collapse of the binary system and the creation of a unified national system, and because the present major discipline reviews conducted (and funded) by the Australian government are themselves to be reviewed, a rigorous evaluation of the nature and scope of the academic standards program is now timely. While the higher education institutions are largely self-accrediting, there are expectations of demonstrable quality control and accountability.

As earlier indicated, reports from the academic standards panels affirm the value of the visiting programme as a mechanism for focusing the attention of departments on their procedures for maintaining and monitoring standards. As a process of peer review, the programme has the advantages of involvement, feedback and interaction in a non-threatening environment. Yet, within the full range of higher education, honours programmes are but a small component. It is worth considering adapting the programme to form the basis of university-based self-regulatory accountability covering the range of undergraduate and postgraduate teaching. This wider framework could be the basis for the future operation of subject panels.

The most recently established panels, biochemistry and English, are aware of the changed context, and the panel chairs have been asked to consider the implications of extending their activities to cover a wider range of undergraduate and postgraduate education. The two panels have agreed in principle to pilot this extended coverage and discussion has turned to practical consequences. Both panels will need an extended time during institutional visits and more time to discuss and review the information they obtain. For biochemistry, it will be necessary to consider practical courses as well as lecture content, tutorials, textbooks, examination format and assessment and reporting generally. For English, which has the largest enrolment in any discipline in Australia and has emerged as the central subject now in arts courses and is a subject taught in all but one of thirty-six Australian universities, each institutional visit would need to be extended, and a sampling frame of institutions will be needed, as it would be impossible to encompass the entire range of undergraduate and postgraduate teaching in every institution in any conceivably desirable time frame. The sampling frame should acknowledge the legitimate diversity of approaches which will characterize the expanded university system, and be based on criteria which can accommodate all disciplines.

A Possible Way Forward

The description of developments to this point is a factual account of what has happened, and an indication of the extent to which the Australian Vice-Chancellors' Committee has endorsed the work of the panels and the programme. Some issues seem likely to surface and to need resolution if the programme is to be extended on a more comprehensive basis. These matters have not yet been resolved, so the following points represent the author's personal perspective and predictions rather than agreed policy.

1 *The need to sample.* The early panels had completed much of their work before the creation of the unified national system increased the number of universities in Australia and considerably extended the responsibilities of the AVCC. When the visiting of, say, fifteen to eighteen departments covered the universities, all institutions could be visited by a single team within a

two-year period. Doubling the number of departments would double the time required, or require two teams, or require a sampling of institutions. The present preference is to keep the reporting time to two years, to avoid creating separate visiting teams (extra expense is one, but not the only, factor) and so sampling will be needed. An attempt will be made to include the different types of institutions, e.g. the older established universities in the capital cities, smaller regional universities, former institutes of technology, former colleges and amalgamated colleges.

2 *The availability of panel members.* Panel members act in an honorary capacity and have substantial teaching and research responsibilities in their home institutions. The task of panel members cannot be made too demanding and yet retain the commitment and willing service of our best academics. A realistic expectation is about three interstate visits, each of two or three days, each covering two or three institutions in an annual cycle. Sampling will need to take account of this. As broadening may extend the duration of visits a little, it may be necessary to increase panel size to a small extent, and to have some flexibility, so that all members no longer necessarily visit all institutions. It is, however, desirable to hold to one panel only in a discipline, and to keep the visiting and reporting program to two years.

3 *Composition of the panels.* So far, panel membership has been restricted to subject experts drawn from the institutions. From time to time it is suggested that it would be preferable to broaden the membership. There are several ways in which this might happen:

i   add a discipline specialist from outside the universities from, for example, a major employer of graduates, or from a research or industrial or commercial organization;
ii   add a nominee of a professional accrediting body;
iii   add an education specialist from outside the discipline who may bring particular expertise in curriculum development, assessment methodologies and for a comparative perspective across a series of panels.

It is likely that some broadening of future panels will occur, the constraints on such developments being less those of principle and more purely practical considerations such as the availability of such people as needed, who pays, etc.

4 *The need for administrative support.* So far, the programme has run with a single coordinator in the AVCC secretariat who has coordinated the appointment of panel members and the visiting programmes of all panels to all universities, prepared budget estimates, acted as a liaison person between the panels and the departments being visited, arranging travel and collecting

information, and has prepared draft reports of each visit, of each year's work by each panel, and a draft final report of each panel.

Broadening the coverage will increase the amount of documentation to be handled and the amount of relevant educational literature to be assembled and put before panel members; and it is likely to enable the development of a systematic national database of quantifiable information on course structures, departmental practices, student numbers, grades obtained, etc. While the administrative costs will increase, more extensive information will become available.

5 *Cost.* To date the programme has evolved at modest cost and in a no-frills, cost effective manner. Costs will increase if the number of panels operating simultaneously increases, and if the visiting is a little extended (though sampled). However, relative to other processes such as the major national Discipline Reviews, this is a highly cost effective process, far cheaper than each department in each university continuously maintaining an external examiner.

Conclusion

Provided the panels and the academic standards programme are seen as a major means, but not the only means, of maintaining consistency, comparability and some interactive dialogue about standards, it is likely to serve the Australian system of institutions well in the coming years. It is developing from a base of experience; it is proving acceptable as a peer review process; and it is, by comparison with other schemes, quite cost effective. The programme will benefit from a broader framework and compass, and, in the author's view, would be enhanced by widening the panel membership to include in each case one or two people with perspectives different from staff in the disciplines within the university sector

References

AUSTRALIAN SENATE STANDING COMMITTEE ON EMPLOYMENT, EDUCATION AND TRAINING (1990) *Priorities for Reform in Higher Education*, Canberra, Australian Government Publishing Service.

AUSTRALIAN VICE-CHANCELLORS' COMMITTEE (1990) *Report of the Academic Standards Panel, Physics*, AVCC.

3   The French Comité National d'Evaluation

André Staropoli

Higher education in France is almost entirely publicly funded. The structure and administration of the system are described here, with particular reference to the universities. In 1985 the President and Parliament created the Comité National d'Evaluation, responsible for the evaluation of each higher education institution. Using quantitative indicators and qualitative peer judgment, the Comité gives public advice on the quality of individual institutions.

Introduction

The institutions, laws, rules and financial structures for higher education are complex, have national (and sometimes regional) idiosyncrasies, and also share some common features, enabling comparisons (or at least connections) to be made. A study of these common features in many countries suggests the following characteristics of modern higher education systems.

1   The state, whether through central or local government, plays an essential part in financing higher education, as regards both teaching and research.
2   The basic tasks of a higher education institution are to educate professionals and impart knowledge. Highly specialized professional instruction and cultural education are therefore provided, either as initial or further training.
3   Pure and applied research or research services are increasingly being undertaken by university teams in conjunction with industry.
4   Access to courses is to some extent selective or at least restricted by available places, so that preparatory education exists in a variety of forms.
5   The 'democratization' of higher education, although spread unevenly, means that an ever-increasing portion of a particular age group receives higher education.

6   Higher education no longer rests solely with universities, but is available in new types of institutions, offering a new range of courses.

The French Higher Education System Today

The French higher education system comprises over 1.5 million students out of a population of approximately 55 million, and has approximately 150,000 teacher-researchers, technicians and administrative staff. Overall expenditure may be estimated at some 50 thousand million francs. The state provides almost 90 per cent of this, and the consolidated expenditure on higher education (including financing by students and their families) amounts to almost 2 per cent of GNP. Expenditure on research and development is estimated at some 2.5 per cent of GNP, of which 10 per cent is for pure research.

Within the French higher education system, we may distinguish:

1   the seventy-eight universities which are attended by almost a million students, i.e. a little over 60 per cent of all those undertaking study at post-secondary level;
2   the University Technology Institutes, attached to the universities, providing higher education of a technological nature lasting for a two-year period; they have some 70,000 students, which is approximately 5 per cent of the total;
3   the advanced technician sections which are responsible to the French Ministry of Education or other ministries, and train advanced technicians over a two-year period; they have approximately 160,000 students, i.e. almost 12 per cent of the total, and are separate from the universities;
4   the 'grandes écoles' (mostly engineering colleges or business schools) which, with their preparatory classes, have approximately 130,000 students, i.e. a little over 8 per cent of the total; and
5   some public and some private colleges which account for approximately 10 per cent of all students.

This chapter focuses on the universities within the French higher education system. As in other European countries, they have traditionally carried out both education and research. In this way they can be distinguished from other post-secondary educational institutions which tend to place emphasis on teaching. This distinction is becoming more pronounced, as is the case in the USA, where Boyer has commented that 'higher education is a profession arising out of several cultures', with research universities, liberal arts colleges and two-year community colleges (Boyer, 1987).

Whether the French system can accommodate increased numbers of students through extrapolation of the existing structure is arguable. Indeed, the pressure for diversification towards pre-vocational education through short educational courses in establishments other than universities should be noted.

Four Major Partners

The state, or more precisely *the government*, is a dominant actor. As guardian of the public interest, in 1984 it defined the role of public service higher education as follows:

> The public service provided by higher education contributes to developing research and raising the scientific, cultural and professional standards of the nation and the individuals composing it; regional and national growth; and reducing social and cultural inequalities. . . .

> The public service tasks in higher education are initial and in-service training; scientific and technological research together with applying its results to best advantage; spreading culture and scientific and technical information; and international cooperation. (Higher Education Act, 1984, Articles 1 and 4).

The state is also the major *financier*, but it is no longer the sole source of funds. The role of all the financial partners must be considered, and their particular awareness of the 'cost-benefit' criterion recognized.

The universities, in the European tradition, are run by the *teaching staff*, and the objective of academics (the 'peers') is the pursuit of excellence. These actors play a very significant role.

Finally, the development of higher education, especially since the 1960s, has brought about a profound change in the relationships between universities and the rest of society. It is not really a question of the university opening up, since the latter has always practised forms of openness, but of developing contractual links with the socio-economic environment. Market demand from *users or 'consumers'* — students, their families and future employers — is an increasingly important factor.

Quality Assurance: Three Levels of Quality Control

Three levels of quality control operate within the French higher education system: administrative, market and academic.

1 *Centralized administrative control.* Concern for the quality of higher education within a system of centralized management is reflected in the ongoing involvement of the French Ministry of Education which has several

departments directly concerned with the appointment and promotion of teaching (as well as administrative staff), the allocation of finances, and the authorization (or 'accreditation') to award national degrees. The role of central government in each of these areas is considered below.

The state finances 90 per cent of the universities' budget, and the salaries of *teaching and non-teaching staff*, who are for the most part civil servants, make up the largest part of this budget. The establishments receive funding for personnel which is managed at a national level. Staff recruitment is by means of competitive examination which seeks to guarantee equality and consistency of training, and also quality. Staff careers are decided by the National Council of Universities (CNU), a body approved by the Ministry, which comprises seventy-four sections made up solely of academics with professorial status. To become professors or be recruited to another university, staff must submit to the CNU a dossier, the main components of which concern their research activities.

As regards *finance*, the Ministry grants each institution a subsidy which is all-encompassing; this takes account of the number of students at the establishment, its surface area (built on and not built on), the numbers of hours of classes to be provided, and the differences in approach among the academic sectors. Some subsidies are allocated directly to programmes, especially for equipment and research. Most proposals are submitted by professors on an individual basis (especially when they are heads of research laboratories); the decision is taken by the Research Director within the Ministry on the recommendation of scientific advisers, and the university is then required to allocate these funds directly to the team or programme concerned.

Establishments are given *authorization to award national degrees* in the various academic branches and at the various levels, by committees of professors reporting directly to the central administration. To gain authorization, an institution has to put forward a proposal and provide proof of its abilities, which are inspected and compared by a committee of experts. As part of this process, the institutional plan which outlines the teaching policy and clarifies the objectives of the institution is discussed with the central government administration.

In addition, the academic advisers of the Ministry's Department of Research and Doctoral Studies (DRED) give an opinion on the quality of higher education, taking many indicators into account, in particular the number of doctoral students and doctorates completed. The central administration draws up regulations binding the establishments, undertakes a regular audit of administrative actions, and maintains direct contact with the various departments of each university establishment.

On the other hand, the central administration does not participate in choosing the students allowed to enter universities. University entrance is not selective: any person holding a 'baccalauréat' is legally entitled to admission.

This is in contrast to the preparatory classes for the engineering and business 'grandes écoles' which take the best pupils, and is also in contrast to the technology institutes and the advanced technician sector which also select their students. As a result, in the universities selection becomes an ongoing process, and failure, withdrawal and transfer rates, particularly during the first two years, are higher than in other higher education institutions.

2 *The universities and the market.* All higher education systems have a mixture of market orientation and public management, and the relative importance of government, university administration and other agencies varies. However, universities are becoming increasingly dependent on outside partners such as local government, business, the students and their families, and employers. These various partners in their relationships with the universities can exert control over the quality of the services offered, in return for their financial support or participation, as outlined below.

Finance from *local government* is sometimes by means of subsidies for students for research and study, but is often in return for a service provided, such as in-service training of personnel. The most traditional relationship with *business* is the provision of services or research sub-contracted by a company to the university. In France the proportion of contracts within the research budget of major universities has become quite substantial, and is similar to the American research universities, as 20 per cent of the research activity of universities comes from contractual financing provided by business, 10 per cent from local government, 30 per cent from research organizations, and some 40 per cent from the various ministries.

There are some fears that this might divert universities from carrying out pure research. Industrial research contracts are certainly different from pure research contracts; the question of ownership of the research results, and the secrecy which a company may wish to maintain around the results may conflict with the prime aim of the university—to disseminate knowledge. It is clear that the principal criterion of success in the relationship with industry is to satisfy the company, which must decide whether or not to renew its financial support. In view of this problem it is important for the university at least to have additional financing available for doctoral students.

France is also witnessing the development of appraisal of education by the *students* themselves. As indicated above, the university sector is not selective, and it has low fees. Students make their own choices and may be more or less attracted by the type and quality of provision at a given university.

As for *employers*, they express their judgment on the quality of degrees by the type of graduates they choose to recruit and from which universities. Increasingly open discussions are being held between the university, administrative and business communities to determine the requirements of economic sectors and the qualifications and training which are desired. The upgrading of the links with employers is also seen in the increased number of training courses on offer to students and the number of company representatives undertaking teaching tasks within universities.

3 *The role of the Comité National d'Evaluation.* Concerns about the dysfunctions of centralized administrative control and the shortcomings of quality control via the market led the French President and Parliament to create the Comité National d'Evaluation (CNE). In 1985 an act of Parliament established the CNE as an independent body responsible for the evaluation of each higher education institution.

The CNE reports directly to the President. It comprises seventeen members appointed from lists presented by authorities representing the academic and scientific community, and the main state jurisdictions: the 'Conseil d'Etat' and the 'Cour des Comptes' as well as the 'Conseil Economique et Social', which is France's third Parliament. The Committee has a General Secretariat with permanent staff and extensive autonomy in managing its own affairs.

The CNE is mandated by Parliament to evaluate each of the higher education establishments and the value of the public service tasks they provide — mainly research, initial education, in-service training and the application to which these are put. The Committee also examines the governance of each institution. It has no responsibility for managing the higher education system. It strives to have a regulatory role and encourages institutions to develop internal assessment procedures and to take responsibility for their own quality assurance.

The Committee has developed an approach which is partly quantitative, collecting and examining data and defining precise indicators, but it takes the view that the qualitative approach, or peer recognition, should remain paramount. In the assessment of teaching and research it is cognisant of two issues addressed by OECD studies which are explored briefly below.

The uncertain nature of the quantitative approach. Within the member states of the OECD, assessment of research tends to follow agreed definitions and criteria which enable some comparisons to be made at an international level (OECD, 1987). A quantitative approach has been tried, based on the definition of indicators, and it is believed that quantitative indicators can provide some useful data as support for experts' judgments. However, the qualitative approach of assessment by peers is regarded as irreplaceable, whether it is 'direct', 'indirect' or 'combined', to retain OECD terminology.

The criteria of quality within the university community. Qualitative assessment is employed systematically in the university world for the recruitment and career progress of teaching staff. This remains the exclusive preserve of the academic community itself. However, for institutional assessment, the use of performance indicators is increasingly widespread. For example, in its 1987 report the OECD quoted the example of the University of Göteborg which since 1979 has prepared departmental profiles using six research indicators (the number of research workers per department; the number and size of contracts; the number of awards made by research councils; the number and quality of international contacts (visiting professors etc.); the number of theses; and the use of non-Swedish external assessors). Such data have been used systematically at Göteborg to help determine departmental financing, and to identify which departments are in difficulty, enabling remedial action to be taken.

Le Comité National d'Evaluation: First Conclusions

The CNE is independent: it can make judgments about the actions of the civil service; it can choose which evaluations to undertake; and it is free to publish the results of its findings. This is what makes the Committee, in the words of the President of the Republic, 'a major innovation in the French system of higher education' (President's installation message, June 1985).

Evaluation has several aspects. For the *decision-makers* — the politicians — evaluation generally relates to the need to have available an analysis of the standing of the institutions, so as to make on-the-spot decisions about levels of support. More fundamentally, the motive for setting up the CNE was awareness at the highest level of the deficiencies of the French higher education system, as it had been established twenty years previously, with a centralized administration and yet at the same time an acknowledgment of the autonomy of the institutions. Thus the President's message explicitly linked evaluation with incentive and quality, stating that 'any system of higher education needs variety and flexibility, not uniformity.'

For the *institutions* themselves, evaluation, when it is performed by a body that has no decision-making authority and is independent of the central administration, satisfies two needs. First, it makes it possible to see the institution's policy orientation more clearly, to appreciate its strengths and weaknesses, and to bring about desirable reforms. In a sense this is the 'audit' role of evaluation. Second, it helps in persuading external authorities to take account of specific problems of the institution, including difficulties with students or with the academic community as a result of inadequate staffing or resources. This is the role of the CNE as 'intercessor'. Finally, for the *general public*, evaluation reflects the desire of the students themselves, the families of current and future students, and the university's contacts in the wider economic and social world to discover the worth of the institution as regards its teaching, research and standing relative to other establishments, field by field, discipline by discipline. They would especially like to know the value of the qualifications, which appear to be increasingly under scrutiny and which determine the likelihood of finding employment, but they are also concerned with the institution's capacity to provide professional training or expert advice.

References

BOYER, E.L. (1987) *College — the Undergraduate Experience*, New York, Harper and Row.
OECD (1987) *The Manual of Frascati*, Paris, OECD.

4   The German Experience

Edgar Frackmann

This chapter considers some parallel developments in higher education and industry, and suggests a framework for the analysis of quality assurance mechanisms. The difference between implicit and explicit quality assurance, between internal and external evaluation, and between input, process and output criteria is explored. It is suggested that quality assurance at a traditional German university may be characterized as implicit and clanlike. However, public pressure and initiatives at the institutional, state and federal level are shifting the emphasis towards more explicit approaches.

A Framework for the Analysis of Quality Assurance Mechanisms

Quality assurance is now high on the agenda of higher education as well as industry. In industry the concern for quality assurance reflects the challenging need to combine consumer orientation with mass production. Consumers have become more conscious about product quality and more 'individualistic' as regards product variety, while industry, for the sake of competitiveness and survival, still has to provide 'mass' products at reasonable production costs and high quality. Higher education only recently entered the era of 'mass production', and thus has to consider whether the quality of its educational functions is still self-evident, as it seemed to be during its 'élitist' era.

Whether in industry or higher education, quality and quality assurance are rather elusive concepts. The quality of a product or service might be defined as the 'congruence of its required with its real characteristics' (Wornhard, 1991). An organization produces or delivers services for consumers. The required characteristics of the products or services (i.e. their quality) first have to be defined. The task of quality assurance is to incorporate the quality requirements and ensure that they are met by all the products and services leaving the organization. Thus quality assurance involves:

identifying what quality is and should be;

monitoring that quality standards are being met (i.e. quality control, which is only a partial aspect of the broader concept of quality assurance); and

improving quality, in the sense of a permanent adjustment of products and services to changing consumer requirements and quality standards.

The main emphasis and expected outcomes of quality assurance processes and mechanisms are on product quality, responsiveness to changing consumer demand, and, as an accompanying variable, productivity at competitive prices (Womack, Jones and Roos, 1990).

Ouchi (1979) offers a conceptual framework for analyzing how 'an organization can be managed so that it moves towards its objectives'. He identifies three different control mechanisms focusing 'on the problems of achieving cooperation among individuals who hold partially divergent objectives', namely:

the *market mechanism*, in which external forces in a competitive environment (i.e. the consumers) evaluate the organization's goal achievement and product quality;

the *bureaucratic mechanism*, in which rules are explicitly set and monitored, either by a system of hierarchical superiors or by functionally separated 'quality control units'. Monitoring takes place according to pre-defined 'rules', which may concern processes to be completed or specific standards of output; and

the *clan mechanism*, in which a high internal commitment to the organization's goals is the driving force. To become a member of a 'clan', 'profession' or 'culture' requires a process of socialization and selection, in which not only skills but also the organization's values are 'learnt'.

Two additional pairs of mechanisms can broaden Ouchi's view of organizational control:

implicit versus explicit control mechanisms. Explicit quality control implies setting rules a priori with bureaucratic mechanisms to check the real product against the pre-defined standards; these mechanisms can constrain flexibility of adjustment to changing consumer requirements. Implicit control mechanisms are less visible; they do not have separate organizational control units or evaluation steps, but are incorporated into the process of production or consumption. Ouchi's clan and market mechanisms involve implicit control.

internal versus external control mechanisms. An organization delivers its products or services to an external environment, and the quality of its products and services is monitored externally, either by the consumer market or by a bureaucracy. But an organization is unlikely to wait and see whether external 'sanctions' endanger its survival; instead, it will try to identify consumers' requirements in advance as guidelines for internal quality definition and quality assurance mechanisms. Regarding the more explicit control mechanisms, an additional distinction is whether quality assurance focuses on input and process 'rules' concerning the 'production process', or on the output of the organization (see Figure 1).

Figure 1.   Possible Quality Assurance Mechanisms

	Implicit	Explicit
Internal	Clan/culture/profession	Bureaucracy (input/process or output rules)
External	Market	Bureaucracy (input/process or output rules)

These distinctions have been introduced in order to compare recent developments in higher education with trends perceived in industry. While quality assurance in higher education seems to be moving from implicit internal mechanisms to external bureaucracy, we witness in industry a shift from internal explicit quality control to more implicit methods, often referred to as 'total quality management' (cf. Joiner, 1990).

Womack *et al.* (1990) investigated the success of the Japanese automobile industry compared with its American and European competitors. They suggest that one of the most important factors contributing to Japanese productivity and product quality seems to originate in the organization of quality control. While visiting a German high quality (but low productivity!) automobile plant, it was noted that: 'At the end of the assembly line was an enormous rework and rectification area where armies of technicians in white laboratory jackets labored to bring the finished vehicles up to the company's fabled quality standard' (p. 90). By contrast, Japanese automobile companies incorporate implicit quality control into the production process itself, the main characteristics of this being to 'deploy responsibility to the working teams, detect and solve defects immediately, trace every problem, once discovered, to its ultimate cause. Problems are thus rather solved in advance, defects are rather prevented than being detected and remedied superficially at the end of the production line' (p. 99). This implicit quality assurance is based on an understanding that 'quality inspection, no matter how diligent, simply cannot detect all defects that can …' occur (p. 57).

Deming (1986) stresses the principles of implicit quality assurance; he does not recommend pre-defined objectives and standards, which may be followed thoroughly, but which may in fact impede flexibility, adjustment and improvement. Instead, the members of an organization or organizational unit should be involved in the goal-setting, based on a corporate culture and commitment to quality and permanent quality improvement. Creating this kind of corporate philosophy or culture is identified as the primary task of management (leadership). What has been described seems to deserve the term 'total quality management' and follows the model of implicit internal quality assurance rather than the model of explicit quality control.

For higher education, this kind of internal implicit quality assurance is not a new concept. On the contrary, the system of 'self-management of academic standards' (*THES*, 1991) seems to be the traditional form of 'organizational control mechanisms' in higher education. Quality has been regarded as falling within the realm and responsibility of the academic community. Hardy *et al.* (1983) describe the functioning of 'professional control' (i.e. control by the profession):

> Professors choose books that tend to be well regarded by their colleagues, they design their courses in ways that reflect their own training, they adopt teaching methods acceptable in their disciplines (and sometimes even sanctioned by professional associations ...), they research subjects that can be funded by the granting agencies (which in turn are subject to professional influence), and they write articles in styles acceptable to the journals refereed by their peers. (p. 413)

With higher education entering the 'mass production' era, public confidence in the institutions' self-management capabilities with respect to quality seems to be somewhat damaged. In industry, the competitive environment and the existence of a market are the driving forces for consumer orientation and quality assurance. Public scrutiny is increasing as to whether higher education quality is controlled sufficiently by *its* environment without a market or external agency to exert quality control. The greater the absence of competition and market forces, the greater the danger of bureaucratic quality control mechanisms.

These analogies between higher education and industry in the analysis of quality assurance may facilitate understanding of recent developments in German higher education.

Quality Assurance in German Higher Education

One might distinguish between higher education systems with an inherent orientation towards equality and equivalence, and systems which 'accept' differentiation and variety (Spee and Bormans, 1991). In equality oriented higher education systems, the main focus of external control is directed towards the monitoring of equivalence and the provision of formal and structural prerequisites that are supposed to guarantee it. Where differences in institutional performance and quality are accepted, the primary focus of quality assurance is to inform the public and the customers about these differences.

The German higher education system seems to be a classical example of a system with equality and equivalence characteristics. The assumption that the performance and degrees of all institutions are equal, of course, is a question of trust, confidence and belief: 'If we don't know that there is variation and differentiation, then variation and differentiation do not exist!' As long as equality seems to be guaranteed, quality seems not to be a problem. One might characterize the underlying philosophy quite succinctly: 'Equality equals quality.'

Two differences are, however, acknowledged. First, the Federal Republic of Germany has eleven (after re-unification sixteen) potentially different state higher education systems. This is a really challenging 'differentiation' in view of the equality pretension of German higher education! Second, German higher education has two different sectors (which will be maintained as such, unlike the situation in the UK and Australia): the more vocationally oriented 'Fachhochschulen', awarding a 'lower level' vocationally oriented degree, and the research oriented universities, awarding traditional university degrees (including doctorates).

In the context of the framework suggested above, the question is whether internal or external forces (such as governments and employers), implicit or explicit mechanisms play a role in German higher education, and whether input and process (structural prerequisites) or output criteria are the main focus of quality scrutiny in such an equality oriented system.

The classical German research university system is characterized by public confidence in its quality. But this seems to be a confidence in the abilities and commitment of individuals rather than in the performance of the institutions. The individual is the individual (eminent) researcher, the core of the German research university concept. Quality is assured by entry and input standards and procedures for the appointment of staff, rather than by output assessment. The 'profession' and the government share responsibility for personnel selection, and this combination of peer and state influence is supposed to guarantee quality. Thus,

> professors are civil servants; they are supposed to *serve*, and to be intrinsically motivated;
>
> although selected by the university, they are appointed by the education minister of the state. The employer is not the university but the state;
>
> university professors must have a second research dissertation (called 'habilitation') as well as a doctorate;
>
> professors at the 'Fachhochschulen' have to have a doctorate, which they cannot earn at the 'Fachhochschulen'. They thus have to undergo their 'socialization' within the university system;

with the 'habilitation', the 'venia legendi' (the right to teach) is formally granted. In other words, teaching ability is assumed to be self-evident for a good researcher, according to the Humboldtian tradition of 'unity of research and teaching'.

Research and researcher evaluation is well established in the German higher education system. What Hardy *et al.* (1983) referred to as 'professional control' is institutionalized in the allocation of public research money. The 'Deutsche Forschungsgemeinschaft' (German Research Foundation) funds research projects, programmes and research units; proposals and research units are evaluated by peers who are elected by scholars of the respective fields (Maier-Leibnitz, 1989). Similar procedures apply for other research foundations in Germany.

While research evaluation takes the quality of research and researchers' performance into account, this is not true for the teaching functions of German higher education; here the emphasis is on *equality* of degrees throughout the country as the centrepiece of 'quality assurance' efforts.

In medicine, pharmacy, law, and teacher education, degrees are awarded by the state and the examinations are state examinations ('Staatsexamen'). State examinations for teachers, for example, are held jointly by professors and representatives from the state school system, and the specifications for the examinations and the whole teacher education programme are passed as a governmental regulation by the state education minister. The sixteen states have a coordinating body ('Kultusministerkonferenz', 'KMK') which is supposed to adjust the specifications.

Other disciplines and programmes have degrees awarded by the university, which is responsible for the examinations and course programmes. The state minister of higher education, however, has to approve the specifications for the examinations; the ministry checks individual university proposals against the general national frameworks for 'Diplom' examinations ('Allgemeine Bestimmungen für Diplomprüfungsordnungen') or, if already existing, against the discipline-specific national frames for 'Diplom' examinations ('Diplom-Rahmenprüfungsordnungen'). These 'national frames' are coordinated and agreed jointly by the conference of education ministers ('Kultusministerkonferenz') and by the German rectors' conference ('Hochschulrektorenkonferenz').

Thus, while the state is responsible for guaranteeing equality, the responsibility for quality is left totally with the university. The state has the task of 'legal monitoring' (in German, 'Rechtsaufsicht'); any other monitoring or evaluation is supposed to take place within the system ('Fachaufsicht').

The qualification level for students to enter universities is high. Thirteen years of school and the high school degree 'Abitur' are prerequisites for enrolment. Universities do not select their students. Selection is left to the school system, and equality and equivalence of the 'Abitur' degrees throughout the country are guaranteed by state coordination within a national framework. Traditionally, the institution is not responsible for the students' educational progress and achievements; the individual student must take care of his/her own educational career. It has been quite usual for students to change institution in the course of their studies (one reason for not holding an individual institution responsible for a student's educational progress). It should also be mentioned that academics cannot be nominated for appointment as professors within their own university ('Hausberufungsverbot'). This mobility of both professors and students is believed to contribute to providing equality and equivalence throughout the country.

Employers seem to have confidence in the German higher education system and its implicit quality assurance mechanisms. Many are graduates of the same system, and would have to mistrust their own qualification if they allow doubts as to the system's quality and reliability. Sharing the values and tradition of German higher education, they seem reluctant to make comparisons between institutions. They are more interested in the differences between individual graduates, and trust in their own judgment, and in recruitment and selection procedures.

In summary, the German higher education system appears to be characterized by the clan/profession-like 'organizational control mechanism', i.e. internal and implicit mechanisms of quality assurance seem to guarantee organizational functioning. External assurance mechanisms focus mainly on the assurance of equality and equivalence throughout the national higher education system. Explicit evaluation in the form of peer review emphasizes only research and research performance. Public confidence in the quality of teaching and the educational functioning of higher education seems to prevail throughout the country. In addition, for both the education providers and the education recipients, it is not the institution but rather the individual who is the focus of scrutiny on quality.

The Changing Context

One might ask whether this description of the German system reflects the reality or just the conceptual elements of a system — a 'closed system', in which harmony and confidence seem to prevail, and in which each participant's behaviour seems to be well suited to contribute to the system's overall functioning. What is it that might 'stir up' such a 'wonderful' closed system? It seems to be 'external pressure' rather than any 'self-curing' mechanism. The key words for this 'external threat' are (as everywhere in Europe): 'internationalization', 'Europe 1992', 'competitiveness of the national industry and the national higher education system'.

Willingly or not, Germans have looked beyond their borders, and what they have discovered has caused some worries. They have found that the duration of studies in German higher education is too extended compared with other European countries (an average of seven years for the first degree). Graduates are often more than 28 years old on leaving university and entering their first employment; they thus spend the most 'productive' and 'creative' period of their lives in education instead of in their occupation. This in turn may damage the competitiveness of German industry and German economic health. Even worse in relation to the 'equality illusion' inherent in the German higher education system, differences in the duration of studies in the same discipline between different institutions have been detected. The result is that, for the first time, institutions are being held responsible for the educational progress of their students.

The discussion on duration of studies in Germany parallels what in other European countries is being handled (perhaps more honestly) as quality problems of the higher education system. The external pressure which German higher education increasingly faces, however, seems to originate not only in international trends and in the visible deficiencies of higher education, but also in additional changes and developments during the last two decades. Some of these are outlined below.

> Like other European systems, German higher education has developed from an élite to a mass education system. Between 1977 and 1989 the number of students enrolled increased by more than 50 per cent (from 913,000 to 1,509,700), representing 21.5 per cent of the 19- to 26-year-old age group in West Germany in 1989. Of the 19- to 21-year-old-age group, 29.1 per cent enrolled in 1989 in higher education.

> The motivation of this increasing proportion of the age group is not simply for 'academic studies'; to a greater extent they expect professional and vocational preparation and orientation (Frackmann, 1990).

> Only a minority of students now change institution during their studies (according to Leszczensky and Filaretow, 1990, less than one-quarter of university students and less than 15 per cent of 'Fachhochschul' students). The majority enrol in institutions of the state in which they passed their high school degree (Lewin and Schacher, 1991). Student mobility thus is no longer a reliable contribution to 'equality' throughout the German system. The responsibility of the institutions for their students is increasing as more students receive their whole post-secondary education in only one institution.

> Between the mid-1970s and the mid-1980s the German higher education system underwent a major 'study reform' ('Studienreform'), which might be considered a failure, compared with its stated objectives. The idea, 'imposed' by law, was to develop nation-wide and discipline-wide 'model specifications for examinations and curricula' ('Musterstudien und Prüfungsordnungen'). The main emphasis of these model specifications was to ensure a more practical orientation (with more emphasis on the

qualifications required by industry and other employers); limit the standard duration of studies; improve the teaching process; and create nation-wide equivalence of programmes and examinations.

In the mid-1980s this approach was abandoned, except for the work on 'frames' for examinations (mentioned earlier), and the task of 'permanent study reform' has been given back to the institutions. The danger of a unitary, inflexible and bureaucratic system of national curriculum planning and of national examinations has been avoided at the price of increasing public expectation that higher education institutions will be responsible for study reform and their students' educational development.

Employers' expectations as regards higher education seem to be rather contradictory and elusive (Teichler *et al.*, 1984; Teichler, 1990; Konegen-Grenier, 1989). On the one hand they expect studies to be oriented towards practical problems, on the other they do not seem to reward total adjustment of curricula to the short-term skill requirements of industrial practice. On the one hand they complain about duration of studies and the age of graduates, on the other they encourage practical experiences of the students, extracurricular activities, and studies abroad, which all contribute to the prolongation of studies. They expect specific knowledge in the discipline, and yet often select their junior managers on characteristics such as international approach, language proficiency, problem-solving capability, communication ability and teamwork. All of these 'qualities' seem to be even more elusive for 'quality assessment procedures' than the more discipline oriented skills and knowledge. German employers seem to prefer a smooth, continuous, incremental and informal adjustment of qualification processes and qualification requirements. They see this being realized through personal contacts between professors and industry departments, through students writing theses based on practical problems, and by means of industrial managers teaching and giving presentations in higher education institutions.

They are unenthusiastic about (bureaucratic) formal adjustment mechanisms such as the 'study reform' approach. German industry increasingly views the responsibility for curriculum planning and educational quality within the institutional realm rather than in government-imposed organizational structures. Their expectations are directed towards more visibility of institutional self-control rather than governmental control mechanisms.

External Pressure and Its Consequences for Quality Assurance

The pressure on German higher education institutions to tackle these problems is increasing. In other European countries some fairly comprehensive and clearcut quality assurance measures were implemented by governments or self-regulating bodies (such as the programme review process in the Netherlands, the foundation of the Comité National d'Evaluation in France, or the funding mechanisms of the Universities Funding Council in UK). In Germany the concern is multi-faceted, is initiated by a variety of public agencies, and in many cases involves no more than proposals and plans rather than real actions. This may be due to some of the features of the German higher education system discussed earlier, i.e. the federal structure of higher education with no centralized power; the deep rooted tradition of the German research university with its principles of unity of research and teaching, and academic freedom; and the traditional attention paid to the individual (researcher or student) in higher education rather than to the institution.

Three particular manifestations of pressure for change are the concern about the duration of studies, a new emphasis on teaching and learning, and interest in information systems. Some of the initiatives in each of these areas are considered below.

Concern about the Duration of Studies

As indicated earlier, reflection on the duration of studies seems to be the starting point of a new concern about teaching and learning and their quality in German higher education in general. Lists of measures and remedies have been proposed including one published by the 'Länder' (state) ministers of education (KMK, 1989). Their main emphasis is on the universities' own understanding of what measures are needed and on which measures should be voluntary rather than mandatory. If the universities themselves take no action, of course, the ministers may impose the remedies.

The ministers expect the universities to improve student counselling facilities, so that students have more information about programmes and labour market prospects. They propose that comparative data on duration of studies in different universities should be made public. Examinations should be better organized so as to become less time consuming. In selecting students for postgraduate studies and student grants, applicants' duration of studies should be evaluated. Finally, teaching and learning resources are to be made more easily available for students, for example, by extending the university library's hours of opening.

The proposal to publish duration of studies for different disciplines and institutions has been taken up by the Science Council ('Wissenschaftsrat', an advisory 'buffer body' consisting of both state and higher education members). The main purpose of this regular and continuous publication is to inform the interested public, make institutional performance differences visible, and promote the institutions' responsibility for their students. Against the background of German traditions of equality and individual responsibility, this effort is very important and remarkable (Wissenschaftsrat, 1990).

The 'Länder' ministers can significantly influence the institutions' educational activities through their approval (or non-approval) of programmes and the specifications for examinations, and they are being encouraged to use this approval process to scrutinize whether these contribute to an unjustifiable extension of the length of studies (BLK, 1988). One of the 'Länder' ministers (Bayern, 1990) has urged the universities to structure and shape programmes to give students more orientation as to what to study, and in which order. Students in this state understood the minister's recommendation as a deviation from the German tradition of an 'individualistic' rather than a 'directed' curriculum (Boys *et al.*, 1988), and as an attack on freedom of higher learning and the freedom of choice. In immediate protests students expressed their will not to be exposed to a school-like system of higher education.

Another recommendation from the same education minister was to establish computerized information systems within the institutions: based on student records, this should assist departments and professors in caring for individual students, detecting their problems such as failure in intermediate examinations, too much time spent in various parts of the study programme, etc.

Two further initiatives go beyond the status of publication and proposal. A German foundation decided to award money prizes for special efforts in reducing the length of studies (Stifterverband, 1990). The prize was divided into two parts: one to reward graduates who received their degrees in a relatively short time, and the other to reward model efforts of institutions, departments or professors for reducing duration of studies or enhancing the quality of education and educational outcomes. The prizes are being awarded once a year during a symposium, to make the models visible to other institutions and individuals.

It is interesting to note that this foundation normally allocates research grants within the German higher education system, and that it is a foundation endowed by German industry. While the initial focus of the award was on duration of studies, it has also contributed to a general awareness of institutions' responsibility for students' educational progress and the quality of educational outcomes.

The higher education minister of Baden-Württemberg is also using financial incentives to encourage universities to shorten the duration of studies. Results of the universities' efforts are evaluated and money from a special purpose fund is allocated accordingly on an annual basis within the state.

New Emphasis on Teaching and Learning

The focus on duration of studies is part of a broader concern about teaching and learning in general. The federal minister for education, in his *Goals for Higher Education 1990*, devoted some paragraphs to this new emphasis

(BMBW, 1990). He announced projects to be financed for the improvement of teaching. Not for the first time he suggested that universities should select their students in order to strengthen their responsibility for them. He encouraged institutions to deliver reports on teaching and the educational function to the public (most institutions already publish a regular research report); and institutions are urged to initiate self-evaluations at departmental and discipline level, based on student surveys. The federal minister advised his 'Länder' colleagues, however, to refrain from administrative (bureaucratic) measures, but rather to rely on performance oriented incentives.

One state minister has allocated 12 million DM in higher education to contribute to a new 'culture' of commitment to teaching and learning. An 'action programme' (MWF, 1991) states the goals of efficiency, structure and didactic dimensions in which the ministry intends to intervene, whereas responsibility for quality is left to the higher education community. Financial incentives will be given by funding additional teaching personnel, teaching laboratories, experiments with new teaching methods (e.g. using information technology and media), good teaching and additional teaching awards, and grants and prizes for graduates with short length of studies. It is also recommended that the universities in granting the 'venia legendi' and selecting professors should scrutinize more intensively the teaching qualification of applicants. Finally, the minister has mandated student evaluation of courses and teachers.

At the same time, students, the 'customers' of the higher educational services, are becoming increasingly aware of their 'rights', and are developing quite remarkable approaches. The Students' Council of the University of Münster identified the German research allocating agency ('Deutsche Forschungsgemeinschaft', 'DFG') as a critical factor in the successful development of German university research. The DFG is organized as a self-managed unit of the academic community, distributing public money, with the main emphasis on incentives and quality assurance in research. The students now suggest a German Teaching Foundation ('Deutsche Lehrgemeinschaft', 'DLG'), distributing public money similarly to the DFG, but with funds devoted to the improvement of teaching and educational outcomes and quality. Innovative teaching, student involvement in curriculum development, interdisciplinary programmes, educational research and teacher training are conceived by the DLG initiators as appropriate 'projects' to be sponsored.

Students also seem to be well informed about American teacher ratings and student reaction questionnaires, and have started conducting surveys and publishing the results in order to 'test' and rank their professors. The economics students of the University of Münster, for example, carried out such a survey as suggested by the education minister of their state. The criteria underlying the teacher ratings were clarity of presentation, speech and diction, conception of the course, the availability of literature, commitment of the teacher, and the role of written tests.

At the beginning of the 1970s many universities established 'centres for higher education didactics'. Unfortunately, they could not develop to their full potential, because in many cases they did not receive adequate status within the professorial hierarchy. The Association for Higher Education Didactics (the professional organization of these centres' staff) has seized the opportunity to link the revival of concern for teaching with their original endeavour. Following a major conference, they published a memorandum (AHD, 1991) in which they propose a new culture of academic reputation to be earned for commitment to teaching. University teachers are urged to make explicit the details of their courses and teaching methods, to keep in touch with alumni to get feedback for university programmes, and to generate immediate feedback from courses and lectures. They encourage teachers to use student reaction questionnaires as teachers' self-evaluation tools. They suggest that institutions as well as 'Länder' education ministers should offer incentive money for good teaching, and grant sabbaticals not only for research but also for the development of new teaching methods. The main concern of the association is to promote the image and reputation of the higher education teacher as compared with the researcher.

Another testimony to the new concern about teaching and learning is the emergence of published rankings, one by the influential weekly newspaper, *Der Spiegel* (circulation 1.2 million), which reported the results of a survey which asked students about teaching and learning in selected fields of study (*Der Spiegel*, 1989). The 'revolutionary' approach of the *Spiegel* ranking in the German context is its emphasis on differences in educational performances of universities, and the idea of asking students to give their judgments.

Information Systems

One of the more comprehensive and continuing approaches to tackling educational deficiencies is the proposal to develop and establish information systems; their role is to provide regular information to the internal and external public about the educational functioning of institutions and about improvements in teaching and learning.

Much of the interest in information system approaches within the institutions can be traced back to a proposal of the Science Council (Wissenschaftsrat, 1985). In its recommendation concerning competition in higher education, the Council urged institutions to deliver a self-description of their resources and performance as information for the public and potential customers of higher education services. The Science Council suggested that performance information on member institutions should be published comparatively by the German rectors' conference. The rectors' conference, however, argued that it is supposed to lobby for *all* institutions, rather than detect differences among them. However, to help provide comparability, the rectors developed and published a framework for the institutions themselves to use in informing the public about their goals, resources, strengths and performances. It suggested that such institutional reports should encompass verbal descriptions as well as facts and figures on the institution as a whole and on its discipline oriented parts (Alewell, 1989). It is interesting to note that the rectors' conference recommended that external performance rankings in Germany (such as the *Spiegel* ranking) should be included in these self-descriptions.

The federal minister of education commissioned an investigation on the use of existing statistical data to give more comparative insight into the educational performances of the institutions (Block, Hornbostel and Neidhardt, 1990). Universities have long-established public information channels such as their annual and research reports, but are now being urged to publish more on their educational performance and to use such 'education reports' as a stimulus for the improvement of teaching and learning.

Institutional managers and academics recognize that concern for teaching and learning is on the public agenda. For example, the President of the Technical University of Berlin has tried to encourage intra-institutional efforts to improve the educational functioning of the university. Faced with significant dropout rates, with duration of studies above the national average, and with a rather low position in the *Spiegel* educational ranking, he was the first to publish duration of studies and age of the graduates in his annual presidential report, and he was the first to conduct student surveys in order to detect weaknesses in programme structure, and the teaching and learning environment (Fricke, 1987, 1991). He also asked the economics department to design and test the feasibility of an educational information system on access, graduations, dropout rates, duration of studies and scores, and which could be developed into a student tracking system, so that teachers and departments could intervene and support students' educational progress before it is too late (Räbiger and Helberger, 1989).

Similar approaches to educational information systems are underway at the Free University of Berlin (Konzept, 1990), the University of Hanover and the University of Stuttgart (Horváth and Müller, 1989).

As mentioned earlier, German industry favours informal liaison between higher education and industry rather than formal 'bureaucratic' mechanisms. The research institute of German industry has suggested that a database could facilitate feedback, by making available better information, for example, on existing forms of cooperation between institutions and industry, on priorities and major emphasis in departmental curriculum and teaching methods, and on company offers of cooperation, etc. Another German industry foundation awarded a prize to a British university, to call attention to a very good model of internal reporting systems used for university management purposes (Bertelsmann Foundation, 1990).

Conclusions

One has to acknowledge that the German public is less willing than in the past to accept internal/implicit quality assurance. What we are witnessing is a whole range of external pressures on higher education in the form of government threats to impose 'bureaucratic' scrutiny, publication of institutional performance differences, prizes and special purpose incentive funding, rankings and changing behaviour and attitudes of employers. Public pressure is directed towards the institutions to make more explicit, not primarily the quality, but rather their internal quality assurance mechanisms and efforts to improve educational quality, as illustrated in Figure 2.

Figure 2.   The Main Traits of Quality Assurance Developments in German Higher Education

	Implicit	Explicit
Internal	on internal/ implicit mechanisms →	to be made more explicit
External	external pressure →	threat of external bureaucratic mechanisms

Public opinion and the 'Länder' governments are still cautious enough not to impose bureaucratic structures and external scrutiny mechanisms; they still rely on the German research university tradition of individual commitment and intrinsic motivation. For their part, German universities do not have organizational structures (such as a formal powerful role of deans or presidents) which would easily allow the implementation of internal explicit quality control mechanisms. The thrust towards a new emphasis on teaching and learning in German higher education thus almost entirely has to rely on individuals' initiatives and reactions to public concern.

Perhaps the potential danger and damage of external bureaucratic interference is taken more seriously in Germany than in other countries. There still seems to be a broad consensus that the internal/implicit model of quality assurance is the most suitable one. What is expected from higher education institutions, however, is that their internal, implicit quality assurance mechanisms should be made more visible to the public.

Referring again to what in industry is termed 'total quality management' and which appears as a development towards more internal and implicit quality control mechanisms within the industrial production process, one might conclude that German higher education may not be totally wrong to keep its emphasis on implicit internal mechanisms. Four lessons might be learnt of the German quality assurance experience:

1   The efforts industry makes to improve and maintain the quality of its products arise from being permanently exposed to the pressure of the market. German higher education is experiencing external pressure, which might adequately replace external bureaucratic intervention, but which does not fully replace the external incentives of competition and market mechanisms. German higher education perhaps needs more competition and market-like mechanisms in respect of financing and budgeting. Competition, which seems to function quite successfully with regard to research, is almost totally absent from the educational services of German universities.

2   Higher education goals and the concept of educational quality are rather elusive; whatever formal quality assurance mechanisms might be implemented (such as reporting systems, accreditation and approval mechanisms, formalized peer review procedures, etc.), one never can be sure whether, after an initial successful and promising phase, they may develop into mechanisms which follow formal requirements but have nothing to do with reality. This might justify the relatively informal approach to quality assurance in German higher education. What seems to be more important and effective is to maintain an ongoing thrust towards quality improvement. It may not be misleading to follow the guiding principle of the more dynamic companies in industry: 'Re-organize every five years!'

3   Stating that internal/implicit models of quality assurance may be the most suitable ones for German higher education does not imply that German institutions have already fully developed the potential of 'total quality management' (and this may be true for German industry as well, cf. Womack *et al.*, 1990).

4   Whatever internationalization and the European single market development may mean in the future, it has already helped Germany to open a rather 'closed' system of higher education and to pave the way for the improvement of educational quality in higher education.

References

AHD (1991) Arbeitskreis für Hochschuldidaktik e. V., *Bielefelder Memorandum zur Stärkung der Qualität der Lehre in den Hochschulen*, Bielefeld.

ALEWELL, K. (1989) 'Diskussionsvorschlag für ein Hochschulberichtssystem', in Westdeutsche Rektorenkonferenz, *Leistungsbeurteilung und Leistungsvergleich im Hochschulbereich*, Bonn, pp. 163–199.

BAYERN (1990) Bayerisches Staatsministerium für Wissenschaft und Kunst, *Maßnahmen zur Verkürzung der Hochschulausbildung*, München.

BERTELSMANN FOUNDATION (1990) *Carl Bertelsmann Prize, Award Ceremony 1990*, Gütersloh.

BLK (1988) Bund-Länder-Kommission für Bildungsplanung und Forschungsförderung, *Verkürzung der Studiendauer*, Bonn.

BLOCK, H.J., HORNBOSTEL, S. and NEIDHARDT, F. (1990) *Leistungstransparenz von Hochschulen*. Ergebnisse aus dem Forschungsprojekt der Hochschulen, Bonn, Bundesminister für Bildung und Wissenschaft.

BMBW (1990) Der Bundesminister für Bildung und Wissenschaft, *Hochschulpolitische Zielsetzungen der Bundesregierung*, Bonn.

BOYS, C.J., BRENNAN, J., HENKEL, M., KIRKLAND, J., KOGAN, M. and YOULL, P. (1988) *Higher Education and the Preparation for Work*, London, Jessica Kingsley Publishers.

DEMING, W.E. (1986) *Out of the Crisis*, Cambridge, Mass., MIT, Center for Advanced Engineering Study.

DLG (1990) Der Allgemeine Studentenausschuß der WWU Münster stellt vor: *Deutsche Lehrgemeinschaft DLG*, Münster.

FRACKMANN, E. (1990) 'Resistance to Change or No Need for Change? The Survival of German Higher Education in the 1990s', *European Journal of Education*, 25, 2, pp. 187–202.

FRICKE, M. (1987) *Rechenschaftsbericht des Präsidenten der Technischen Universität Berlin*, Berichtszeitraum 01. März 1986 bis 28. Februar 1987, Berlin.

FRICKE, M. (1991) 'Auch künftig überzeugende Lösungen', *TU Berlin intern*, Februar 1992.

HARDY, C., LANGLEY, A., MINTZBERG, H. and ROSE, J. (1983) 'Strategy Formation in the University Setting', *The Review of Higher Education*, 6, 4, pp. 407–433.

HORVÁTH, P.X. and MÜLLER, B. (1989) *Analyse der studiengangspezifischen Fach-studiendauer an der Universität Stuttgart — Eine flächendeckende Untersuchung*, Stuttgart.

JOINER, B.S. (1990) 'Total Quality Management. Ständige Verbesserung — der gemeinsame Nenner', *Technische Rundschau*, 48/90, pp. 70–71.

KMK (1989) Sekretariat der ständigen Konferenz der Kultusminister der Länder in der Bundesrepublik Deutschland, *Zusammenfassende Darstellung der von der Kultus-ministerkonferenz beschlossener Umsetzungsmaßnahmen zu den Empfehlungen ... zur Verkürzung der Studienzeiten*, Bonn.

KONEGEN-GRENIER, C. (1989) *Trainee Programme. Berufsstart für Hochschulabsol-venten*, Köln, Deutscher Instituts Verlag.

KONZEPT (1990) *Konzept für Bericht über Lehre und Studium an der Freien Universität Berlin*, Berlin.

KULTUSMINISTERKONFERENZ (1989) Kultusministerkonferenz und Westdeutsche Rektorenkonferenz, *Allgemeine Bestimmungen für Diplomprüfungsordnungen — Universitäten und gleichgestellte Hochschulen*, Bonn.

LESZCZENSKY, M. and FILARETOW, B. (1990) *HIS Ergebnisspiegel 1990*, Hannover.

LEWIN, K. and SCHACHER, M. (1991) *Regionale Mobilität von Hochschulabsolventen und Studienberechtigten mit Berufsausbildung zwischen Ländern der Bundesrepublik Deutschland*, Hannover.

MAIER-LEIBNITZ, H. (1989) 'The Measurement of Quality and Reputation in the World of Learning', *Minerva*, 27, 4.

MWF (1991) Ministerium für Wissenschaft und Forschung des Landes Nordrhein-Westfalen, *Qualität der Lehre. Aktionsprogramm*, Düsseldorf.

OUCHI, W.G. (1979) 'A Conceptual Framework for the Design of Organizational Control Mechanisms', *Management Science*, 25, 9.

RÄBIGER, J. and HELBERGER, C. (1989) *Vorschläge zu einem Berichtssystem für die Fachbereiche über die Effektivität von Lehre und Studium*, Berlin.

Edgar Frackmann

SPEE, A. and BORMANS, R. (Eds) (1991) 'Performance Indicators in Government-Institutional Relations', Paris, OECD/IMHE, Draft.

DER SPIEGEL (1989) 'Die neuen Unis sind die besten', *Der Spiegel*, 50/89.

STIFTERVERBAND FÜR DIE DT. WISSENSCHAFT (1990) *Memorandum und Aktionsprogramm zur Studienzeitverkürzung*, Essen.

TEICHLER, U., BUTTGEREIT, M. and HOLTKAMP, R. (1984) *Hochschulzertifikate in der Betrieblichen Einstellungspraxis*, Bonn, BMBW.

TEICHLER, U. (1990) *Europäische Hochschulsysteme: Die Beharrlichkeit vielfältiger Modelle*, Frankfurt a. M.

THES (1991) 'The Quality Agenda', *The Times Higher Education Supplement*, 25 January 1991.

WISSENSCHAFTSRAT (1985) *Empfehlungen zum Wettbewerb im deutschen Hochschulsystem*, Köln.

WISSENSCHAFTSRAT (1986) *Empfehlungen zur Struktur des Studiums*, Köln.

WISSENSCHAFTSRAT (1990) *Fachstudiendauer an Universitäten 1988*, Köln.

WÖRNHARD, M. (1991) 'Neue Formen des Qualitätsdenkens', *Neue Zürcher Zeitung*, 3 April 1991, p. 37.

WOLF, H. (1990) 'Total Quality Management. Qualität — so gut wie nötig?', *Technische Rundschau*, 16/90, pp. 38–42.

WOMACK, J.P., JONES, D.T. and ROOS, D. (1990) *The Machine that Changed the World*, New York, Rawson Associates.

5   The Hong Kong Initiative

Allan Sensicle

This chapter describes the establishment and work of the Hong Kong Council for Academic Accreditation (HKCAA) against a background of significant investment in a rapidly expanding tertiary sector. It addresses the implications of a government initiative, the object of which is to ensure independent advice on the quality of tertiary education. It also sets out the criteria and procedures employed by the HKCAA to ensure that Hong Kong's tertiary education is of a standard and quality comparable with the best internationally. Additionally, it touches on quality in relation to the expansion of tertiary education, the autonomy of institutions, the appropriateness of performance indicators and the disadvantages and advantages of external accreditation.

(Many of the terms used in discussing quality assurance have different meanings from country to country. To avoid confusion some definitions are offered in Annex 1.)

The Hong Kong Context

Hong Kong is British territory, founded 149 years ago. It is situated at the south-eastern tip of China. Its total area is just over 1000 sq km and is a maximum of 38 km from north to south and 50 km from west to east. Its population is approaching 6 million and it is one of the most densely populated areas in the world. Over 96 per cent of the population is Chinese (Hong Kong Government, 1990).

Hong Kong ranks eleventh in the world's leading trading economies. The wealth and energy of its people provide an excellent foundation for investment in, and expansion of, its education system. Those who live in Hong Kong and its frequent visitors cannot fail to notice Hong Kong's progress as a complex developed society. There is considerable urgency to ensure for its inhabitants that its strong economy, efficient infrastructure and government are further strengthened and consolidated in advance of transferring Hong Kong's administration to the People's Republic of China in 1997. Of paramount importance to such developments is higher education.

Allan Sensicle

Education in Hong Kong

In addition to the pressing need to ensure that the education system of Hong Kong is comparable with the best internationally, Hong Kong people and the government have always attached a great importance to education. It is the largest single budget item currently comprising around 17 per cent of the total. This amount will increase dramatically during the next decade as government improves the quality of education and expands tertiary opportunities.

There are nine years of free and compulsory education starting at the age of 6. The minimum school leaving age is 15; however, at age 16+ most pupils take the Hong Kong Certificate of Education Examinations. About a third of 16-year-olds go on to complete a two-year course which leads to the Advanced Level Examinations, success in which may provide entry to the institutions of higher education. At present about 20 per cent of these pupils obtain places on degree courses but it is planned to increase this to around 55 per cent by 1995.

Education is one of the leading issues in Hong Kong and generates passion and debate. The people of Hong Kong consider that education is the most reliable path to a successful career, and almost all parents are ambitious for their children to have the best education available. Degree level education is most parents' goal for their children and this reflects attitudes which give rise to some of the characteristics of Hong Kong people which may seem remarkable to visitors from the West. These include singlemindedness, diligence, a tendency not to question and to learn by rote. Such generalizations need to be considered cautiously, but they are not without foundation and are important factors when organizing, developing and implementing education in Hong Kong.

Currently Hong Kong has eight degree awarding bodies:

The City Polytechnic of Hong Kong (6500 full-time equivalent students) was founded in 1984. It offers degree and sub-degree courses and largely follows the British polytechnic model.

The Chinese University of Hong Kong (over 8000 students) was founded in 1963 following an amalgamation of several separate colleges that had been started by refugees from China. It is organized, to some extent, in the American university tradition.

The Hong Kong Baptist College (over 3000 students) was founded in 1956 and has grown rapidly in size and quality, particularly since the early 1980s when it first was given government permission to offer degree courses. All students are on degree programmes. The college is in the American liberal arts tradition, but courses have a similarity to the British pattern.

Hong Kong Polytechnic (nearly 14,000 full-time equivalent students) was founded in 1972 on the pattern of a British polytechnic. It offers degree and non-degree courses.

Hong Kong University of Science and Technology is still being built and developed, and admitted its first students in 1991. Many of the staff recruited have links with the USA and this may influence the nature of courses it provides.

Lingnan College was established in Hong Kong in 1967. From 1991 it will begin to offer degree level courses.

The Open Learning Institute of Hong Kong (over 16,000 part-time students) admitted its first students in 1989. It uses distance learning methods closely modelled on the UK Open University system. Much of the study material is from the UK, but some additional material is obtained from Canada, New Zealand and Australia, and new courses are being developed locally. Its 'open' principle of student admission attracts many mature and non A-level entrants.

The University of Hong Kong (nearly 8000 students), founded in 1911, offers a wide range of graduate and undergraduate programmes in the British university tradition.

In addition to these eight tertiary institutions it is anticipated that the Hong Kong Academy for Performing Arts will offer degrees in a couple of years' time.

The Binary System

Many countries throughout the world have a 'binary system' of tertiary education. This means that the system is split into two parts, 'universities' and 'other tertiary institutions'. Depending upon the country and/or social perception, 'other institutions' may be considered either superior or inferior to the 'universities'.

Hong Kong has a binary system similar to that in the UK, with universities and other tertiary institutions (referred to here as 'polytechnics' for convenience). The former are self-accrediting, while the polytechnics are subject to external accreditation and have developed from a largely sub-degree course base. Hong Kong's tertiary system is influenced by the UK, and UK developments are watched with keen interest. In making comparisons and considering the future, however, there are some important differences, among them the following:

1   unlike the UK, which at present has two funding bodies for tertiary education, Hong Kong has one funding body for the whole of the tertiary sector;

2 unlike Hong Kong tertiary institutions, the polytechnics in the UK are not autonomous degree awarding institutions; and

3 Hong Kong has relatively few institutions, physically quite near but not necessarily collaborating closely.

There are other differences, such as the relatively short time in which the polytechnic sector has been in existence in Hong Kong as compared with the UK. Also, both American and Chinese influences affect, in varying amounts, the form of education in the tertiary institutions.

Internationally there is a trend away from binary systems in tertiary education towards unitary systems: such moves can be for economic, administrative, political, or educational reasons, or a combination of one or more of these. The Australians have already abolished their binary line, and in 1991 in the UK a government White Paper proposed a new framework for higher education (DES, 1991) which will end the binary system, establish unitary funding councils, give polytechnics degree awarding powers and university title, and establish a single quality assurance unit to audit the whole tertiary sector.

In recent years the case for limiting the title of 'university' to some tertiary institutions has become weaker. The UK White Paper uses the following argument for removing the title of 'polytechnic':

> The title of polytechnic has never been widely understood. The British academic world realises that the polytechnics are higher education institutions achieving the same academic standards and giving the same quality of education as most universities. Many able school leavers and their parents still tend, however, to regard the title as a reason for making them a second choice to a university when seeking a place in higher education. In their international contacts, polytechnics still find that they have to explain that they are not further education or sixth form or technical colleges.

This argument can apply equally well to the non-university tertiary institutions in Hong Kong. It should be noted that, in common with other countries operating similar binary systems, the professions and the public sector consider university and polytechnic degrees on a par, for the purpose of appointments.

Expanding the Tertiary Sector

The Hong Kong government has an ambitious tertiary education development policy (Hong Kong Government, 1989). Expansion of this sector was first announced by the Governor in 1988 and then revised in October 1989 to set a more ambitious pace of development, with the aim of doubling the number of first year first degree places to 15,000 by 1994/95. By then, six out of ten sixth form leavers will be able to study some form of higher education in Hong Kong. This will be 18 per cent of the age group, compared with around 8 per cent in 1990/91. Among the reasons for such expansion are the demand for a more highly qualified workforce and the loss of graduates through emigration.

After the 1989 announcement, the territory's tertiary institutions, which are heavily funded by government, set out to develop new degree courses, research plans and departmental expansion. The two polytechnics are being allowed to increase their proportion of degree work from 40 to 65 per cent of all courses by 1994/95. (The Baptist College already has 100 per cent degree programmes.) A third university, the Hong Kong University of Science and Technology, opened in Autumn 1991, when Lingnan College also had its first intake of degree students.

Numbers and Quality

In different societies between 5 per cent and 35 per cent of the population receive degree level education. The variance relates to higher education policy, the perceived need for graduates and to the available resources. Within the past thirty years many countries have embarked on programmes of expansion in tertiary education, as, for example, in the UK following publication of the 'Robbins Report' (DES, 1963). In such times of expansion it has been necessary to address the question of the quality of education and whether it would be sacrificed for quantity. In general, quality *on average* is likely to go down, and the most able students are selected by the institutions at the top of the 'pecking order'.

It would theoretically be possible to achieve the expansion in Hong Kong simply by increasing class sizes in existing courses. This will happen, but the institutions are additionally responding to the need to introduce *new* courses. Such large, rapid and widespread change can be de-stabilizing. Institutions can lose their direction, and standards can slip; and an accreditation agency can help by providing external reference points. As a practical expedient, it can use the same panel for reviews of similar courses at different institutions, and this is a valuable means of ensuring comparability between institutions.

Quality Assurance and the Role of the HKCAA

During the early 1980s the Hong Kong Polytechnic and the Hong Kong Baptist College were moving towards a position where they could offer degree courses. To support them, and to ensure appropriate standards would be applied, the Hong Kong government requested an established accreditation organization in the UK, the Council for National Academic Awards (CNAA), to advise on standards in the institutions and the appropriateness of their offering degree courses. The CNAA was invited because the organization of tertiary education in Hong Kong has, in general, been closer to the English model than any other.

In 1983 the CNAA was engaged by Hong Kong's University and Polytechnics Grants Committee (UPGC) to advise on the academic quality of degree courses proposed or offered by the non-university institutions. The UPGC is appointed by Hong Kong's Governor. It advises government on the development, and funding requirements, of higher education in Hong Kong and administers government grants for the tertiary institutions.

The rapid increase in the development of tertiary education made the government realize that continued reliance on an overseas organization was no longer appropriate and that it would be desirable to consider the establishment of a Hong Kong system. To this end it was decided, in principle, in 1987 that a Hong Kong Council for Academic Accreditation (HKCAA) should take over the work previously undertaken by the CNAA and that there should be a phased evolution of a Hong Kong system of academic accreditation. In the same year a Provisional Hong Kong Council for Academic Accreditation (PHKCAA) was established to prepare for the HKCAA. In 1989 the PHKCAA submitted its final progress report to government, which confirmed that the HKCAA should be set up. An ordinance was drafted and on 8 June 1990 the HKCAA came into being (see Hong Kong Government, 1987, 1989, 1990).

In developing accreditation in Hong Kong, lessons were learned from the experience of others. Those setting up the HKCAA investigated accreditation systems elsewhere. The UK system was well-known through the association between Hong Kong and the CNAA. The US system was examined carefully and some features assimilated into the Hong Kong initiative. Quality assurance systems in Australia, Canada, France, Germany and the Netherlands were also studied.

The USA

Accreditation in the USA is described in Chapter 11. There are over 100 different accreditation organizations with different philosophies and standards. They include those concerned with particular subjects and professions, and those covering groups of institutions by subject, geographical area or academic level. The agencies range from large influential ones such as the Accreditation Board for Engineering and Technology (see Chapter 12) to the small and relatively recently established Accreditation Board for Colleges of

Oriental Medicine and Acupuncture. Such organizations are under one umbrella body, the Council on Postsecondary Accreditation (COPA), which acts as a focus for discussion and respectability for them. Other low standard accreditation organizations exist but do not have COPA recognition.

Although there are significant variations in the US accreditation organizations, there is one common thread in their activities. Accreditation is normally approached from the point of view of an external agency evaluating whether an institution is meeting its *own* aims and objectives.

The United Kingdom

Accreditation and validation developed in the UK through the establishment in 1966 of the CNAA as a degree awarding body for the non-university tertiary institutions. At first its procedures were considered by the institutions to be strict and unpopular external methods of judgment. However, they are now highly regarded and have evolved towards a 'partnership' between the institutions and the CNAA.

Aspects of CNAA activities have moved nearer to the US approach of an institution testing itself; and in recent years the remit of the CNAA has brought it closer to a general accreditation and academic audit role (DES, 1985; CNAA, 1989; DES, 1990).

In 1990 the UK university sector established an Academic Audit Unit, set up for the purposes of quality assurance in the universities. In 1991 legislation for a new framework for higher education with unitary funding and quality assurance arrangements was introduced (see Chapter 10).

Hong Kong

The HKCAA is a quasi-autonomous non-governmental organization (although independent, it receives the majority of its funds from government and is financially accountable to it). It provides authoritative advice to the government on the standards of degree courses in non-university tertiary institutions in Hong Kong. It carries out this task through academic accreditation, that is, by validating and revalidating any courses conducted by institutions and by reviewing the general standards of institutions.

The role of the HKCAA is to:

1 recognize an institution as having the ability to validate or revalidate courses conducted by it, subject to periodical reviews;
2 establish and maintain relationships with accreditation agencies outside Hong Kong and to keep under review systems of academic accreditation world-wide;

3   disseminate information on academic standards and degree courses and good accreditation methods and practices;

4   conduct seminars, conferences and other forms of developmental activities, and to assist in maintaining and monitoring academic standards;

5   advise the government on all matters pertaining to academic accreditation; and

6   carry out other functions connected with accreditation as may be permitted or assigned by government.

Some of the basic principles on which the HKCAA operates are as follows:

1   degree awarding institutions in Hong Kong should primarily be responsible for their own academic standards;

2   academic freedom and autonomy should be a right which carries with it the responsibility for achieving and maintaining the highest standards and quality of tertiary education;

3   institutions' confidence in their own internal methods of quality control develop best when tested by some external peer review;

4   an accreditation authority must be capable of helping to strengthen the institutions' own procedures in order to increase the validity and reliability of standards; and

5   the external agency should adopt a constructive positive approach, helping the institutions to develop their own courses, standards and goals.

Three other elements underlie Hong Kong's accreditation activities, namely the appointment of experienced professionals to administer the HKCAA, the use of an international register of specialists for forming review panels, and a governing Council which includes in its membership people of international experience and high reputation.

Accreditation Procedures

Some of the procedures, criteria and standards used by the HKCAA for controlling and maintaining quality in tertiary education are discussed here. (See Annex 1 for interpretation of terms.)

Course Validation

Course validation is a process carried out within the institution (internally) and by the HKCAA (externally), whereby a proposal is examined against criteria related to the standards and aims of the course (HKCAA, 1991). It aims to establish whether a course is equivalent to degree courses elsewhere and to assist the institution and the academics concerned (the course team) to develop, maintain and, if necessary, improve it.

Accreditation agencies and learned societies throughout the world list criteria for degree courses. The now defunct Australian Council on Tertiary Awards (ACTA) produced some useful guidelines in 1986 (ACTA, 1986). In terms of 'quality' in engineering education, the UK Engineering Professors Conference prepared some key questions which are applicable to a number of disciplines (1988). The CNAA and the HKCAA annual handbooks also provide guidance and checklists (CNAA, 1989; HKCAA, 1991).

The HKCAA recognizes that both internal and external processes are means whereby those responsible for a course can ensure it is of the highest possible standard within the scope of the institution. The institutions themselves carry out internal course validation, cognisant of the fact that they should establish, maintain and improve the standards of their courses, as part of their responsibilities.

Normally, the external validation process is conducted by the HKCAA, using an expert team of appropriately qualified people from Hong Kong and overseas. Detailed information on the course is considered by this team against a framework of principal issues. An important requirement is reassurance that the proposal has the full support of the appropriate government funding authority.

Following a validation exercise the HKCAA makes recommendations. These may be that the course should be approved as presented; that the course should be approved with conditions to be met and/or with advice to be taken into account; or that the course should not be approved. If the course is approved, a date for revalidation (typically six years later) is also specified.

Revalidation

Revalidation has the same purpose as and a lot in common with validation but with the benefit of some years of implementation of the course. It considers whether standards have been maintained and whether developments have occurred. It focuses upon an active course, its academic health and its relationship with the community.

Professional Accreditation

Institutions often seek accreditation for particular courses, from an appropriate professional body. The initiative for seeking such accreditation rests with the institution, and the processes and outcome of professional and academic accreditation can be quite different. The HKCAA policy is to work with professional bodies on accreditation when the tertiary institution perceives such joint action to be to its advantage. Such joint action does not necessarily result in common decisions.

Institutional Review

An institutional review must be appropriate to the institution and its current stage of development. Reviews can have varying status; they can be intended to comment on whether a currently non-degree awarding institution is ready to take the step to degree awarding status; they may be intended to ascertain whether an institution is continuing to maintain its standards; or they may be intended to assess the institution's readiness to take full responsibility for the standards of its own courses (institutional accreditation). Finally, a review may be a periodic event for an institution which has already been accredited (i.e. has achieved institutional accreditation).

One very important feature of an institutional review is that it is conducted by the HKCAA on the assumption that the institution is involved in a continual process of self-review. It provides an opportunity for an institution and an external peer group to share experiences of institutional practices and developments.

Further details of institutional reviews administered by the HKCAA are in Annex 2 and in the HKCAA *Handbook* (1991). It should be noted that guidance is in the form of a series of questions which encourages the institution to evaluate itself.

Institutional Autonomy

Tertiary institutions throughout the world have varying degrees of autonomy. Some are completely independent, being able to award their own qualifications and only being accountable in vague terms to the community which they 'serve'; others can be subject to varying levels of external control. With increasing sensitivity about the very high cost to governments and taxpayers, increasing awareness of the huge investment of a country's future in ensuring that the most able young people are developed and educated, there has been a significant world-wide trend towards accountability in tertiary education.

In the UK, for example, at present there are autonomous tertiary institutions (universities) and other institutions (polytechnics) which are subject to an external awarding body's control. There has been a relaxation in the latter of tight validation and accreditation methods, moving more towards self-regulatory systems subject to periodic inspection and testing.

The polytechnics, traditionally lacking autonomy, have become more independent. They are subject less to external scrutiny and soon will be awarding their own degrees. Conversely, there has been no external quality control agency for the universities, which have traditionally depended on external examiners to monitor the quality of student output, together with internal quality control mechanisms developed under the Reynolds code (CVCP, 1986). As already noted above, they are now subject to an Academic Audit Unit, set up to provide external quality control, and the 1991 White Paper proposes considerable strengthening of external auditing.

It is inevitable that tension exists between accountability and autonomy. However, the HKCAA believes that the system of peer judgment embodied in the Hong Kong model, with an emphasis on a positive and cooperative partnership between an accreditation authority and the institutions, can contribute to the strength and quality of the tertiary education system and the local institutions.

Performance Indicators

Evaluations of any kind require comparators, and the HKCAA's guidelines go into detail about factors which provide such comparability. A fashionable approach to comparability these days is to use performance indicators as a technique for measuring quality. However, performance indicators are tools which are employed to do a task, and should not be confused with the task itself. There is often a failure to define the purpose of the indicators and a tendency to accord most importance to those factors which can be measured most easily.

To illustrate the dangers of a preoccupation with performance indicators, consider an exercise purported to have been carried out by some experts who undertook an efficiency audit of the French railways, using profitability of its various components as performance indicators, to quote from a 'report':

> They found that first and second class carriages, considering their passenger load and the cost of the tickets, were paying their way. The same was true to a lesser extent of sleeping cars because of a lesser occupancy. The dining cars, which were breaking about even, should be kept because of the convenience to the public.

> But they discovered that all trains had at the front (or exceptionally at the back) a heavy vehicle which carried neither goods nor passengers with the exception of one or two people, who not only did not pay their fare but were actually given money by the company. The financial utility of this vehicle was clearly nil and it was proposed to do away with it.

Comparability is indeed very important and without some way of achieving it, standards are very difficult to ascertain. The HKCAA does not use a performance indicator approach but does consider (as the majority of those involved in any sort of evaluation) some markers which allow for direct comparability. For example, in course reviews, student-staff ratio can be one indicator of whether resources are adequate to maintain appropriate staffing levels.

The HKCAA encourages institutions to have a good understanding of the criteria and standards set. Where this is coupled with confidence to respond within a supportive accreditation mechanism operated by peers, progressive quality assurance can be implemented. The HKCAA believes this is more professional, flexible, searching and evolutionary than basing a quality assurance method on a rigid set of performance indicators.

The External Agency

The advantages and disadvantages of using external accreditation agencies can, to some extent, relate to the type of external agencies, to whom they are accountable and their philosophy. The following indicates some general disadvantages and advantages.

Disadvantages

One major disadvantage of an external accreditation agency is the possible conflict between it and the institutions undergoing accreditation. Any external agency, no matter how benevolent and how laudable its aims, can be seen as authoritarian. Another disadvantage, an inevitable consequence of external accreditation, is that it places considerable demands on an institution to make its case, involving a significant amount of preparation of documents and paperwork. This is time-consuming and costly for the institutions.

Advantages

One advantage is the discipline engendered in institutions evaluating their standards through the imposition of quality assurance methods to maintain and control quality. No matter how good the intentions of the institution might be about the quality and development of itself and its courses, it is easy for it to let slip the mechanisms and awareness of quality assurance without the formality of accreditation and the need for external recognition and accountability. A significant further advantage is the help, support and encouragement which an external agency can provide towards the development of institutions as strong, self-critical and coherent academic communities.

An objective of the Hong Kong initiative is to provide a focus for comparability and equivalence to enable the institutions to look outside themselves and be aware of good practice and development, in other institutions at home and overseas. In addition, an external agency can be seen as a resource, providing a forum for discussion and the exchange of ideas on matters of academic development. It can act as a liaison between other interested parties, such as professional bodies.

Institutional Accreditation

To respond to validation by an external agency, institutions need to set up significant internal quality control mechanisms. In so doing, as an institution develops, it can achieve, for the majority of its courses, an understanding and acceptance of the methods and procedures of quality assurance. Such development can enable it to evolve into a 'self-regulating' institution. This should allow it to move away from course-by-course validation towards institutional accreditation (see Annex 2) whereby it gains responsibility for the quality assurance of its own courses, subject to periodic institutional and/or sectoral (i.e. subject area) review by an external agency.

There are advantages of institutional accreditation, one being the requirement for less paperwork as only an internal submission is prepared. Far more important, however, is the confidence engendered within the institution as it becomes more a progressive and coherent self-critical academic community.

A major disadvantage of institutional accreditation can be seen as providing an opportunity for institutions to become lax in their weakest areas of operation. However, appropriate periodic institutional and sectoral reviews should, in the long term, provide the impetus to remedy this disadvantage.

The Future

One special aspect of the Hong Kong initiative is its international approach. Generally accreditation mechanisms are confined to the institutions and academics within the country concerned. The dynamic and outward looking nature of Hong Kong and its strong links with the rest of the world inevitably involve an international dimension. It is believed that the involvement of experienced and respected academics from both home and overseas provides the best input to a rapidly developing and strong tertiary system. In addition, this international approach is expected to help establish Hong Kong tertiary education and its quality assurance activities firmly on the world scene.

Annex 1. Interpretation of Terms

Certain specific terms relating to accreditation have been interpreted for the purposes of the chapter as follows:

Academic accreditation means any evaluation, assessment or other activity to determine whether or not the academic standards of any institution of higher education are comparable with internationally recognized standards.

A *degree course* means a programme of study, the successful completion of which is marked by the conferring of a degree or other equivalent award. In general, degree courses refer to courses of study taken by a country's most able students over a period of years from their late teens to their early 20s. (Typically, in Hong Kong over three years from 18 to 21.)

Validation is an evaluation of a particular degree course conducted or proposed to be conducted by an institution of higher education, to determine whether or not the academic standard of the course is comparable with internationally recognized standards.

Revalidation is an appraisal of the progress of an existing degree course to determine whether it continues to be of a standard comparable with internationally recognized standards.

Institutional review is a review of the academic and general standards of an institution of higher education (see also Annex 2).

Institutional accreditation is an assessment to determine whether an institution of higher education is competent to take responsibility for the validation and revalidation of the degree courses conducted or proposed to be conducted by it.

Annex 2. Review of Institutions

Institutional Reviews

Purpose and method. An institutional review is the process of evaluating an institution of higher education to determine whether it can sustain a suitable academic environment in which the standard of degrees remains comparable with those recognized internationally. It is based on an institution's self-evaluation and the HKCAA's knowledge of that institution.

An institutional review must be appropriate to the institution and its current stage of development. The review could be intended to comment on whether a currently non-degree-awarding institution is ready to take the step to degree-awarding status. For another institution that already awards degrees, the review may be intended simply to ascertain whether the institution is continuing to maintain this standard. Alternatively, the review may be intended to assess the institution's readiness to take full responsibility for the standards of its own courses (institutional accreditation); or it may be an occasional review of an institution that already has this responsibility.

Institutional reviews are conducted by the HKCAA on the assumption that the institution is involved in a continual process of self-review. The external review then enables the institution's own assessment of its performance to be scrutinized externally. It also provides an opportunity for an institution and an external peer group to share their experiences of institutional practices and developments, and (where relevant) permits the HKCAA to consider the institution's progression towards institutional accreditation.

An institutional review is conducted by the HKCAA using a panel of appropriately qualified academics (from Hong Kong and overseas) and local lay people. In consultation with the HKCAA, the institution prepares a submission which is considered by the panel, which then visits the institution. At the institution, the panel consults the senior staff, and makes whatever other investigations it deems appropriate.

Principal issues to be considered in an institutional review. The main matters considered by the HKCAA are:

1 *institutional structure*: Is the institution an academic community? Are there opportunities for staff and students to contribute to the formation of academic policy? Can the priorities among various institutional activities be successfully determined and action initiated?

2 *government and management*: What is the committee structure? What are the committees' terms of reference and policies? Is the academic board effective in guiding academic policies? Are the committees and boards properly accountable? Is the management structure effective? Does the institution have adequate processes for internal review?

3 *course development and design*: Are the academic staff able to make a full contribution to the design and development of courses? Does course development benefit from the research and consultancy work done by the staff?

4 *the development of new work*: Is there adequate management in formation and employment data? Is there an intelligent and integrated approach to academic and resource decisions? Is academic planning responsive to the changes in institutional profile and educational philosophy and vice versa?

5 *academic staff*: What is the quality of the teaching staff and how is it monitored and maintained? How do the staff respond to subject and course developments? What are the expectations of the staff for development? Do the staff provide a stimulus for student learning?

6 *scholarly activity*: Does the institutional environment encourage research and innovation? What is the staff's record in this respect as indicated by, for example, level of research grants, publication in international journals, acquisition of patents, etc.? Does the environment encourage consultancy and collaboration with industry in research and development work? What is the extent of such activity?

7 *students*: Is the environment suitable for undergraduate teaching? Are the learning resources and teaching methods appropriate? How are the students selected for entry to the institution and courses? How are they guided in relation to their academic programmes? What are the standards of student counselling, medical care, accommodation, and recreational and other communal facilities?

8 *course evaluation and standards*: Is there regular monitoring of courses? Are validation and revalidation procedures and mechanisms employed? Are they adequate and are they properly applied? Are appropriate standards set for

courses and are these standards achieved? How is student assessment carried out? What criteria and methods of assessment are employed?

9   *resources*: Are the present and planned resources (fiscal, accommodation, equipment, furniture, books, software, etc.) realistic? Do they match the future development of the institution? Is resource administration and management of an appropriate standard? Are there suitable research facilities?

10   *new technology*: Does the institution take sufficient account of new technologies?

11   *collaboration*: Does the institution actively seek and exploit collaborative teaching and research with industry and local and overseas institutions?

12   *past reviews*: Has the institution taken account of advice given or recommendations made following past reviews?

Based on this general list, the HKCAA draws up a set of guidelines specifically related to the institution under review and to the terms of reference of the review.

Information required for institutional review exercises.   The documentation provided by the institution is expected to be in the form of:

1   the institution's self-evaluation;
2   previous institutional review documents, if any, with details of how any specified conditions have been met;
3   academic development proposals;
4   academic regulations;
5   committee handbooks;
6   lists of selected publications of institution's staff; and
7   report on academic support facilities.

Outcome of institutional review.   An institutional review panel prepares a report on the institution considered. The report may conclude that the institution:

1   is not yet ready to mount courses at degree level (such an outcome would normally be accompanied by conditions and/or recommendations on appropriate measures that could be taken by the institution to move towards this goal);
2   is ready to introduce degree level courses;
3   continues to have the ability to sustain a suitable environment to maintain an appropriate degree standard (but its courses will be validated and revalidated externally);
4   is ready to be accredited (and take full responsibility to validate and revalidate its degree courses); or
5   continues to have accredited status (and will be subject only to occasional institutional review).

The report of the review is presented to the body that invoked the services of the HKCAA for its decision on the actions to be taken as a result of the review. The review would also normally be the subject of consideration and action by the HKCAA and the institution. Such action includes the monitoring by the HKCAA of the fulfilment of any conditions specified or recommendations made. The usual period between institutional reviews is five to seven years.

Institutional Accreditation

It is intended that, for any institution, the HKCAA should gradually change its activities away from monitoring the institution's individual courses and standards and towards affirming its ability to maintain its own standards. The process of accrediting an institution to do this is a cumulative one, involving the acquisition by the HKCAA of detailed knowledge of that institution over a period of time through the execution of course validations and revalidations and institutional reviews. It is likely that this process would culminate in an institutional review for which the major term of reference would be to ascertain whether the institution is ready to be so accredited. Clearly, such a review would involve detailed consideration of the institution's own quality control and assurance mechanisms.

Any institution that has full responsibility for its own degree courses will be subject to occasional review, as this enables formal external interaction, and the sharing of ideas and experiences of practices and developments in tertiary education.

References

AUSTRALIAN COUNCIL FOR TERTIARY AWARDS (1986) *Guidelines for the National Registration of Awards for Advanced Education*, Canberra, Australian Government Publications Service.

COUNCIL FOR NATIONAL ACADEMIC AWARDS (1989) *Handbook*, London, CNAA.

COMMITTEE OF VICE CHANCELLORS AND PRINCIPALS (1986) *Academic Standards in Universities (Reynolds Report)*, London, CVCP.

DEPARTMENT OF EDUCATION AND SCIENCE (1963) *Higher Education (Robbins Report)*, London, HMSO.

DEPARTMENT OF EDUCATION AND SCIENCE (1985) *Academic Validation in the Public Sector Higher Education (Lindop Report)*, London, HMSO.

DEPARTMENT OF EDUCATION AND SCIENCE (1990) *Report of the Review of the Council for National Academic Awards (Bird Report)*, London, DES.

DEPARTMENT OF EDUCATION AND SCIENCE (1991) *Higher Education: A New Framework*, London, HMSO.

HONG KONG GOVERNMENT (1987) *The Report of the Planning Committee on Academic Awards to His Excellency the Governor of Hong Kong*.

PROGRESS REPORT OF THE PROVISIONAL HONG KONG COUNCIL FOR ACADEMIC ACCREDITATION (1989) Hong Kong Government.

HONG KONG COUNCIL FOR ACADEMIC ACCREDITATION BILL (1990) Hong Kong Government.

HONG KONG GOVERNMENT (1989) *A Vision of the Future*, Annual Address by His Excellency the Governor of Hong Kong to the Legislative Council, 11 October 1989.

Allan Sensicle

HONG KONG GOVERNMENT (1990) *Hong Kong 1990*.

HONG KONG COUNCIL FOR ACADEMIC ACCREDITATION (1991) *Handbook 1991–92*, Hong Kong, HKCAA.

UK ENGINEERING PROFESSORS CONFERENCE (1988) *Quality in Engineering Education: Interim Report*.

6   Towards an Indian Accreditation System

Ashoka Chandra

Accreditation of Indian higher technical education is to be entrusted to a statutory National Board of Accreditation. This Board's organizational structure, criteria of accreditation and procedures are described. Its mandatory quality assurance system will be separate from 'recognition', 'approval' and the award of degrees. Accreditation in the general higher education sector will be voluntary, but institutions will be expected to comply. It will be undertaken by an Assessment and Accreditation Council, a new independent body to be established by the University Grants Commission.

Background

As a step towards evolving a new national policy on education, the Government of India brought out in August 1985 a document entitled *Challenge of Education: A Policy Perspective* (Ministry of Education, 1985). This presented a review of the education system, and highlighted its inadequacies and the constraints faced by it; it also offered the perceptions and suggestions of educational planners, teachers, students, parents, intellectuals and citizens interested in education on 'reshaping the education system to enable it to meet the challenges of the future and also to improve its efficiency and quality'. The document was used to trigger a nation-wide debate among different educational and user constituencies. The discussions were carefully recorded and analyzed and the collated views contributed significantly towards evolving the 1986 National Policy on Education.

One major issue which emerged was concern for the quality and standards of higher education, both technical and general. In the early 1980s Indian technical education had witnessed a mushroom growth of institutions, many of which were sub-standard, operating purely on profit considerations with little regard to delivering education according to the prevalent norms and practices. The Indian Parliament debated the issue and it was felt that the All India Council for Technical Education (AICTE), a national body which advises on and supports the development of technical education, should be given statutory authority in order that it might protect and improve standards.

There was also concern about the highly centralized system of general higher education which was considered inimical to experimentation, innovation, motivation and the pursuit of excellence. A report of the University Grants Commission (UGC) (1987) found that colleges were constrained by the 'command and control' style of management of their parent universities, and were finding it difficult to respond adequately to their environment and to maintain a sense of enthusiasm and creativity. These colleges followed courses and systems of instruction and evaluation approved by the universities; deviation was not permitted. The parent university had considerable control over their governance, faculty recruitments, admissions and assessments (Singhal, 1989), leaving the colleges with little autonomy. It was felt that an alternative style of management should be evolved giving autonomy to the colleges and greater authority and status to the working academics; this freedom should be accompanied by a system of accountability, and performance appraisal of institutions, with standards and norms set at the national or state level.

The concern to regulate, protect and improve standards in higher technical education, together with the need to give autonomy to the general higher education institutions, culminated in the formal recognition of the need for development of accreditation systems for each of these two sectors of Indian higher education.

In the field of technical education (which covers engineering technology, management, town planning and architecture, pharmacy and applied arts), the 1986 National Policy on Education stated:

> The All India Council for Technical Education will be vested with statutory authority for planning, formulation and maintenance of norms and standards, accreditation, funding of priority areas, monitoring and evaluation, maintaining parity of certification and awards, and ensuring the coordinated and integrated development of technical and management education. Mandatory periodic evaluation will be carried out by a duly constituted accreditation board. (Ministry of Education, 1986a)

In 1987, Parliament passed the AICTE Act which gave the AICTE powers to:

(i)   lay down norms and standards for courses, curricula, physical and institutional facilities, staff patterns, staff qualifications, quality instructions, assessment and examinations; and

(ii) set up a National Board of Accreditation (NBA) to periodically conduct evaluation of technical institutions or programmes on the basis of guidelines, norms and standards specified by it and to make recommendations ... regarding recognition or de-recognition of the institution or the programme.

Meanwhile for higher general education, the Program of Action for implementing the National Policy on Education argued the case for self-regulation:

Excellence of institutions of higher education is a function of many aspects: self evaluation and self improvement are important among them. If a mechanism is set up which will encourage self assessment in institutions and also assessment and accreditation by an Assessment Council, the quality of process, participation, achievements etc will be constantly monitored and improved. (Ministry of Education, 1986b)

It was proposed that the University Grants Commission should establish an Accreditation and Assessment Council as an independent body to act as a catalyst for maintaining and raising quality. This Council would evolve its own criteria and methodology and would be expected to analyze and evaluate institutions and their performance so as to facilitate self-improvement.

In addition to these two initiatives, mention should be made of other activities related to accreditation. For example, the government Department of Electronics, in association with the AICTE, prepared a concept paper (1990) on the accreditation of computer courses in the private sector. Faced with the problem of shortage of computer personnel at all levels and recognizing that the shortfall could not be made up by the government supported approved institutions, the Department proposed a scheme for encouraging private institutions to produce computer manpower, with accreditation to ensure that these training institutions produced people of the requisite quality.

Similar concerns about the quality of available manpower had led several decades ago to the establishment of a Board of Assessment for examining and recognizing Indian and overseas educational qualifications, with regard to eligibility for government employment. The Board of Assessment continues to perform this important function; whereas its efforts cannot be considered as accreditation in the sense this term has come to be understood, recognition of qualifications by the Board often involves a visit to the institution and assessment of the quality and relevance of the educational programmes.

Industry is also seeing accreditation as an important strategy. Recently, the Manufacturers' Association in Information Technology (MAIT), an apex national body of computer hardware, software, peripherals and training organizations, initiated a scheme to 'empanel' training organizations that meet a set of minimum norms pertaining to experience, infrastructure and facilities for training. Empanelled institutions will be allowed the use of MAIT's distinctive logo and will be required to follow a code of ethics both in promotion and implementation of their operations.

However, it is the two main initiatives to set up accreditation systems for Indian higher technical and higher general education which are described more fully below.

Accreditation in Higher Technical Education

As stated earlier, the 1986 National Policy on Education and the AICTE Act of 1987 envisaged mandatory periodical evaluation of higher technical education by a National Board of Accreditation (NBA) (AICTE, 1990). The concept of accreditation, the roles, responsibilities and composition of the NBA and its policies, procedures and criteria have been a matter of considerable discussion throughout the technical education system. The structures and functioning of the American Accreditation Board for Engineering and Technology and the UK Council for National Academic Awards have contributed significantly to thinking on the NBA, although there are of course differences in the planning and management of technical education in India.

The process of setting up the NBA is not yet complete, nor has actual accreditation activity started; what is described below should be seen more as a declaration of intent and a start on the road to establishing a fully operational accreditation system.

Accreditation has been seen as a process of quality assurance whereby an approved institution or programme is critically appraised at intervals not exceeding six years by a group of external peers. The AICTE has developed highly specific norms for different kinds of programmes and institutions, and has laid down minimum standards for various courses. The NBA will use these norms and standards in its accreditation of courses or programmes leading to the award of a degree or diploma in technical education and offered on a full-time, part-time, sandwich or correspondence basis.

Accreditation does not seek to replace the system whereby degrees are awarded by the parent university or by the State Board of Technical Education. Accreditation is seen as an independent process whereby the quality of an institution or a programme is assessed and assured by the NBA; it is intended to assist prospective students, educational institutions, professional societies, potential employers and government agencies in identifying institutions and their programmes which, apart from meeting the minimum norms and standards prescribed by the AICTE, achieve a certain quality as certified by the NBA. In this sense, accreditation is akin to the grant of a quality mark for the purpose of guiding and protecting the consumer. Accreditation is also expected to provide guidance for the improvement of existing institutions and programmes and for the development of new programmes. In essence, accreditation is expected to stimulate the process of bringing about continual improvement in the system of technical education in the country.

The NBA will also assist the AICTE in reviewing and evolving fresh norms and standards; and on request, it will assist the Council on matters pertaining to approval, recognition, inspection or funding. Accreditation is separate from the process of 'approval' or 'recognition'. The AICTE Act provides that no institution or programme can be established without the prior approval of the AICTE on the need and viability of the proposed institution or programme. Such approval is given by the AICTE after consulting the concerned agencies — the promoters, the state government and affiliating university — and ascertaining that favourable conditions exist for the institution/programme to meet the minimum norms specified by the AICTE. Recognition on the other hand is given by the AICTE for some specific purpose, for example, recognition of programmes making graduates eligible for admission to higher programmes of education, recognition for employment in government or public sector organizations, recognition to practise a profession, and finally recognition of institutions as eligible for financial assistance from the AICTE. While these functions of approval and recognition are separate from accreditation, valuable information may be generated during accreditation which has a bearing on the process of recognition or on evolving norms for the purpose of approval.

An important function of the Board will be to provide feedback to educators and administrators about the need for adjustments and corrections to practices and procedures in the educational process. One expectation is that the Board will constantly monitor the efficacy of its own work and evolve new methods and techniques for evaluating institutions and their programmes. The NBA will establish policies, procedures and guidelines for accreditation, administer the accreditation process, take decisions on accreditation and review decisions in case of appeal. It will also disseminate information on the accreditation process and advise institutions, universities and the State Boards of Technical Education on commendable and innovative practices for the promotion of excellence.

A twenty-seven member Board is envisaged, reflecting the various groups interested in maintaining the standard of technical education. Members will be appointed for three years. Policy-makers, professional societies, industry, research and development establishments, educationists, major segments of technical education and government will all be represented, with very clear guidelines to ensure that all major constituencies are covered.

The Chairperson of the Board will be nominated by the AICTE and shall be an outstanding educationist in this field. Other members will be nominated by the Chairperson from the agreed constituencies, and each shall be a person with a significant record of professional contribution at national or international level. The Executive Director of the Board will be a full-time officer and a member of the Board, with a three-year appointment which may be extended by another term.

Sectoral Committees to consider the reports submitted by the visiting teams will be established, to cover degree and diploma programmes in engineering and technology; architecture, town planning and applied arts and crafts; management; and pharmacy. Other discipline areas may be added as necessary. The Sectoral Committees will comprise experts from educational institutions and the professions, and will be chaired by eminent educationists nominated by the Board.

The NBA Secretariat will need enough staff to administer the accreditation of over 100 institutions and 800 programmes every year. All institutions and programmes approved by the AICTE from which at least two cohorts of students have graduated will be evaluated at regular intervals not exceeding six years. Accreditation of full-time, part-time, sandwich and correspondence programmes will be undertaken independently and separately. The Board will communicate its findings and recommendations to the institution concerned and give reasons for its conclusions; and the Board will publish a list of accredited institutions and programmes together with a short description of the contents of programmes for the information of interested groups. Institutions will be asked to indicate in their publications whether the institution and each of its programmes are accredited, not accredited or awaiting accreditation by the Board.

Accreditation will be a three-stage process. The institution will first be asked to respond to detailed questionnaires, one for the institution as a whole and the other for each individual programme to be assessed. Information will be sought on institutional structure, management, finances and facilities, programmes offered, curriculum content, teaching staff, teaching loads, teaching methods, student numbers and admission criteria, examination system, timetabling, staff development and appraisal schemes, student training and placement schemes, facilities for co-curricular and extracurricular activities, and the mechanisms for self-assessment of the quality of education in the institution.

The questionnaire will also ask the institution to specify its long- and short-range goals and to give a self-appraisal on the extent to which these goals are being achieved along with the major constraints being encountered. The institution will be asked to indicate how the pattern and philosophy of its educational effort have changed during the past five years, and to note major developments or progress achieved, as well as plans for the future.

A separate questionnaire relating to individual programmes will ask about the objectives of each curriculum and research programme; the availability of well qualified faculty and trained supporting staff — technical and non-technical; the adequacy of support services such as laboratory, computer, fabrication and instrumentation facilities; the requirements for each type of programme in terms of credit hours, lectures, tutorial work, laboratories, workshops, etc.; and the division of the curriculum into foundation courses, core courses, professional courses related to specialization, project work and required field experience. Programme information will be requested on the academic profile and achievement of the faculty, and on strategies for developing a professional outlook among the students. This includes student participation and membership in technical and professional societies, exposure to industrial practices and practitioners, opportunities for developing students' understanding of the ethical, social and economic factors involved in the practice of the profession and finally opportunities for faculty-student interaction.

The second step is an on-site visit by a team appointed by the Chairperson of the Sectoral Committee, comprising a chairperson and two experts for each programme to be evaluated of which one should be an educationist and the other from industry, research and development organizations or professional societies. When the institution is to be evaluated along with the programmes, an additional member will be nominated specifically to look at aspects relating to the institution as a whole. The visiting team will verify the written information supplied by the institution and assess factors that cannot be adequately covered by questionnaire such as the institutional philosophy, intellectual environment, opportunity for free enquiry, decision-making process, enthusiasm and dynamism of the faculty and students, the calibre of staff and student body and the quality of work performed by them.

A three-day timetable is contemplated. First the team will meet together for a day to assign specific tasks to each member. On the second day the team will meet the head of institution and team members will spend time with appropriate departments and individuals. In the evening the team will meet to review their findings, exchange notes, discuss weak points and cross-check information. Should any unusual conditions be discovered in a particular department, arrangements can be made for further discussions on the following morning. Recommendations will be drafted during the third day; the entire team will then have a meeting with the head of the institution to summarize the conclusions, discuss the strengths and weaknesses observed and check the factual accuracy of the findings, although the recommendations concerning accreditation will not be disclosed at this stage. By the evening of the last day the team will have finalized the report.

The third stage in the process is an oral presentation of the report to the Sectoral Committee by the Chairperson of the visiting team, leading to specific recommendations from the Sectoral Committee to the NBA. Final action on accreditation rests with the Board, which will inform the AICTE and provide any necessary feedback information regarding the institution and the programmes. If accreditation is given, it is normally for a period of six years unless there are special circumstances such as uncertainty of financial resources, which might result in a shorter accreditation period. Some programmes or institutions will not be granted accreditation and the Board may additionally make recommendations to the AICTE about recognition or de-recognition of the institution/programme(s) for specific purposes. There is provision for appeal and review against a Board decision through the appointment of a special NBA committee which would invite the institution to present its case for review. This committee may visit the institution, if necessary.

Among the criteria for accreditation one of the more important is the institution's commitment to its goals. The institution should not only be able to specify its goals in very clear and specific terms; it should also be able to convince the Board that various conditions necessary for the achievement of its goals have been created and that central administrative systems are operating satisfactorily. The quality of the administration will be judged by its strategies for fostering a climate of mutual support and confidence among the various components of the institution and for creating efficient channels of communication between faculty and administration. Faculty recruitment policies and practices, linkage with industry and professional societies, counselling and guidance to students, and adherence to guidelines for admissions are other aspects to be examined.

Curricular objectives provide another important criterion for accreditation. It is expected that curricula will lay adequate emphasis on developing competence in oral and written communication, an attitude of creativity, the ability to tackle open-ended problems, the competence to examine critically alternative solutions and the appreciation of such factors as safety considerations, reliability, ecology, aesthetics, ethics and social impact.

Faculty and student body provide another two important criteria for evaluation. Strength of faculty has to be adequate to support the full range of institutional activities such as classroom instruction, supervision of laboratory work, conduct of examinations and evaluation, research, student counselling, laboratory development, curriculum planning, development of instructional resource material, institutional development, consultancy, participation in continuing education programs and interaction with professional societies, industry and community. Competence of faculty will be judged on the basis of academic and professional attainments, and performance appraisal systems will draw on peer group assessment and student opinion. As far as the student body is concerned, the standard of admission to programmes, quality performance in the institution and the post-institutional performance of the alumni will provide important indicators.

Some of the distinguishing features of accreditation proposed for the higher technical education system are that it is mandatory, is based on highly specific norms and standards prescribed by the AICTE, and is backed by legal authority to seek information and to visit institutions. The NBA operates within the framework of the AICTE but it is the final decision-making authority on accreditation, and is the only body with the legal power to accredit institutions/programmes in the field of technical education. The cost of accreditation will be borne by the Board, not by the institutions.

Accreditation in General Higher Education

As already indicated, responsibility for establishing an autonomous accreditation body for general higher education lies with the UGC, which has developed proposals for an Accreditation and Assessment Council (UGC, 1987). As with the technical education system, accreditation is seen as a means of self-regulation by the academic profession, involving a process of self-study by the institution followed by an on-site evaluation by a team of professional educators. Accreditation will indicate that, in the judgment of responsible members of the academic community, the institution's own goals are soundly conceived and appropriate, that education plans have been intelligently prepared and are competently conducted, that the institution is accomplishing the majority of its goals substantially and that it will continue to do so in the foreseeable future.

Although the accrediting agency is expected to develop criteria and guidelines for assessing institutional effectiveness, the Accreditation and Assessment Council 'will not enforce any given norms and standards'. Its main function will be catalytic; it will analyze and evaluate institutions and their performance to facilitate self-improvement.

The initial impetus for accreditation assessment will come from the UGC through its selection of a group of about twenty good institutions for initial candidature. Until such time as twenty such institutions are accredited, there will be a provisional Accreditation Association made up of candidate institutions. After twenty institutions are accredited, they will constitute the core of the Accreditation Council and candidate institutions thereafter will have observer status. The Council will be an autonomous, self-governing body which will meet once a year. At this meeting representatives of each institution/association will elect commissioners who will constitute the Accreditation Commission, the body which will take final decisions on accreditation. The Commission will comprise fifteen members serving three-year terms with about one-third of the positions vacated each year. The Accreditation Commission will be served by a Secretariat headed by a Director of Evaluation and a small complement of staff; the Director will be responsible for the codification of the principles, guidelines and methods of functioning of the accreditation agency.

The criteria for accreditation will include institutional mission and objectives, systems for evaluation and planning, organization and governance, nature of programmes and instructional process, faculty, student services, library and learning resources, physical facilities, financial resources and concern for ethical practices. Accreditation will be a voluntary function and the institution seeking accreditation will be responsible for meeting the costs involved.

Ashoka Chandra

Some Distinguishing Features of Accreditation in India

Some significant features of accreditation in India are government involvement, the extent to which accreditation is mandatory, and the use of quantitative as well as qualitative criteria.

Government Involvement

Two models of accreditation are emerging, the National Board of Accreditation in the area of professional education, and the Accreditation and Assessment Council in the field of general education. Both models differ from the USA where accreditation is seen as a non-governmental function and where even indirect involvement or influence of the government (e.g. through linking government grants with accreditation status) is viewed with concern. In India, however, government has traditionally been involved in educational action and reform, so it is not surprising that it has taken a major lead in the promotion and development of accreditation. Nevertheless, conscious of the need to keep accreditation decisions separate from government influence, all substantive action has been deliberately delegated to autonomous national agencies (the AICTE and the UGC) which in their turn propose setting up the National Board of Accreditation and the Accreditation and Assessment Council respectively, each of them independent of the mother agencies. Government will be represented on the NBA, but the assessment process itself will be confined to the visiting group of peers. This limited government involvement is appropriate given the Indian cultural and societal context; indeed, it is expected that the government will actively promote accreditation in technical education through legislation and meeting the costs of accreditation, and in general higher education through linking government support to the accreditation status of institutions or programmes.

Mandatory Accreditation

Sometimes one of the characteristics associated with accreditation is its voluntary character. Institutions may be free to decide whether they wish to seek accreditation and may be able to choose which accreditation agency to use. The voluntary character also means that accreditation relies on the services of volunteers. The staff complement of accrediting agencies is generally small, but thousands of volunteers participate each year in the accreditation process — in self-studies, on accreditation review teams and on committees, boards and Councils. Most volunteers receive no compensation for their services except remuneration for travel expenses; the rest receive token honoraria (Harcleroad, 1963).

In India the accreditation of higher technical education is to be mandatory rather than voluntary. No approved institution of technical education can choose to opt out. The AICTE and the NBA have the authority to demand information from the institutions and the right to visit and inspect; accreditation of both institutions *and* programmes is expected. The NBA can also appraise unapproved institutions if the AICTE requires it to do so. There are no accreditation agencies to choose from. The NBA alone will provide accreditation in the field of technical education. Even where other statutory bodies exist such as the Council of Architecture or the Pharmacy Council with authority for granting licence to practise the profession, the accreditation of institutions and programmes remains within the purview of the AICTE and hence the NBA. The possibility of conflict between the AICTE and other statutory bodies on this matter has been avoided through formally negotiated 'memoranda of understanding' ratified by the respective statutory bodies. Because of the mandatory nature of AICTE accreditation, institutions are not required to pay any fee or costs.

The Indian UGC's Accreditation Council on the other hand has no legal authority to collect information. Accreditation is not mandatory, and theoretically it would be open to institutions not to seek accreditation. The UGC however will 'encourage' accreditation and will exert indirect force by making central grants conditional on accreditation status after the lapse of a certain initial period. Costs are to be borne by the member institutions through membership fees.

Both the mandatory model of technical education and the 'encouraged' accreditation model of general education are different from the voluntary accreditation model of the US. In the context of recent anxieties about standards (especially in technical education), accreditation in India is seen as a policing function to shield students, the public and employers from inappropriate institutions. Since such exploitative possibilities and pressures are greater in technical education where there is high student demand because of the close relationship with employment, the AICTE has had to be particularly determined in its protectionist role. However, with regard to voluntary peer participation, the Indian practice will be like other accreditation agencies. The AICTE and the UGC set up hundreds of committees of various kinds every year and experience little difficulty in getting voluntary participation from the academic as well as professional community.

Criteria

The AICTE has laid down detailed quantitative norms, whereas the UGC does not propose to be so prescriptive. In technical education, where the nature and practice of the profession largely determine the competences, level of skills, and their mix — perhaps as part of a licensing requirement — too large a liberty cannot be taken with educational goals and conditions for their achievement. Consequently, although the visit guidelines may be qualitative, the professional accreditation norms of the AICTE tend to be specific and quantitative. These quantitative norms do have the advantage of being checked unambiguously and objectively, and assessments are therefore seldom challenged. However, they also tend to be applied mechanically and uniformly, and it is difficult to apply quantitative norms in the context of an institution which is engaged in unusual programs or adopting innovative practices: genuine innovation, experimentation and autonomy in setting educational goals may suffer in the process. On the other hand, qualitative norms are liable to be misused or misinterpreted in the hands of unscrupulous institutions or individuals. It will be important to avoid mechanical or uniform application of quantitative norms and to complement these with qualitative guidelines and standards. The AICTE has also emphasized defining norms and standards not in terms of inputs but in terms of educational outputs and competences.

Summary

Accreditation is a relatively new development on the Indian educational scene but one which is being pursued with some vigour both in higher technical education and in higher general education. The two systems agree on the broad accreditation concepts. However, they have developed two separate models somewhat akin to the models of specialized accreditation and institutional accreditation respectively in the USA. The AICTE has prepared detailed plans for establishing a National Board of Accreditation which is expected to be operational very soon. The UGC's efforts towards an Accreditation and Assessment Council are also likely to come to fruition shortly. Both the AICTE and the UGC, which are national statutory agencies with jurisdiction over technical and general education respectively, were set up under the same provision of the Indian constitution which gives the central government responsibility for coordination and maintenance of standards in higher and technical education. Both agencies see accreditation as a major instrument for meeting this responsibility and both are embarking on a learning curve as they establish and operationalize their respective accreditation instruments.

References

ALL INDIA COUNCIL FOR TECHNICAL EDUCATION (1990) *National Board of Accreditation*.
DEPARTMENT OF ELECTRONICS, GOVERNMENT OF INDIA (1990) *Accreditation of Computer Courses in the Private Sector*.

HARCLEROAD, F.F. (1963) *Accreditation: Voluntary Enterprise*, San Francisco, Calif., Jossey Bass.

MINISTRY OF EDUCATION, GOVERNMENT OF INDIA (1985) *Challenge of Education: A Policy Perspective*.

MINISTRY OF EDUCATION, GOVERNMENT OF INDIA (1986a) *National Policy on Education*.

MINISTRY OF EDUCATION, GOVERNMENT OF INDIA (1986b) *Program of Action*.

MINISTRY OF HUMAN RESOURCE DEVELOPMENT, GOVERNMENT OF INDIA (1987) *All India Council for Technical Education Act No. 52*.

SINGHAL, S. (1989) *The Organization and Management of Accreditation System: Some Issues*, New Delhi, Zakir Hussain Centre for Educational Studies, Jawaharlal Nehru University.

UNIVERSITY GRANTS COMMISSION (1987) *Report of the Accreditation and Assessment Council*.

7　The Netherlands:
　　The Inspectorate Perspective

Jan Kalkwijk

The Dutch government is becoming less interventionist in its policy for higher education, and has encouraged the higher education institutions to develop their own quality assurance mechanisms. As a result, the universities have collaborated to introduce an external assessment scheme. This involves regular peer review, by visiting committees of experts who evaluate clusters of related disciplines across the universities. The Inspectorate of Higher Education scrutinizes the process and output of this quality assurance scheme, and the conclusions of its first meta-evaluation are reported here. In Chapter 8 Dr Vroeijenstijn offers the universities' response to some of the points raised by the inspectorate.

Introduction

In the last decade an interesting development with regard to quality assurance (QA) in higher education (HE) has taken place in the Netherlands. Government has fundamentally changed its guiding philosophy with regard to HE. After a long period of direct government interference, the conviction has grown that there was no proper basis for many such interventions. Therefore, government has decided to minimize its role and give the institutions maximum responsibility for their own decisions. The intention is to increase the autonomy of the HE institutions, provided they can demonstrate that education and research meet quality requirements. The principles of this governmental policy were explained in a special paper entitled *Higher Education: Autonomy and Quality* (Ministry of Education and Science, 1985). This has been discussed in parliament and accepted as a basis for legislation (for background information, see Kells and van Vught, 1988; Maassen and van Vught, 1989).

　　Prior to the introduction of this new legislation, government and the HE institutions agreed to set up systems of QA, which take account of the typical features of the university and polytechnic sectors. The universities gave priority to comparative quality assessment of academic disciplines across institutions, using visiting committees of external experts, and resulting in public reports. Initially, the polytechnics concentrated on setting up individual systems of internal quality control for whole institutions, with no public reports. However, in 1989 they decided to adopt procedures similar to the universities. At the time of writing, the experiences of the polytechnics were not yet available on any large scale, so attention here is paid primarily to the developments in the universities.

Agreements between Government and Institutions of HE

In 1986 the Minister of Education and Science (MES) and the HE institutions reached agreement about the establishment of QA systems for the respective sectors of education, confirming that:

1   The HE institutions would set up QA systems that include both internal and periodic external evaluations. The institutions co-operating through their respective intermediate organizations accept responsibility for developing a coordinated and public external quality assessment system, in which all elements of their core tasks, namely teaching, research, and in some cases public services, have to be evaluated.

2   The institutions of HE, coordinated by their respective organizations, would present a rolling evaluation scheme, outlining intended evaluation activities, procedures and criteria, and the way in which the results of evaluations will be used for future evaluations.

3   The QA system should meet requirements of flexibility and consistency, the use of independent visiting committees of peers, systematic data collection, public reporting of the results of evaluation, and the use of protocols concerning the appointment and working procedures of visiting committees.

In principle this aims at improvement and accountability in the core tasks of education, research and public services.

At the same time the agreement confirmed that the MES also has responsibility for the quality of education, which may necessitate additional evaluations by government. The MES takes account of the evaluations carried out under the auspices of the institutions, and in a process of meta-evaluation, evaluates the carefulness with which the institutions carry out their evaluations and how the results are used by the management of the institutions. If deemed necessary, the MES has the power to undertake additional evaluations.

Present Legislation

The meta-evaluation task of government is carried out by the instrument of the MES, the Inspectorate of Higher Education, as laid down in the respective acts on scientific (1986) and higher vocational education (1985).

This is the first time in their existence that the universities have been confronted with inspection of the quality of their activities. They consider it with respect but also with reservation, and in general they question the need for such a strategy. In view of the new government philosophy that there is no need to interfere strongly with the universities, the personnel capacity of the HE inspectorate is small.

The situation for the polytechnics is quite different; they have had an inspectorate for many decades which until recently was very much involved with these institutions. The new government policy means a big reduction in this inspectorate's responsibilities and a considerable re-orientation. As a result of this different history, and because the polytechnics also include teacher training institutes, for which the MES has a specific, constitutional responsibility, the number of inspectors for the polytechnics is still much larger than for the universities.

Future Legislation

The arrangements described above are included in the Higher Education and Research Bill (MES, 1990) which is under discussion in the Dutch Parliament. The Bill contains some clauses dealing specifically with QA in HE, for example:

1 The institution board (i.e. the management board of the educational institution) takes care of regular quality assessment of the activities of the institution, as far as possible in cooperation with other institutions. Independent experts have to be involved, and their findings have to be made public.
2 The MES supervises (through the inspectorate) the execution of the article mentioned above. The MES can also carry out additional evaluations (again through the inspectorate).

These two articles must be considered as a condensation of the earlier agreements about QA between the MES and the institutions. These agreements will remain fully applicable after the acceptance of the Bill, but are subject to modification in the light of experience.

A point of consideration is the power for the MES to intervene. One possibility has already been mentioned, namely the additional evaluation by the MES if the regular evaluation by the institutions does not proceed satisfactorily. Realistically it must be concluded, however, that in countries as small as the Netherlands the practical possibilities of establishing fresh, independent visiting committees, for instance, are limited.

The Bill also gives the MES the power to terminate a discipline in an institution on grounds of quality, when:

> the quality of education or research in a certain discipline (is) considered unsatisfactory over a number of years; or
>
> the system of quality assurance is not in agreement with the relevant legislation.

The addition of the clause 'over a number of years' is fairly important. It implies that the institution will have an opportunity to take adequate measures to improve the situation. Only if the institution fails to bring about this improvement can the MES terminate financing. Up to now the quality aspect has never played a part in such decisions, and these articles are meant to put some pressure on institutions to maintain at least a threshold quality of education.

In one version of the Bill it was indicated that the findings of visiting committees would be published in a register to be controlled by the inspectorate. The idea was to present concise reports on the quality of education and research so as to be more accessible to the public. In this way these evaluation results might help the client (i.e. the future student or employer) to make choices based on the quality of the product. After extensive discussions this was deleted from the Bill, although the idea has not been abandoned. The possibility of publishing such findings in a kind of consumers' guide is currently being examined, with the content of and control over such a publication yet to be decided.

The QA System for Education Developed by the Universities

The institutions have to develop internal and external quality assessment, but have been left free to design their own quality assurance systems on condition that peers are involved in the external assessment procedures. To some extent internal quality assessment already had the attention of the institutions, but in general there was no clear institutional policy. After 1985 a number of institutions adopted a uniform approach to QA; others continued to leave development entirely to each department. This has led to a variety of methods of internal evaluation, although several common features can be noted, for instance, in the recording of student progress, course and curriculum evaluation, programme guidance and the like. Coordination between institutions to develop common systems is rare.

The respective coordinating organizations of the universities and polytechnics, VSNU and HBO-Raad, have concentrated on developing an external QA system for education. For research (only applicable to the universities) the government had already made a start some years earlier (see below). Education therefore had highest priority. VSNU and HBO-Raad followed different paths: the VSNU chose a system in which clusters of related disciplines had to be evaluated by independent experts (peers); the HBO-Raad chose to develop a QA system for whole institutions. After a test period the cluster approach was deemed more satisfactory, leading to a reconsideration, and the HBO-Raad has now more or less adopted the VSNU approach; the polytechnics are therefore lagging behind a little, with their first public reports issued during 1991.

Vroeijenstijn describes the VSNU system in some detail (see Chapter 8; see also Vroeijenstijn, 1989, 1990). The most significant element is that the whole range of disciplines taught at the universities is reviewed nation-wide by independent experts (peer review) every five or six years. Each discipline is reviewed by the same 'visiting committee'. Such a visiting committee has about seven members and includes professional experts from society as well as academics. Each visit takes up two days, and during that time discussions can be held with faculty, staff and students. The findings of the visiting committee are reported in a public document. Members of visiting committees do not get a salary. The other costs of the visits are carried by the VSNU, which takes care of all administrative procedures including the secretarial support for the committees.

To facilitate the work of the visiting committee, the discipline has to prepare a self-study or self-evaluation. Together with the regular information normally issued to the students, this is the most important background source for the visiting committee. The self-study itself is a public document.

The VSNU *Guide to External Quality Assessment* (1989) sets out its procedures in detail, and includes directives for departments about aspects to be dealt with in the self-study. Here the most important points to be considered are the objectives of the discipline, the linkage with secondary education, the arrangements for the first year selection phase (Dutch universities are not allowed to carry out selection on entrance), the doctoral programme, the efficiency and real duration of study, faculty and staff available, teaching and laboratory facilities, and the internal quality system. The visiting committee is expected to analyze critically the self-study with regard to the points mentioned above, but they are free to discuss other items if they consider this appropriate. There is no specific format required for the report of the visiting committee.

The process of external evaluation started in 1988 with a confidential trial. This resulted in a public report, but the individual locations could not be identified, and the report was discussed with the MES and the inspectorate. The first official round was in 1989 with reports of the visiting committees published in 1990, giving the inspectorate the opportunity to fulfil its function of meta-evaluator.

For reasons of efficiency it was necessary to cluster related disciplines. To give some idea of these clusters, the visiting scheme for 1989 is given as an example (the numbers in brackets refer to the number of separate cases):

geography: social geography (4), physical geography (3), pre- and proto-history (3), and demography (1);

mathematics and computer science: mathematics (9), computer science (9), and technical mechanics (1);

languages: comparative linguistic sciences (2), Slavic linguistics and literature (2), Russian linguistics (1), Semitic linguistics and cultures (10), Indian and Iranian linguistics and cultures (2), Indonesian linguistics and cultures (1), Chinese linguistics and culture (1), Japanese and Korean linguistics and culture (1), African linguistics, and Finoegric linguistics and literature (1);

industrial design and aerospace engineering: industrial design and aerospace engineering.

Public reports of these four clusters are available, together with five further reports from the 1990 phase of visits.

The QA System for Research

The agreement on QA also applies to research (at the universities). The QA system for research developed quite independently and differently from the one for teaching, and started somewhat earlier. In 1983–85 the MES initiated a system of conditional financing of research, with the aim of supporting only research of sufficient quality. The universities were invited to submit proposals for research with a minimum of five full-time equivalent faculty members per year. After approval by peers, the MES guaranteed financing for a period of five years, after which the quality of the programme was to be re-assessed leading to budget reallocations. Under the new non-interventionist philosophy, the coordination of this assessment has been transferred from government to the VSNU, that is to the universities themselves who are expected to take adequate measures if a programme gets a negative judgment.

During 1988–90, 1100 programmes were assessed, of which only 6 per cent received a negative judgment. For this exercise the VSNU involved the Royal Academy of Science, the National Council for Agricultural Research and the Royal Institution of Engineers. The peers who carried out the assessments remained unknown to the universities.

A thorough evaluation of this system of conditional financing is not yet available, nor has the inspectorate carried out its meta-evaluation, but some conclusions can already be drawn, viz:

1 Scientific production in the form of papers in professional journals and congress contributions has significantly increased.
2 To some extent it appeared possible to identify research of unacceptable quality, and the impression is that universities connect serious consequences to negative judgments, varying from complete termination to modification. A complete picture, however, is not yet available.
3 The evaluation procedure did not attempt to identify research of excellent quality. So the results cannot be used as the basis for research policy.
4 The evaluation procedures appeared to be complicated and very time-consuming. The universities are looking for methods to reduce the external efforts, for instance by strengthening the role of the internal quality system.
5 The formulation of many relatively small research programmes with subsequent re-approval after five years appears to have promoted rigidity in budget allocation.
6 The separate evaluation of teaching and research activities is considered redundant in view of the specific tasks of the universities, namely teaching and research. Combination with the external quality assessment system for education should be considered.

Some of the points touched upon above are treated in a recent VSNU publication (1990).

Meta-Evaluation

The Inspectorate of Higher Education has to assess the carefulness with which the entire QA system is set up by the institutions, and proposed a scheme whereby it considers the reports of the visiting committees (Bresters and Kalkwijk, 1990). This scheme takes account of the agreement between the MES and the institutions, described earlier, and has added two other principles:

the QA system should be transparent, which means that the criteria used to assess the performance of any activity of an institution should be clear;

the system should contain some follow-up, that is, the institutions involved have to make clear in what way they will react to the findings of the assessments.

In addition, the inspectorate has formulated terms of reference whereby its scrutiny of the VSNU external evaluations should review the content of the evaluations (curricula and teaching, research, and public services), the evaluation procedures (the evaluators, sources of information, procedures and instruments, periodicity of evaluation), and the conclusions and recommendations of the visiting committees.

For each of these areas, the inspectorate suggests a number of issues which should be considered by the VSNU teams. For instance, with respect to curricula and teaching, the following questions apply:

> Have the objectives of the educational programme been defined? Are they relevant and valid with respect to the objectives of the institution, the labour market, related disciplines on the national and international level?

> Is the content of the curriculum in agreement with the objectives mentioned above?

> How is the teaching process assessed? Is it adequate in view of the objectives and the curriculum?

> What is the relation between input and output in terms of numbers of students and the levels attained by them?

> What is the quality of the personnel, of the other facilities such as libraries and laboratories, of the management, etc.?

For the evaluators it is required that they are independent, have a sound knowledge of the educational system, are authoritative experts of the disciplines to be reviewed and have some insight into the labour market for the graduates, and that one of them should be a foreigner.

These requirements overlap considerably with the VSNU *Guide* and are used by the inspectorate as a check on the coverage by VSNU teams. The inspectorate scheme has been applied to the 1989 reports of the visiting committees, and the 1990 reports are under review. To carry out this evaluation of the evaluations (the meta-evaluation), all written information in the form of study guides, self-studies, etc. is made available to the inspectorate, but additional visits to the institutions are not paid. In this respect the inspectorate tries to maintain its reticent position. The first meta-evaluation (Inspectorate of Higher Education, 1990) yielded some important conclusions which are discussed below.

Discussion and Conclusions

1   At the request of the MES, the HE institutions have accepted responsibility for ensuring the quality of education by the introduction of QA systems in HE. An essential element is the use of independent professional experts, who are able to give judgments about the quality of teaching and research. In particular for the universities

this has meant a drastic rupture with the past when academic quality was taken for granted. The polytechnics were already accustomed to some kind of supervision by means of an inspectorate.

2   HE has the 'ownership' of the QA systems to be developed. Without any doubt this has promoted the acceptance of the systems by the institutions (in particular the universities), which in general fear the interference of the MES. The latter can be understood, in the light of several retrenchment operations in HE during the 1980s, even though such actions were not based on judgments about quality. The issue of ownership by HE is a point of discussion elsewhere (*THES*, 1991).

3   The policy of the MES with regard to QA in HE has generally induced a positive reaction. More and more the conviction is growing that QA is an important issue. Many institutions have succeeded in formulating a general policy for internal QA in the sense that their departments are obliged to obey a minimum set of conditions in this respect. Although detailed insight is not yet available, institutions seem to be developing a useful evaluation culture.

4   The mere visit of a body of outside experts evaluating the performance of an institution often generates an internal debate on the quality of education. The product of this debate, the self-study or self-evaluation, is sometimes very honest and critical. The opposite also sometimes holds: in some cases the self-study resembles a public relations document, which does not help the task of the visiting committee.

5   Although the schedule of operations of all visiting committees is the same and editing is in the same hands (VSNU), the way of reporting is rather different. The VSNU seems reluctant to prescribe a uniform format for reports, perhaps ignoring the fact that generally the professional experts are not professional evaluators.

6   For the first time in history (sometimes abundant) information about the quality of education (and research) in HE has become available. The self-studies and visiting reports are made public, but this does not mean that they are easily accessible to the public. Their content is very diverse, but — more serious — they are so voluminous that extensive distribution is impossible. The possible introduction of a register containing concise quality reports for the disciplines examined may offer a solution to this.

7   Most visiting committees have so far failed to formulate their own terms of reference with respect to the contents of the discipline. Thus the basis of certain statements is often not clear. It might be argued that this is not necessary and that it is the privilege of the peers to assume that their opinion is authoritative and therefore decisive. On the other hand in this way academic discussion is

avoided in the visiting report, and this is against the tradition of a university. It does not matter whether or not consensus is reached in a visiting committee. It is far better to show the discussion than to 'forget to present' it. At least the next visiting committee (operating five to six years later) needs a starting point. If it is not acquainted with the terms of reference of the previous committee, its task is significantly hindered.

8   The visiting committees demonstrate a reluctance to give hard critical statements, and if they do, an unknown multiplier has to be applied. The question arises whether committee members are too much involved in the national network of their own discipline in a small country as the Netherlands. In other words, the members may be formally independent but in practice their contacts and interests can be so intertwined that some judgments may be biased.

9   So far the reports of the visiting committees aim primarily at the improvement function of the QA system. The accountability function is not yet well developed, and it is difficult for the reader to get a clear view of the quality of education in a specific discipline at a specific location. This aspect needs to receive more attention in the future.

10   The existence of separate QA systems for education and research can be questioned. There are good reasons to merge them, arising from the relationship between research and education in the universities. For instance, a condition for good teaching staff is that they also execute good research; if they do not, a question should be raised about the quality of education as well. Furthermore, the post-doctoral programmes are research oriented: to consider their quality without taking account of the quality of the research involved is meaningless. Finally, the experts on the visiting committees are also capable of evaluating research quality as they generally have a research background. On the other hand, the status of teaching at the universities is often much lower than that for research. Teaching is often regarded as a chore by university staff, as was recently reported by one visiting committee. To put sufficient emphasis on teaching, it may be wiser to maintain separate QA systems for education and research for the time being. The present policy of the MES is to continue with these in view of their recent start, although the VSNU is proposing some pilot projects for joint education and research evaluation (VSNU, 1990).

References

BRESTERS, D.W. and KALKWIJK, J.P. TH. (1990) 'The Role of the Inspectorate of Higher Education', in *Peer Review and Performance Indicators* (*Quality Assessment in British and Dutch Higher Education*), pp. 59–70, Utrecht, Lemma BV.

INSPECTORATE OF HIGHER EDUCATION (1990) *External Quality Assurance in Scientific Education 1989* (in Dutch).

KELLS, H.R. and VAN VUGHT, F.A. (Eds) (1988) *Self-regulation, Self-study and Program Review in Higher Education*, Culemborg, Lemma BV.

MAASSEN, P.A.M. and VAN VUGHT, F.A. (Eds) (1989) *Dutch Higher Education in Transition*, Culemborg, Lemma BV.

MINISTRY OF EDUCATION AND SCIENCE (1985) *Higher Education: Autonomy and Quality*, Policy paper to the Second Chamber of Representatives (in Dutch).

MINISTRY OF EDUCATION AND SCIENCE (1988, modified in 1990) *Higher Education and Research Bill* (in Dutch).

THES (1991) 'The Quality Agenda' [Editorial] *The Times Higher Education Supplement*, January.

VROEIJENSTIJN, A.I. (1989) *Autonomy and Assurance of Quality: Two Sides of One Coin*, Proceedings of International Conference on Assessing Quality in Higher Education, Knoxville, University of Tennessee.

VROEIJENSTIJN, A.I. (1990) *Self-regulation Based on Self-Assessment and Peer Review*, Proceedings of Twelfth Annual European AIR Forum.

VSNU (1989) *Guide to External Quality Assessment*, Utrecht (in Dutch).

VSNU (1990) *Research Policy Paper*, Utrecht (in Dutch).

8 External Quality Assessment, Servant of Two Masters? The Netherlands University Perspective

Ton Vroeijenstijn

This chapter considers the differing expectations of external quality assessment (EQA) in the Netherlands. The system of EQA at the Dutch universities involves peer review by visiting committees followed by a meta-evaluation by the inspectorate (see Chapter 7). It is suggested that the government and the inspectorate are expecting too much from the work of external experts and the reports they publish. Visiting committees cannot serve two masters. Assurance of quality is more important than the exact measurement of it.

Introduction

Opinions about the way external quality assessment (EQA) in the Netherlands is developing differ. Since 1988, Dutch universities have become acquainted with a new phenomenon: committees of external experts visit faculties, reviewing degree programmes in a discipline. Thus far nineteen committees have reviewed seventy-seven degree programmes (about 50 per cent of all degree programmes at Dutch universities), involving 118 faculties. Nine reports have been published; another four are in preparation.

How is one to judge these developments? For an outsider it is not easy. The Association of the Universities in the Netherlands (VSNU), which is in charge of the development, organization and coordination of the EQA system, believes it is developing satisfactorily (Vroeijenstijn, 1990). But the Ministry of Education and Science (MES) and the Inspectorate for Higher Education have a good many question-marks about it (Paardekooper and Spee, 1990; Spee, 1990; Inspectie, 1990; Kalkwijk, 1991). The government seeks a more precise definition of quality and stresses the need to clarify criteria and standards and to use more performance indicators. The universities emphasize the role of peers and dialogue with the faculty.

How can we explain those diverging views? For a sensible answer, we first have to ask why quality assessment is carried out and to consider the relationship between autonomy and quality assessment.

Why External Quality Assessment?

The 1960s were the time of equality, the 1980s and 1990s are the era of quality. Quality stands at the centre of interest in all sectors of society, including education. All the parties concerned have an interest in quality — government, employers, students and the universities — but not everyone has the same ideas about it. We need only to look at the different suffixes used, for example, quality assessment, quality review, quality control, quality measurement, quality improvement.

There are different motives for quality assessment. A threshold quality may be required before a programme or an institution can be accredited. In other cases the comparative quality of different programmes (for ranking) is sought, for example, because the government may want to know where to allocate the money or when reallocation is necessary. Quality assessment can also be used to discover weak and strong spots and, in doing so, to improve the education offered.

Government is interested in EQA, because it has a constitutional obligation to assure the quality of education, and because it is called to account to Parliament for the money spent on higher education. Government also wants to find out how far its own aims are being realized, for example, in moving towards mass higher education, or as regards the role of universities in technological developments, or in increasing the participation rate for women.

For the government, EQA means collecting as much objective information as possible with regard to the state-of-the-art of higher education institutions and their quality, and the minister strives for a set of performance indicators on which to base decisions. Behind this view of EQA lie three presuppositions, namely that quality can be defined; that performance indicators have a relation with quality; and that quality can be quantified and objectified. We will return to this subject later.

Looking at governmental policy papers, we find they use the terms 'quality control' and 'quality measurement'. Control and measurement are summative in nature and convey the idea of punishment or reward. 'Quality control is inherently punitive, imposing sanctions for inadequacy, but at the same time it implies that once a minimum acceptable level has been reached no further effort for improvement is needed' (Lynton, 1988).

The government is interested in demonstrating to the public at large and Parliament in particular that it is in control and makes justifiable decisions with regard to the allocation of money, termination of programmes, etc. So government's problem is how to 'prove' that the right decisions are being made wherever changes in the boundary conditions might affect quality. If those effects could be measured and compared, such a 'proof' comes into view. Performance indicators are thus regarded as very helpful in assessing the outcome of governmental and institutional policies (Vroeijenstijn and Acherman, 1990).

The universities' concerns are whether it is possible to offer high quality education within the conditions set by the government (especially following some severe budget cuts and a government-imposed maximum length of programmes of four years), and how to convince the public that the faculties are providing the best quality possible under the circumstances. The goal is quality improvement where possible, and the main question is how to ensure that teaching is adapted to changing boundary conditions. To quote Henry Minzberg (1983): 'Change in the professional bureaucracy (like universities) does not sweep in from new administrators taking office to announce major reforms, nor from government technostructures intent on bringing the professionals under their control. Rather, change seeps in by the slow process of changing the professionals....' So the question is how to change the attitude of professionals with regard to their contribution to a particular educational programme. In other words, to whom will they listen? The obvious answer is that they are willing to listen to their peers, and the basic answer to programme improvement is peer review, rather than 'control' by administrators, inspectors or the like.

Figure 1 summarizes the views of government and the universities. Facing the summative approach of EQA from the government side stands the more formative approach of the VSNU. Here the starting-point is that EQA especially aims at quality improvement. This opinion finds support in the literature about EQA (Cook, 1989; Kells and van Vught, 1988). The most important function is an analysis of strengths and weaknesses and the formulation of recommendations for improvement; the most important instrument for this is the peer review. The universities also emphasize the accountability function of EQA, and believe that the outcome of EQA should play a role in the process of self-regulation and internal steering and quality assurance.

Comment on EQA

The discussion of EQA is dominated by the following notions: quality, criteria and standards, performance indicators and peer review. The MES view is that quality should be defined plainly, criteria and standards should be formulated clearly, and that performance indicators should be used more. Each of these comments is considered below.

Figure 1.   Views of the Government and Universities on EQA

Nature of EQA	Government Summative	Universities Formative
Aims	* accountability to Parliament * steering/planning of HE: are the aims of the government with regard to HE reached? * constitutional 'assurance of quality' * information for students and employers	* quality improvement * accountability * self-regulation * quality assurance
Instruments	* inspectorate * performance indicators	* self-assessment * peer review

Quality Should Be Defined Plainly

One of the Dutch student unions has commented that a system of EQA can only start when quality is defined clearly (LSVB, 1990). The inspectorate claims that the reports of the visiting committees do not give 'a clear view of the quality of education in a specific discipline at a specific location' (Kalkwijk, 1991). The Higher Education and Research Plan 90 (Ministerie van O&W, 1989) describes one of the tasks of the inspectorate as 'the development and maintenance of a good system for standardization and measurement of quality' (Bresters and Kalkwijk, 1990). Such remarks imply that it is possible to define quality. But quality is like love. Everybody talks about it and everybody knows about what (s)he is talking about. Everybody knows and feels when there is love. Everybody recognizes it. But when we try to give a definition of it, we are standing with empty hands. In the literature we find several descriptions of the concept of quality. 'Quality is determined by the degree to which the previously set objectives are met' (de Groot, 1983). Sometimes quality is defined as 'fitness for purpose' (Ball, 1985). Quality is also defined in terms of added value (McClain *et al.*, 1989). Another often used description is 'Something has quality when it meets the expectations of the consumer/user; quality is the satisfaction of the client.'

Talking about a concrete product we want to buy, for example a computer, it is easy to define quality: it has to do with what we expect it will do. There will be no misunderstanding. But talking about education, we have trouble. Who is the client? Who is the consumer? The government, talking about quality, looks first to the pass/fail ratio, the dropouts and enrolment time. Employers, talking about quality, will refer to the knowledge, skills and attitudes obtained during the period of study: the 'product' that is tested is the graduate. Quality of education has a totally different meaning in the eyes of the students. For them, quality is connected with the contribution

Figure 2.   Aspects of Quality and Stakeholders

Stakeholder Aspect of quality	Students	Employers	Government	University
Input (for example):				
* student intake			*	*
* selection	*		*	*
* budget	*		*	*
* academic staff	*			*
Process (for example):				
* aims/goals	*		*	*
* educational process	*			*
* educational organization	*			*
* content	*			*
* counselling	*			*
Output (for example):				
* pass/fail rate	*		*	*
* the graduate	*	*	*	*

to individual development and preparation for a position in society. Education must link up with the personal interest of the student. But the educational process also has to be organized in such a way that (s)he can finish the course in the given time.

We must conclude that quality is a very complex concept (see Figure 2). We cannot speak of 'the quality'; we have to speak about *qualities*. We must make a distinction between the quality requirements set by the student, the university discipline, by the labour market/society and by government. But there are not only different qualities; we must also consider different aspects of quality. So there is quality of input, process quality and quality of output. Quality assessment must take account of all these dimensions. It is a waste of time to try to define quality precisely, and the ultimate supplier (the faculty) must make allowances for the different wishes and requirements of all its clients. Sometimes the expectations will run parallel, but they can conflict.

Criteria and Standards Should Be Formulated Clearly

If one looks at what is said about quality, it will be equally obvious that it is impossible to identify one set of criteria for quality in higher education. The parties concerned will have their own criteria and norms derived from their own objectives and/or demands. This means that government will formulate different criteria than, for example, employers. And the criteria will differ from discipline to discipline. The expectations of the labour market will play a totally different role in assessing philosophy or assessing electrical engineering.

The criteria from different partners may actually be in conflict. Government can put forward as one of its criteria: 'the program must be organized in such a way that students can finish the program with a minimum of dropout and in the given time'; or 'the success ratio of the first year should be 70 per cent.' But this criterion may clash with a student criterion that 'the program should give enough options and enough time for personal development.'

Criteria can also be mutually conflicting: is it possible to deliver graduates in four years with the expected academic standards? For example, in engineering, students, employers and the academic world say that it is not possible to complete the study in less than five years, but government has set as a criterion that it must be done in four years.

We can conclude that we have no scale at our disposal to measure the quality of education and that standards and criteria are a matter of bargaining between the parties concerned. An absolute value for the academic level or the quality of graduates does not exist. It is a matter of communis opinio: what is generally accepted as good quality.

Performance Indicators Should Be More Used in EQA

There already exists much literature on the concept of performance indicators (Ball and Halwachi, 1987; Cave *et al.*, 1988; Segers *et al.*, 1989; Goedegebuure *et al.*, 1990; Dochy *et al.*, 1990; Sizer, 1990; Kells, 1990; Spee and Bormans, 1991). There are two opposing parties: government strongly emphasizes their importance and is optimistic about the possibility of determining the right indicators. In general, institutions of higher education are very reserved and sceptical about them.

We can make a distinction between quantitative and qualitative performance indicators. The former are often simply basic data, concerning numbers of students, numbers of staff, dropout, student-staff ratio. They tell us nothing about quality or performance. One faculty has a pass rate of 80 per cent, another 60 per cent: does this say something about the performance of the faculty? The quality of education? Is the performance of university Y with a pass ratio of 80 per cent superior to the achievement of university X with a ratio of 60 per cent? Or has university Y lowered its level? Or is university X more selective in the first year? These performance indicators do not give answers but do raise questions.

The so-called qualitative performance indicators can be seen as elements to be taken into account when looking at the quality. In their research report for the MES, Segers *et al.* (1989) suggested performance indicators for quality assessment, which parallel closely the VSNU checklist for the assessment of faculties (see Annex). Although the term 'performance indicator' will not be found in the *Guide to External Program Review* (VSNU, 1990), faculties are expected to describe these aspects in their self-assessment and they are used as the basis for discussions with the visiting committees.

It will be clear that these performance indicators can never speak for themselves, but must be interpreted by experts. Where they seem to be object-ive, they are not really performance indicators, but only statistical data or management information. Ideally, this concept should be set aside, and we should simply seek agreement on which data can be used for assessment and which aspects of quality should be inspected.

External Quality Assessment and Institutional Autonomy

The idea of summative EQA fitted like a glove in a centrally steered higher education system and at a time when government was considered capable of directing higher education developments by detailed regulations. In 1985 a new era began with the publication of the MES policy document, *Higher Education: Autonomy and Quality* (Ministerie van O&W, 1985). Much has already been published about the contents and the consequences of this docu-ment (see, for example, van Vught, 1988, 1989). Maassen and van Vught (1989), give the following analysis:

> In [this] policy document the minister presented a new governmental strategy towards higher education. The new attitude indicates an important break with the traditional governmental strategy, which was a strategy of detailed planning and control. In the years before 1985 government tried to steer the higher education system with stringent regulations and extensive control mechanisms. Government saw itself as an omnipotent actor who thought to be able to guide the higher education system according to its own objectives. The new strategy appears to be an important change. By strengthening the autonomy of the higher education institutions, government claims to create fruitful conditions for the enlargement of the adaptive power and flexibility of higher education institutions to respond to the needs of society. By strengthening the institutional autonomy government also claims to stimulate the levels of quality and differentiation of the higher education system. The new governmental strategy is based on the idea that the increase of institutional autonomy will result in an improvement of quality of the higher education system.

The question arises whether this autonomy is real, fake or limited. The universities were promised autonomy and self-regulation, but at the same time government has set bounds to this freedom: 'Certain forms of behaviour by the institutions cannot be allowed' (Maassen and van Vught, 1989). Government has its own goals for higher education and still wishes to steer its development. Instead of handing responsibility to the universities and stepping back, government has an attitude of 'remote control'. Instead of being autonomous, the Dutch university is in imminent danger of becoming a puppet on a string.

This ambiguous attitude is also expressed in the approach to EQA. Are the faculties right, saying that it was a smart move of the Minister of Education and Science to force the universities to set up a system of EQA, having in that way a cheap inspectorate? Or is the autonomy real, that is to say self-regulation of the higher education system instead of state regulation? EQA and autonomy are two sides of one coin: in return for 'home rule', the universities must be accountable for the quality they deliver. They must show society (Parliament and government) that they take quality seriously. But it also means that the government has to trust the universities. In a good dialogue the government can make explicit its aims for the higher education system. In that case the universities are not the annexes of the ministry but equal partners, not colonies but members of the commonwealth.

Daily practice sometimes contradicts the new doctrine which is still not formalized in legislation. The government (and the Ministry of Education and Science) wish to be as close as possible to the universities and to keep their finger on the pulse. It is not easy to loosen the grip and to have confidence that the universities can cope with more freedom.

EQA at the Dutch Universities

Dutch universities have accepted the challenge of the new philosophy and in 1986 introduced a system of quality assessment for the universities (Stuurgroep HOAK, 1986; Vroeijenstijn, 1989). By the end of 1991 seventy-seven degree programmes had been reviewed, which is about half of all degree programmes in the Netherlands (see Figure 3).

Characteristics

The system of external quality assessment as it takes shape little by little in the Netherlands has the following characteristics:

> it is based on faculty self-assessment and visiting committees of external experts;
>
> it is discipline (or programme) oriented. For example, the review of geography includes social geography, physical geography, urban planning, demography and pre- and protohistory;

Figure 3.   Disciplines Reviewed in 1988/91

Year	Discipline	Faculties
1988 (trial)	history	7
	physics and astronomy	9
	mechanical engineering	3
	psychology	7
1989	geography	7
	mathematics and information technology	10
	non-Western languages	6
	industrial design	1
	aerospace engineering	1
1990	biology	7
	law	9
	economics	7
	philosophy	9
	electrical engineering	3
1991	medicine	10
	Western languages	6
	political sciences and public administration	7
	theology	6
	geology	3

initially it is concentrating on teaching; it is anticipated that in the future research and service will be included;

it is nation-wide: all faculties with programmes in the field are visited by the same visiting committee;

it is cyclical: after a cycle of five years it starts again with the first discipline;

it covers the whole university system: in five years all university degree programmes will be assessed;

it is public: the visiting committee submits a report to the VSNU, who make the report public.

These characteristics of Dutch EQA meet most of the requirements of Cook (1989) and Kells (Kells and van Vught, 1988): the system is institution-based, rather than government-based; external and internal evaluation are complementary; self-evaluation is the cornerstone of the system; and the assessment of quality takes as its starting point the goals and objectives formulated by the faculty. However, the Dutch system differs in two respects: quality assessment of education and of research is still done separately; and the results of the studies and the visits are not confidential, because one of its functions is public accountability.

Ton Vroeijenstijn

Functions

For the Dutch universities the aims of quality assessment are:

1 to contribute to *quality improvement*. Quality assessment first and foremost aims to discover weaknesses and to enhance and improve quality. In the first place this is done through critical self-assessment by the faculty or institution. Peer review is an additional instrument for internal quality assurance, because problems can be discussed with external experts. Based on discussion and interviews, the visiting committee formulate recommendations for improvement.

2 *self-regulation* based on quality. Up till now, governments often sought to steer higher education by detailed interference and state regulations. The new philosophy of greater autonomy, now evident in several countries, means that the universities themselves ask whether their goals and aims are realized and whether the process for realization of goals and aims is under control. This self-regulation should increasingly take the place of state regulation.

   Self-regulation must be based on a good system of quality assessment and quality assurance. It is in the first place the faculty who have to make decisions about their 'mission' and the possibility of achieving it. The outcome of self-assessment and the recommendations of peers should be discussed by the faculty. But the faculty cannot do the job on its own. The university itself should be involved through negotiation with the faculty concerned, based on the results of the past quality assessment.

3 *accountability* to the public. Quality assessment is not only to guarantee quality but also to provide accountability to society. The committees of external experts study the self-assessment of the faculty and hold discussions with staff and students. In their public reports, the committee give their account of the faculty's goals, its capacity for realizing them, and of the system of internal quality assurance.

The Self-assessment

External quality assessment is never an end in itself, but rather an extension of internal quality control. The hinge linking external and internal quality assessment is the self-assessment study. This is an internal evaluation carried out in the faculty prior to the visit by the external specialists. The self-study report is intended to stimulate internal quality management; to prepare internally for the visit; and to provide basic information for the visiting committee.

   The layout and content of the self-study report are related to the task of the visiting committee which is to form an opinion about the programme in terms of the content, educational process, organization and management of the programme, and is graduates. The chapters of the self-study report broadly correspond with these areas of attention (see Annex for the VSNU detailed *Checklist for the Self-study*).

In dealing with the individual points, a description is not enough; there must also be analysis, and the faculty/discipline's position on the question must be stated. This offers an opportunity to go more deeply into strong points and areas of concern. Finally, after the description and analysis, strategies for dealing with any shortcomings must be indicated.

From 1988–90 about eighty self-study reports were submitted and about thirty of these (in mathematics, information technology, geography, industrial design and aerospace engineering) have been reviewed to see whether they fulfil expectations. Are they analytical and critical and likely to lead to action by the faculty? Or are they simply an expression of strategic behaviour and a public relations document?

The review of these thirty self-studies suggests that only 10 per cent show a self-assessment approach. The majority are very descriptive; self-reflection is weak or sometimes missing, and many of the reports create the impression that they were only written for the visiting committee. Not all self-studies have clarified the problems the faculty has had to deal with. In general, the faculty has followed the VSNU checklist and has tried to answer the questions for the visiting committee, but few have asked the basic questions necessary for a good self-assessment, namely:

What are our goals, aims and objectives? Are they clearly stated? Are they useful? Why do we do what we are doing? Does consensus exist on the interpretation of the goals, aims and objectives?

Is the programme designed in view of the realization of the goals? Is the programme functioning well? Are there any problems? Do we control the input, the process and the output?

Are the constraints for realization of the goals satisfactory?

Are the goals realized? How can we collect data systematically? What is the meaning of those performance indicators? (Kells, 1988; Maassen, 1989).

Although it is possible that a defensive attitude can account for the strong descriptive character of the early reports, it seems more likely that it is caused by inexperience with self-assessment.

The self-study is a very important source of information for the visiting committee. Most committees said the self-studies were very useful and were a good starting-point for the interviews, but many complained that quantitative data frequently used different definitions for the calculation of success ratios.

It is too early to speak of real self-assessment. But realizing a good self-evaluation is also a process of learning by doing. Comparing the self-studies of 1989 with those of 1990, we already see an improvement. Starting without a real tradition of self-assessment, we should not expect too much. Rome was not built in a day.

The Visiting Committee

It is very important that the whole discipline has confidence in the visiting committee. The faculty deans, meeting in the Disciplinary Board of the VSNU, nominate outstanding experts using agreed criteria. Each committee has about seven members to allow for division of the work and to cover for any temporary absence. In the choice of experts, every effort is made to cover the specializations within a discipline as fully as possible. This is particularly true if a number of (sub)disciplines are combined. The experts are drawn from universities, potential employers and, insofar as they exist, professional organizations. A balance between those who have retired and those who are still working is sought. The presence on the committee of someone with knowledge of educational processes is also important. It is further assumed that there will be at least one foreign expert on the committee. The secretariat of the visiting committee is provided by the VSNU office.

The distribution between 'potential employers' and the academic world has presented no problems. Big industries like Philips and Shell are very willing to take part in the committees. Up to now it has not been difficult to find (Dutch-speaking) experts from abroad, and the distribution of the foreign experts is as follows: Belgium (19); USA (5); Germany (4); United Kingdom (5); Austria (1); Switzerland (1). In four cases a foreign expert was chairman of the committee. Figure 4 shows the distribution of different categories from 1988 to 1991.

Terms of Reference

The tasks of the visiting committee are:

1 to form an opinion on the basis of information supplied by the faculty and by means of discussions held on the spot about the standard of education, the quality of the educational process, organization, and the standard of the graduates; and
2 to make suggestions on quality improvement.

The phrase 'form an opinion' should not be interpreted as 'sitting in judgment' and handing out a sentence in terms of 'good' or 'bad'. Nor is it a

Figure 4.   Origin of Visiting Committee Members, 1988/91

Dutch retired professors	43
From a Dutch university	21
Potential employers/professional organizations	36
Foreign experts	35
Educationalists	13
Total	148

matter of approval of an educational programme; the committee is not directed towards accreditation or programme recognition. The aim of the visit is rather to discuss with the faculty the points of strength and of weakness indicated in the self-study. The committee can, as a group of expert outsiders, hold up a mirror to the faculty. The fact that the committee does not pass sentence is not to say that it cannot make critical comments. What is needed is criticism which is fair without being judgmental.

The starting-point for the committee must be the objectives which the faculty has set for itself. Here it is impossible to evade the question whether these objectives are generally accepted as appropriate for a particular programme. Nor will the scholarship of the educational programme escape attention. Comparisons with courses abroad also have their place.

As already indicated, the committee bases its work in the first instance on the self-study of the faculty. The committee makes use of the published prospectus of courses, and studies examination papers, theses, syllabuses. If there are any, the committee will look to preceding evaluations in the faculty.

Comment on the EQA System

Dutch universities have chosen external quality assessment aimed at quality improvement and based on peer review. The experiences thus far show that faculties are willing to talk with their peers, and to listen to the opinion and advice of the visiting committee. The interviews are often very open and frank, and although the committees rarely bring up new items (and no wonder if the self-evaluation is done well), the outsider view can give a different dimension to a problem.

By peer review we lose the possibility — if it exists! — of measuring the exact quality at a certain moment. Ranking is out of order. But the process of peer review and its outcomes have much influence on quality. The results of the visit give the faculty a starting-point for improvement. Sometimes the committee is a catalyst for innovations by breaking a deadlock. Sometimes faculties can take direct action, based on the recommendations of the committee, unless negotiation with the executive body of the university is needed.

Although external quality assessment by the VSNU is developing well, there are some points which require special attention.

For the time being, the emphasis is on education. In the near future there must be a connection between assessment of education and research.

It is all very well to assess quality at department level, but what about the contribution of central services and the institution as a whole? It will be necessary to complement the departmental reviews with a review of central services and general management.

The visiting committees concur about the lack of good quantitative information from the faculties. In the near future a good data system has to be developed.

It will be necessary to monitor what the faculties do or can do with the outcome. Is this intensive investment in time worthwhile?

Special attention must be paid to attuning all the quality assessment activities being carried out by different groups. The faculties are in danger of being squeezed to death by all the attention for quality.

The Inspectorate and the Meta-Evaluation

The government and institutions of higher education have agreed upon the role of the inspectorate. The inspectorate laid down its ideas with regard to meta-evaluation in the report, *The Inspectorate of Higher Education and Its Meta-evaluative Task in the System of Quality Assessment in Higher Education* (Inspectie, 1989), stating that 'The Inspectorate supervises the system of quality assessment and informs the Minister on its validity with respect to process and output. The task of the inspectorate is called meta-evaluation' (Bresters and Kalkwijk, 1990). Regrettably, this report has not been discussed with all parties concerned with EQA.

The inspectorate has described meta-evaluation as the assessment of 'the carefulness with which the entire quality assurance system is set up by the institutions' (Kalkwijk, 1991). The agreed criteria for meta-evaluation are that EQA must cover all activities; it must be regular; external experts must be involved; and reports are public. The inspectorate itself has added that the system must be transparent and there must be a follow-up (Bresters and Kalkwijk, 1990).

In 1990 the inspectorate published its first meta-evaluation of EQA. This was an analysis of the reports of the visiting committees of 1989 and was based on a list of 'hall-marks', formulated by the inspectorate (Bresters and Kalkwijk, 1990; Kalkwijk, 1991). Although the VSNU published reports are important, they reveal only a small amount of what happens during the process of external quality assessment. A meta-evaluation should perhaps be asking:

Are the goals and aims of EQA formulated clearly?

Is the EQA process appropriate for realizing those aims?

Do the products meet the formulated requirements?

The inspectorate's list of 'hall-marks' (which also has not been discussed with the universities) overlaps with the VSNU checklist (VSNU, 1990); but this checklist is intended for quality assessment rather than for the assessment of the EQA system, and it does not really contain the right points for a meta-evaluation. Goals and aims of a faculty are properly the object of assessment by a visiting committee, and the conclusion in a VSNU report that 'the committee has paid attention to the goals and aims' should suffice. However, in commenting on the report of the geography visiting committee, the inspectorate is critical because the discussion that led to the committee's judgment is not included. Yet chartered accountants do not need to explain why they approve the books of a firm. Experts are hired for their expertise, and it does not make sense to publish all the discussions which take place during the course of a visit.

The inspectorate's meta-evaluation appears to be based on aims for EQA, which have not been made explicit or on which no agreement has been established. It seems to be using the framework of a summative, governmental-based view of EQA, suggesting that society needs an independent organization that can provide unbiased information about the higher education system (Bresters and Kalkwijk, 1990). In this light it is clear why the inspectorate recommends more detailed and more informative reports.

In Chapter 7 Dr Kalkwijk has summarized some other comments from the inspectorate's meta-evaluation, and these are addressed below.

1 *The reports of the committees are not uniform.* The inspectorate suggests that this is because 'the VSNU seems reluctant to prescribe a uniform format for reports.' This is not quite true: a format *is* suggested, but every discipline has its own problems, and every committee has its own interpretation of the task. Internal consistency of a report is important, and the VSNU sees to it that all committees deal with the most important issues. EQA is not a bureaucratic process, but a formative exercise; it should not be necessary to compare the results of the assessment of electrical engineering with the results for philosophy.

2 *The reports are not easily accessible for the public.* The reports are specifically written for the faculties, for the people concerned, not for the public in general. Students, employers and the public in general have access to the contents of the reports and media accounts of them, but are not the main audience.

3 *So far, the committees have failed to formulate their own terms of reference.* The terms of reference are fixed and laid down in the VSNU *Guide*, and since 1990 the committees also have to describe their *frame* of reference. There is an extensive discussion in the preliminary meeting of every visiting committee, for example, as to the minimum requirements of, say, the biology curriculum. But there is no attempt to formulate an 'ideal curriculum' and to test all the programmes against this ideal.

4 *The committees dislike giving hard critical statements.* It is true that the committees of 1989 were very cautious with hard critical statements, but the faculties concerned knew exactly what was intended. The prudence was, in the first instance, caused by uncertainty about the attitude of the government. Would the minister really stay back? Now that it is clear that there will be no direct interference, the reports are becoming more and more plainspoken.

5 *The experts are not independent.* It has been suggested that members of the visiting committee may be too much a part of the national network since the discipline is very much involved in their nomination. However, this approach is purposely chosen, because faculties must have confidence in the committee. They can hardly deny the judgments and recommendations of people who have been appointed as experts by the faculties themselves. They will accept the results and act on the recommendations more readily when they come from accepted peers rather than from experts 'parachuted' in from outside. It may be necessary to have experts with no connections at all for summative assessment, especially when decisions must be made about allocation of funds or closing down a department, but not when the assessment is formative, when it is important to have people to whom faculties are willing to listen. The 1989 and 1990 reports offer sufficient evidence that the experts are not defenders of the faculty or discipline, but are independent critics. There are many remarks and comments which support the policy of the minister rather than the policy of the faculty.

6 *Accountability must be improved: it is impossible to get a clear view of the quality of education in a specific discipline at a specific location.* The question arises as to who needs this insight in a specific discipline at a specific place in the framework of the promised autonomy and self-regulation. The students? The employers? The reports give interesting information for 'consumers' (the students) about the state-of-the-art in the discipline at a specific place, but they are not intended as a *Michelin Guide.* The comment of a committee that 'faculty *X* is very careful with student counselling; faculty *Y* leaves the students to their fate' cannot be translated into a quality judgment. The student must decide whether (s)he wants to be given a hand or wants to be left alone.

This criticism of the VSNU reports may be made with another task of the inspectorate in mind: 'to be informed about the state of affairs in higher education' (Bresters and Kalkwijk, 1990). But a visiting committee is not an instrument for the inspectorate. The reports of the committees are one of the many sources of information which the inspectorate can use.

Concluding Remarks

The Dutch universities find themselves in an interregnum: the new philosophy of autonomy and more self-regulation is not yet converted into legislation. Universities are planning, acting and thinking in the spirit of the new philosophy, in advance of the new law. Yet they are confronted with a government which still appears to want to regulate them. When the government really takes the policy-document *Higher Education: Autonomy and Quality* seriously, and withdraws from direct interference, there will be the following consequences:

1 In the new philosophy, the constitutional obligation for quality assurance is delegated to the universities. They will be responsible for assuring the maintenance and improvement of quality by a continuous, structured system of EQA, based on self-assessment and peer review. The role of the inspectorate is to inspect the EQA system as implemented by the universities, looking with an outsider's critical eye at the system to prevent it from in-breeding, dilution or degeneration. To do this, the frame of reference for the meta-evaluation has to be changed and must be discussed with the parties concerned.

2 The minister must make clear what type of information he needs for accountability to Parliament. This should be provided by universities in their annual reports on education, research and finance.

3 The minister must decide what type of indicators can be used to evaluate if the goals and aims for higher education are being realized. Then he and the universities must agree on the necessary information.

4 Sources of information for students and employers, including the reports of the visiting committees, need to be 'unlocked' and made accessible.

The developments of EQA in the Netherlands suggest that it does work to enhance quality. Faculties are jolted, cobwebs are blown away. Education stands in the spotlight again. We must be very careful, however, not to over-tax the EQA system with summative as well as formative functions, remembering that:

a visiting committee is not a cheap inspectorate;

a visiting committee is not a supplier of information for the minister, student or employer;

a visiting committee is the mirror and sounding-board for the faculty;

a visiting committee cannot serve two or more masters; With one, the job is already heavy enough.

Annex: Checklist for the Self-Study (VSNU, 1990)

Chapter 1. The place in the organization

- the discipline oriented approach of external quality assessment does not always correspond to the way in which the unit to be visited fits, in organizational terms,

into the university organization; it is therefore desirable to begin the self-study with a chapter describing the specific organizational structure and the position of the faculty/discipline within the university structure; the departments involved in designing the programme should also be listed;
- which committees are involved in the discipline? What are their tasks and how are they made up?

Chapter 2. The students

- the size of the student intake;
- the characteristics of the student intake (sex, age, geographic origin, previous education/professional experience);
- the prevention of and problems with deficiencies; problems with previous education;
- activities related to information and recruitment;
- intake trends in recent years; significant shifts in the intake;
- success rates of the propaedeutic and the degree phase.

Chapter 3. Brief description of the programmes

General
- have objectives been formulated?
- has the required level of ability and knowledge among graduates been laid down?
- do the objectives differ according to the programmes?
- to what extent do the objectives differ from those of similar programmes at other universities?
- to what extent are the objectives achieved?
- are the objectives still appropriate in changed circumstances?
- are there plans to modify the objectives?
- are there plans to profile the programme or strengthen its current profile?

The propaedeutic course
- what is the general structure of the propaedeutic stage? Which subjects are taught? What are the relative proportions of the subjects?
- are there requirements in terms of a mutual relationship between the subjects?
- does this propaedeutic stage differ from that of other institutions?
- which subjects play a role in the orientational and selective function of the propaedeutic stage? What is the assessment of the orientational, selective and referral function?
- is the propaedeutic stage satisfactory in the light of the follow-on courses?
- what were the grounds for choosing this structure for the propaedeutic stage?
- have there been structural changes to the course in recent years?

The degree phase
- how is the degree phase organized? What is the relation between joint courses and main subjects?
- which main subjects are available?
- how, in general, are the various main subjects organized? what are the core components of the programme and what are the optional components?

- what is the extent of the fixed programme? What is the variation in optional elements?
- the profiling of the various main subjects *vis-à-vis* other institutions; what led to the decision to profile a particular main subject? Does the profile meet the expectations?
- are there problem areas in the main subjects?
- organization of practical work, projects and master thesis.

Other courses offered
- postgraduate courses (vocational and teacher training);
- so-called short courses;
- service and contract courses;
- research assistantships;
- how many students go on to postgraduate study? Does the standard of postgraduates meet expectations?
- experience with service and contract course.

Part-time programmes
- are part-time courses also offered in the programme?
- if so, how does the part-time programme differ in terms of material and structure?

Chapter 4. The educational process

- what forms of teaching are used in the acquisition and transfer of knowledge (scope of lectures, organization of seminars, tutorials, practical work, etc.)?
- how is the computer used in the courses?
- in terms of educational theory and didactics, is the programme designed in such a way that it can be completed in the allotted time without too much difficulty?
- are there specific problem areas, for example, the transition from a structured propaedeutic stage (or basic course) to the degree phase (or graduation phase), student traineeships, writing a master thesis, final paper?
- how are students assessed? a) in what way (multiple choice, open questions); b) when (sessionals, finals)?

Chapter 5. Programme organization and programme management

Educational policy
- how is the educational policy formulated? Which committees are involved?
- is the policy relating to the discipline linked to the institutional policy? Connection with development plans?

Personnel policy
- what is the policy in respect of the ratio of teaching to research? How large is the teaching load?
- what is the policy in respect of deploying staff in the propaedeutic course and the main subjects?
- what is the policy in respect of staff deployment in seminars, supervision of master thesis, practical work and/or work experience?
- are there factors which make it difficult to pursue a good personnel policy?

Internal quality management
- how is attention given to internal quality management? Is there systematic evaluation? Which evaluation system is used?
- how is educational innovation handled? How is education support organized? Is there cooperation with the Center for Research and Development in University Education (RWO Center)?
- how is attention given to the professionalization of the staff (management courses, educational/didactic training)?

Study progress, study supervision and study counselling
- have the study hours involved in the propaedeutic course and/or the degree phase been measured in recent years? If so, what were the findings?
- have the results led to changes in programme design and/or study supervision?
- is the study progress recorded? Do these records lead to the early recognition of problems and to remedial and/or preventive actions aimed at the individual student or programme design?
- has there been an investigation into the reasons for exceeding the term of enrolment? If so, what were the findings? What were the resultant measures?
- how is study counselling organized and what is its effect?
- how is study supervision organized and what is its effect?
- programme information a) for prospective students, b) during the programme and c) as preparation for entering a profession?

Facilities
- educational facilities (lecture halls, areas for practical work, etc.);
- the situation in respect of laboratories;
- the situation in respect of libraries;
- the situation in respect of computer equipment;
- the size of the budget for facilities.

Interaction between central and faculty level
- how is the interaction organized between the faculty/discipline and the Executive Board of the university in respect of education and, in particular, of promoting quality?
- how does the faculty's educational policy relate to the institution's educational policy?
- does the faculty profit from facilities provided by the central level for promoting quality?

Chapter 6. The graduates

- do prospective employers set standards which the graduate must meet? Can the future profession be clearly defined? Have these definitions changed over the years?
- where do the graduates end up?
- what is the unemployment rate among graduates?
- are there contacts with alumni?
- how do the alumni regard the programme?
- are contacts with prospective employers structural or incidental?
- what is the policy for gearing the programme as much as possible to the labour market?

References

BALL, CHRISTOPHER (1985) 'What the Hell is Quality?' In his *Fitness for Purpose*, Guildford, SRHE.

BALL, C. and HALLWACHI, J. (1987) 'Performance Indicators in Higher Education'. *Higher Education*, 4–16.

BRESTERS, D.W. and KALKWIJK, J.P. TH. (1990) 'Quality Assessment in Dutch Higher Education: The Role of the Inspectorate', in GOEDEGEBUURE, LEO C.J., MAASSEN, PETER A.M. and WESTERHEIJDEN, DON, F. (Eds), *Peer Review and Performance Indicators: Quality Assessment in British and Dutch Higher Education*, Cheps, Utrecht, Lemma BV.

CAVE, M., HANNEY, S., KOGAN, M. and TREVET, G. (1988) *The Use of Performance Indicators in Higher Education: A Critical Analysis of Developing Practice*, London, Jessica Kingsley Publishers.

COOK, CHARLES M. (1989) 'Reflections on the American Experience', in MINISTERIE VAN O&W, *Verslag van de Conferentie Kwaliteitsbewaking Hoger Onderwijs*, Noordwijkerhout, 3–4 mei.

DOCHY, F.J.R.C., SEGERS, M.S.R., WIJNEN, W.H.F.W. (Eds) (1990) *Management Information and Performance Indicators in Higher Education: An International Issue*, Assen/Maastricht, Van Gorcum.

GOEDEGEBUURE, LEO C.J., MAASSEN, PETER A.M. and WESTERHEIJDEN, DON F. (Eds) (1990) *Peer Review and Performance Indicators: Quality Assessment in British and Dutch Higher Education*, Cheps, Utrecht, Lemma BV.

GROOT, A.D. DE (1983) 'Is de Kwaliteit van onderwijs te Beoordelen?' in CREEMERS, B.P.M., *et al.* (Eds), *De Kwaliteit van Onderwijs*, Groningen, Wolters Noordhoff.

INSPECTIE HOGER ONDERWIJS (1989) *De Inspectie Hoger Onderwijs en Haar Meta-evaluatie taak Binnen het Stelsel van Kwaliteitszorg in het Hoger Onderwijs*, De Meern.

INSPECTIE HOGER ONDERWIJS (1990) *Externe Kwaliteitszorg in Het Wo 1989* [External Quality Assessment in the Univerities, 1989], De Meern.

KALKWIJK, J.P. TH. (1991) 'Quality Assurance in a Higher Education in the Netherlands', Paper presented at the HKCAA International Conference Quality Assurance in Higher Education, Hong Kong, 15–17 July 1991.

KELLS, H.R. (1988) *Self-study Processes: A Guide for Postsecondary Institutions*, New York, Macmillan.

KELLS, H.R. (1989) 'The Future of Self-regulation in Dutch Higher Education', Paper presented at the meeting of the Association for University Governance and Management (VUB&M) Utrecht, Cheps.

KELLS, H.R. (1990) 'The Inadequacy of Performance Indicators for Higher Education: The Need for a More Comprehensive and Development Construct', *Higher Education Management*, 2, 3, Paris, OECD.

KELLS, H.R. and VAN VUGHT, F.A. (1988) 'Theoretical and Practical Aspects of a Self-Regulation System for Dutch Higher Education', *Tijdschrift voor Hoger Onderwijs*, 6, 1, February.

LYNTON, ERNST A. (1988) 'The Role of Self-study in Quality Assessment of Institutions of Higher Education', in Ministerie van O&W, *Verslag van de Conferentie Kwaliteitsbewaking Hoger*.

LSVB (1990) *Onderwijs is Meer*, Utrecht, LSVB.

MAASSEN, PETER A.M. and WEUSTHOF, PETER J.M. (1989) 'Quality Assessment in

Dutch Higher Education', in Maassen, PETER A.M. and VAN VUGHT, FRANS A. (Eds) *Dutch Higher Education in Transition*, Culemborg, Lemma BV.

MAASSEN, PETER A.M. and VAN VUGHT, FRANS A. (1989) 'Is Government Really Stepping back?' in: Maassen, PETER A.M. and VAN VUGHT, FRANS A. (Eds), *Dutch Higher Education in Transition*, Culemborg, Lemma BV.

MAASSEN, PETER (1989) 'External Evaluation in Higher Education', In Ministerie van O&W, *Verslag van de Conferentie Kwaliteitsbewaking Hoger Onderwijs*, Noordwijkerhout, 3 en 4 mei, Zoetermeer.

MCCLAIN, CHARLES I., *et al.* (1989) 'Northeast Missouri State University's Value Added Assessment Program: A Model for Educational Accountability', in KOGAN, M. (Ed.), *Evaluating Higher Education*, London, JKP.

MINISTERIE VAN O&W (1985) *Hoger Onderwijs: Autonomie En Kwaliteit*, 's Gravenhage, Staatsuitgeverij.

MINISTERIE VAN O&W (1989) *Ontwerp Hoger Qnderwijs en Onderzoek Plan 1990*, 's Gravenhage, SDU.

MINZBERG, H. (1983) *Structure in Fives: Designing Effective Organizations*, New York, Prentice Hall.

MOODIE, GRAEME C. (Ed.) (1986) *Standards and Criteria in Higher Education*, Guildford, SRHE.

PAARDEKOPER, C.M.M. and SPEE, A.A.J. (1990) 'A Government Perspective on Quality Assessment in Dutch Higher Education', in GOEDEGEBUURE, LEO C.J., MASSEN, PETER A.M. and WESTERHEIJDEN, DON F. (Eds), *Peer Review and Performance Indicators: Quality Assessment in British and Dutch Higher Education*, Cheps, Utrecht, Lemma BV.

SEGERS, M.S.R., DOCHY, F.J.R.C. and WIJNEN, W.H.F.W. (1989) *Een Set van Prestatie-Indicatoren Voor de Bestuurlijke omgang Tussen Overheid en Instellingen voor Hoger Onderwijs*.

SIZER, JOHN. (1990) 'Performance Indicators and the Management of Universities in the UK', in DOCHY, F.J.R.C., SEGERS, M.S.R. and WIJNEN, W.H.F.W. (Eds) (1990). *Management Information and Performance Indicators in Higher Education: An International Issue*, Assen Maastricht, Van Gorcum.

SPAAPEN, JACK (1989) 'External Assessment of Dutch Research Programmes', in KOGAN, M. (Ed.), *Evaluating Higher Education*, London, JKP.

SPEE, A.A.J. (1990) 'What Is New in Quality Assessment in the Netherlands?' Paper presented at the Twelfth Annual European AIP Forum on Quality and Communication for Improvement, Lyon, 9–12 September 1990.

SPEE, A.A.J. and BORMANS, R. (1991) 'Performance Indicators in Government Institutional Relations', OECD, Thirtieth Special Topic Workshop Performance Indicators in Higher Education, Paris, 24–26 April 1991.

STAROPOLI, A. (1988) 'External Evaluation in Higher Education', in MINISTERIE VON O&W, *Verslag van de Conferentie Kwaliteitsbewaking Hoger Onderwijs*, Noordwijkerhout, 3 en 4 mei, Zoetermeer.

STUURGROEP HOAK (1986) *De Opzet van een Visitatiestelsel: Een Voorstel voor een (Proef) Protocol*, Utrecht, VSNU.

VROEIJENSTIJN, A.I. (Ed.) (1981) *Kwaliteitsverbetering Hoger Onderwijs*, Voorburg, CRWO/CBOWO.

VROEIJENSTIJN, A.I. (1989) 'Autonomy and Assurance of Quality: Two sides of One Coin', in BANTA, W. TRUDY and BENSEY, MARGERY W. (Eds), *Proceedings of the*

International Conference on Assessing Quality in Higher Education, Cambridge July 24–27, Knoxville, University of Tennessee (a revised version is published in *Higher Education Research and Development*, 9, 1, 1990).

VROEIJENSTIJN, A.I. (1990) 'Self-regulation Based on self-assessment and Peer Review', Paper presented at the Twelfth Annual European AIR Forum, 9–12, Lyon, Utrecht; VSNU.

VROEIJENSTIJN, A.I. (1991) 'From the Northsea to the Baltic: How to Transfer Dutch Experiences in Quality Assessment into the Finnish Universities'? Paper presented on the conference 'Quality Assessment in Higher Education in Finland', Helsinki, 21–22 March 1991.

VROEIJENSTIJN, A.I. and ACHERMAN, J.A. (1990) 'Control Oriented Quality Assessment versus Improvement Oriented Quality Assessment', in GOEDEGEBUURE, LEO. C.J., MASSEN, PETER A.M. and WESTERHEIJDEN, DON F. (Eds), *Peer Review and Performance Indicators: Quality Assessment in British and Dutch Higher Education*, CHEPS, Utrecht, Lemma.

VSNU (1990) *Guide to External Program Review*, Utrecht, VSNU.

VUGHT, F.A. VAN (1988) 'A New Autonomy in European Higher Education?' in KELLS, H.R. and VAN VUGHT F.A. (Eds), *Self-regulation, Self-study and Program Review in Higher Education*, Culemborg, Lemma BV.

VUGHT, F.A. VAN (1989) 'Higher Education in the Netherlands', in MAASSEN, PETER A.M. and VAN VUGHT, FRANS A. (Eds), *Dutch Higher Education in Transition*, Culemborg, Lemma BV.

WESTERHEIJDEN, D.F. (1990) 'Peers, Performance or Power: A. Reflection on the Dutch Quality Assessment System in Higher Education', GOEDEGEBUURE, LEO C.J., MASSEN, PETER A.M. and WESTERHEIJDEN, DON F. (Eds) *Peer Review and Performance Indicators: Quality Assessment in British and Dutch Higher Education*, CHEPS, Utrecht, Lemma BV.

9 Evaluation Criteria and Evaluation Systems: Reflections on Developments in Sweden and Some Other OECD Countries

Marianne Bauer

Dr Bauer argues that evaluation systems in higher education vary with the political culture and the institutional system in which they function. Furthermore, variation in evaluation criteria within and between countries makes comparative evaluation problematic, and yet it is increasingly demanded. She draws on OECD studies of performance indicators and evaluation systems, and describes quality assurance approaches in the Swedish higher education system. She concludes that the emphasis should be on development and improvement rather than on accountability and control, and that industrial analogies of quality assurance may not be appropriate for higher education systems.

When studying evaluation systems for higher education in different countries, one is struck by their great variety. One might perhaps expect higher education, with its long tradition of international contact, to have arrived at a fairly uniform system of quality control, just as the evaluation of research, with its peer reviews in connection with the filling of appointments, project applications and publication, forms part of an international pattern.

In France, the Netherlands and the UK, for example, each of which devoted great efforts during the 1980s to developing national systems for the evaluation of higher education (and research), markedly different approaches have been employed. In Northern Europe such closely related countries as Denmark, Finland and Sweden are in the process of building up quite varying approaches to the follow-up and evaluation of higher education activities. An evaluation system, no matter how well-developed, cannot be bodily transferred from one country to another.

In a recent study where eleven OECD countries (nine European plus Australia and Ontario, Canada) report on the development and use of performance indicators in their evaluation system (Kells, 1990), the lists of indicators proposed or used in these countries present a fair number of similarities. This, however, is because indicators tend to focus more on quantifiable behaviour than on essential qualitative dimensions. On the other hand, there are great differences in the intended uses of these performance indicators, due to differences between the evaluation systems.

Perhaps the greatest value of the eleven descriptions in this OECD study lies in the very fact that together they reveal a whole spectrum of evaluation systems which vary according to the political culture, national traditions and educational systems in which they function. These variations in evaluative approach relate among other things to whether the systems of higher education are unitary, binary or even more differentiated, to their being more or less academic or vocational, and to their being entirely governmental or a mixture of governmental, quasi-governmental and private institutions. The variation in higher education system in turn depends on national traditions and basic education policy.

Subsequently, and as part of the same OECD project, a sub-study of five countries was undertaken to investigate such connections more closely and also to analyze the role of performance indicators in government-institutional relations (Spee and Bormans, 1991). Denmark, Norway, Sweden, the Netherlands and the UK were included in this analysis. For each country, a brief description was given of the political culture, the main features of the higher education system, higher education policy and funding of higher education, quality assessment and the development of performance indicators.

Two types of political culture were identified. In one, 'the systems are based on equality of treatment of institutions with funding based on their needs so as to ensure equality of opportunity for students and equivalence of quality of study programmes and courses, by taking account of regional and special institutional factors ... [these] are moving from a centralized to a devolved system of institutional management within a system of national planning ... implying the need for comparable quality assurance systems' (p. 31). This group includes Sweden and Norway.

The other type of political culture emphasizes the desire 'to stimulate variety of provision, based on diversity of institution, selectivity of funding, devolved institutional management, and implying comparative quality judgements' (p. 31). This group includes the Netherlands and the UK. In Denmark the system seems to be under transition from the first to the second culture.

Important concepts like 'equivalence' and 'variety' thus influence higher education policy. Among other things the report notes that 'countries which place emphasis on equivalence of courses and programmes and equality of opportunity will stress internal quality procedures. When countries shift their attention towards diversity and variety, more attention is paid to differentiated allocation of resources and comparative quality ratings' (p. 17).

In the positive perspective of a growing international exchange of students, teachers and graduates, there is a growing demand from universities and colleges for quality assessment, and a growing need for opportunities of international comparison. This can lead to greater homogeneity of evaluation systems, and during work on the OECD study we were able to observe a movement away from extremes. In Sweden, at one end of the continuum in the study, changes have occurred recently in the interest taken in quality assessment and selective funding; while in the UK the incipient transition from élite to mass higher education seems to be prompting a greater interest in quality and resources in all tertiary education, and not only at élite institutions, so that market forces cannot be allowed to operate entirely without restriction. Similarly, the initially very different approaches in the Netherlands and the UK appear to be moving towards a more similar view of the use, respectively, of performance indicators and peer review.

Fears have been expressed of increasing uniformity of higher education systems resulting from the heavy growth of international exchanges. I have not heard anyone advocate this. If anything, pluralism and flexibility are the buzzwords. But there are perhaps strong forces operating in that direction nonetheless, a kind of international academic drift in which all institutions strive for similar goals. If so, steering instruments such as systems of evaluation and funding will have to be fashioned with great care.

Differences among national evaluation systems, then, are justified if we are not aiming to develop all higher education in the direction of international uniformity. Evaluation systems not only can but should differ. But perhaps one can imagine some array of internationally valid criteria of high quality in education, applicable whatever the type of evaluation system used.

In this context the Swedish National Board of Universities and Colleges has commissioned an initial attempt at directly comparing Swedish study programmes in business administration and economics with their counterparts at a Finnish, a French, a Dutch, an English and two German higher education institutions. On the basis of descriptions of the education systems of the five countries and equivalent descriptions of the eleven study programmes, the latter have been assessed by a committee of experts from six European countries.

The report (European Foundation for Management Development, 1991) begins by saying that there is no best school in absolute terms, i.e. that there are no universal criteria of high quality. The quality of a programme hinges on its capacity for understanding the needs of its environment and catering for those needs from its available resources. Every country's education system, then, must offer educational opportunities which, taken together, meet the nation's requirements. The ability of the education system to accomplish its task depends partly on variations among different higher education establishments and partly on the characteristics of each individual establishment. Instead of trying to place the study programmes in rank order by some conceivable set of criteria, the reviewers try, by bringing out and analyzing certain characteristics of the Swedish study programmes, to show how the Swedish system, compared with other European education systems and schools, responds to present and future needs.

Goals and criteria, however, vary not only with types of education policy, education systems and higher education institutions, but also among national, institutional and departmental levels. To relate the inputs and performance of an individual higher education establishment to its role in the national education system, one needs a distinct description of goals which can counteract homogenization and academic drift, and guarantee fair evaluation. Thus goals need to be developed at both national and institutional levels and differences elucidated, so that meaningful criteria can be discussed for various levels and types of institution.

Although goals and criteria are closely interconnected, there seem to be ever so many goals but few criteria! This is because goals are located in the future and are often expressed in positive and rather vague terms, whereas criteria are concerned with present performance, are associated with critical appraisal and require concrete formulation. Universities and colleges, therefore, find it relatively easy to accept general goal formulations but react vehemently when these are translated into universal criteria for their own activities.

This is also connected with the positivist epistemology which characterized a number of earlier evaluation models and in some places appears to be returning (Henkel, 1991). This epistemology tells us that the goals defined at top level have to be broken down and operationalized stage by stage at each subordinate level and finally linked to quantitative indicators which, in turn, can be aggregated and accumulated in concise tables and fed back to the top level again. The objection to this model — apart from its inadequate view of knowledge — is that it neglects all goals but those of the central level and is therefore an insufficient basis for the development of criteria at subordinate levels.

This justifiable criticism of the formulation of goals and criteria should lead not only to opposition from the higher education community but also to that community itself giving an account of the qualities of its activities, based on a more qualified view of knowledge. Universities and colleges, therefore, must themselves define their goals and, in connection with them, propose criteria of goal achievement for different levels. In bottom-heavy organizations like those of higher education, indicators and criteria have to be built up from underneath.

To shed more light on the relationship between evaluation systems, evaluation criteria and forms of information, an example from Sweden follows. By way of background, it is important to know that Sweden is a country with a long historical tradition of powerful centralized steering and belief in rational planning. In higher education as in other fields centrally framed rules and regulations have been looked on as instruments of justice and equality, cardinal values of Swedish society. The government and Parliament have now decided to convert management of the whole of the public sector from management by directives and instructions to management by objectives and results. This change will make feedback of results and quality control a good deal more important than before and will require procedures for systematic follow-up and evaluation.

The higher education evaluation system now being built up in Sweden rests on the following basic principles:

it must primarily be aimed at promoting quality and in the second instance at the improvement of accounting and control;

responsibility for follow-up, evaluation and quality assurance being systematically conducted rests with the higher education system itself, each level from departments to the National Board of Universities and Colleges having its part to play;

horizontal interaction, i.e. between units at the same level — from individual teachers to departments and institutions — is encouraged, and in the long run could develop into a network of exchange for quality assurance and development;

it must be information-efficient, i.e. follow-up and evaluation must comprise the minimum amount of information necessary, not the most information possible;

follow-up will be based on the annual collection and compilation of basic statistical data, so that developments can be followed both at national level and for various universities and colleges or different faculty areas, thereby serving as a signalling system which can indicate areas of activity in need of analysis and evaluation;

on the other hand, evaluations, i.e. studies in greater depth which can provide explanations for the state of a study programme or a research field and, accordingly, a basis for suitable measures for improvement, will not be uniformly conducted for the entire higher education system but will be applied at different levels as necessary. This flexibility is recommended because the main purpose is the promotion of quality, and it is important that timing, method and procedure are geared to the highly variable activities of higher education rather than to accounting regulations;

every university and college is to supply the government, at three-yearly intervals, with an in-depth analysis of results which will form the basis of its funding requests for the coming three-year period. This analysis will among other things contain the results of the evaluations and other quality audits which the unit has carried out. A similar analysis of results will be performed at national level by the National Board.

The type of information required by government on how centrally defined goals are fulfilled affects the actual evaluation activities undertaken by higher education establishments. For example, in Sweden the question is how government and Parliament are to verify that higher education in Sweden is maintaining good quality. At least four levels of information are conceivable:

graded quality by means of quantitative indicators (ranking);

minimum quality guaranteed by pre-defined criteria;

reporting only of the forms of local quality control (assurance);

no information; full confidence in local quality control.

These four levels of information reflect different views of both the knowledge to be transmitted and the allocation of responsibilities within the higher education system. Moreover, they exert a great deal of influence on the types of criteria which will be demanded and on the way in which universities and colleges will go about their evaluation.

The lowest level — no information, full confidence that universities and colleges will not neglect their quality — sounds nice but can mean that people at top decision-making level only pay attention to quantitative results, rather than to the quality of study programmes. There is also the risk that some higher education units may not maintain an acceptable quality. The second level implies a kind of meta-control in that all higher education units are to give an account of the forms of quality control they have established and confirm that these are operating.

At the third level of information an explicit account is demanded of qualitative criteria, but only in order to make sure that no study programme falls below the minimum acceptable standard. At the fourth level, finally, quantifiable quality indicators are required which will make it possible to put performance or units in rank order, with all the risks of misleading or misinterpretive results which the quantification of elusive qualitative aspects can entail.

The type of information best corresponding to emphasis on the higher education units' own goal descriptions within the framework of their roles and tasks in the national education system is the requirement that they should give an account of their own quality control and quality assurance procedures and of the adequacy of the same. Steering of this kind is based on a two-way contract between the higher education establishment and government which articulates the shared but differing responsibilities of the parties for the focus and quality of activities.

Sweden is mainly concentrating on levels two and three; the institutions, which are primarily responsible for the quality of education, will report on the workings of their quality control and assurance, while comparative studies of all study programmes will be undertaken at national level with a view to guaranteeing an acceptable level of quality at all institutions.

This makes far heavier demands on each higher education institution's awareness of its purposes and performance, which in turn will stimulate the development of relevant and accepted criteria. In other words, the entire evaluation system will become *quality-promoting* and *development-oriented*, instead of focusing on accounting and control. This is the main purpose of evaluation systems for higher education.

We have borrowed many of our evaluation concepts from industry, like 'quality control' — meaning control of the final product — and, as in the title of this book, 'quality assurance' — meaning continuous scrutiny during the whole process. It is time now not to rely entirely on these industrial metaphors with their many unintended implications; we should develop our own concepts for higher education, starting with the most important characteristic of education, the fact that our material is living and thinking students who act and react, a fact that demands more dynamic evaluation and development procedures than routine quality control and prescribed assurance procedures can bring about.

Sweden is striving to build up a *quality-driving evaluation system* — meaning a more dynamic system, where students and staff are in the centre of a system that does not simply pass on information from the basic units to the government, and in which horizontal exchange is often more important than vertical.

Thus the sole criterion of good quality in higher education which universities and colleges in all countries could have in common is the establishment of properly working systems of quality assurance, with development and evaluation adapted to varying traditions, education systems and policies.

In my view we should not go to the trouble of trying to develop either international systems of evaluation or common quality criteria or indicators, which are liable to lead to greater uniformity and less abundance in our study programmes. On the other hand there is every reason to continue the interchange of experience on different procedures for strengthening the responsibilities of our universities and colleges and their capacity for developing quality in the highest education which our nations can offer — an education having a crucial bearing on the society which can be created for the future.

References

European Foundation for Management Development (1991) *Business Administration and Economics Study Programmes in Swedish Higher Education: An International Perspective*, Brussels.

Henkel, M. (1991) *Government, Evaluation and Change*, London, Jessica Kingsley, Publications.

Kells, H.R. (Ed.) (1990) *The Development of Performance Indicators for Higher Education. A Compendium for Eleven Countries*, Paris, OECD.

Spee, A. and Bormans, R. (Eds) (1991) *Performance Indicators in Government-Institutional Relations*, Paris, OECD.

10   The UK Academic Audit Unit

Peter Williams

The Academic Audit Unit (AAU) provides external and independent assurance that UK universities have adequate and effective mechanisms and structures for monitoring, maintaining and improving the quality of their teaching. As its first Director, the author describes the origins, scope, and method of the Unit which was established by the Committee of Vice-Chancellors and Principals of the United Kingdom (CVCP) in 1990. He continues with an account of the Unit's first eight months' work, to the completion, in May 1991, of a series of five pilot audits, and ends with some comments on proposals for future quality assurance arrangements in British higher education.

Background

British universities, by virtue of the Royal Charters or private acts of parliament by which they were established, are responsible for the degrees they award and for their own academic standards. Other institutions of higher education in the United Kingdom, such as the polytechnics and colleges of higher education, at present have no degree awarding powers: the qualifications they offer are validated and awarded either by the Council for National Academic Awards (CNAA) or by the universities. This particular distinction of the binary line in the UK is soon to end (see below), but its present existence is of some importance in an understanding of the background to quality assurance issues in the British universities.

Until the mid-1980s little formal attention was given to the quality of the programmes of studies offered by the universities. A general assumption of their excellence prevailed, and favourable comparisons were made with international standards. This view was reinforced at home, for example, by the fact that the charter under which CNAA operates enjoins it to ensure that the standards of its awards are comparable with those of the universities. Within the universities themselves, the assurance of quality, other than in research, has for a long time relied principally on the external examiner system, with its claim of ensuring comparability of academic standards, within disciplinary boundaries, between institutions.

Beyond that, a high degree of self-confidence (if not complacency) within the universities, legitimized in their eyes by the selective student entry system and impressive graduate success rate, militated against any significant internal or external scrutiny of the quality of the teaching function. Difficult questions were dismissed by reference to academic freedom and autonomy, and by an insistence that none but the expert practitioner was in a position to pass judgment on academic matters. Few outside the system were bold enough to dispute this in public.

Against this background, the changes in the regulation of public life in the United Kingdom, which followed the general election of 1979, posed a particular challenge and potential threat to the universities. All areas of publicly funded activity became subject to scrutiny and disciplines which they had not experienced before. Many of these had previously been the preserve of private enterprise and made use of the values and methods of the market-place. Accountability and value-for-money became the watchwords of Whitehall; the vocabulary of the management consultant and the management techniques of industry were increasingly referred to in its corridors. Explicit references to quality and standards — though rarely defined — became more common.

The cultural changes in public life, for which the new government acted as a catalyst, have been lasting and profound. The university world first felt them in 1979 and again in 1981 when public financing of higher education was severely reduced. This was followed by a series of criticisms from a variety of quarters which portrayed the universities as unaccountable, unresponsive, non-relevant, badly managed, and generally ill-fitted to meet the needs of the new entrepreneurial world. The universities were not alone in receiving this treatment: in the early 1980s most 'establishment' citadels — finance, education, the health service, the law, local government, the civil service (only the accountants seem to have been spared) — found themselves similarly in the dock. Whatever the validity of the criticisms, traditional university administrations were frequently ill-equipped to handle the new demands which were being made of them, requiring, as was the case, sharper financial management, a more streamlined decision-making process, and more conscious — and consciously articulated — academic strategies. On occasion, the very justification of the universities seemed to be at stake.

The universities responded to these assaults individually and on a system-wide basis. The CVCP, which is an independent association of the heads of UK universities, established a series of thematically based efficiency studies jointly with the University Grants Committee (the Jarratt Report), which largely vindicated current practice, but which advocated rapid development in the universities towards a more managerially oriented style of administration. It also set up, in 1983, an Academic Standards Group, under the chairmanship of Professor Philip Reynolds, then Vice-Chancellor of the University of Lancaster (the Reynolds Committee), to look at the whole question of academic standards. There were various reasons for doing this, not least the fear that unless the universities themselves could be seen to be monitoring their own standards, then another body would be given the job of doing so. In the UK context this would probably have meant HMI (Her Majesty's Inspectorate), which has long had powers of inspection of non-university higher education institutions. But there was also a strong belief in some quarters that universities' staff ought to be more concerned about the quality of their work and the courses they offer, and that this concern should be an integral part of the professional obligations of the academic staff employed to provide those courses. The Reynolds Committee report, which appeared in 1986, covered a wide range of topics relating to quality and academic standards, and included three formal codes of practice (on external examiners, postgraduate training and research, and research degree examination appeals), as well as two papers on external and internal involvement in the maintenance and monitoring of academic standards, which offered universities yardsticks for self-comparison. This report can fairly be said to have started the widespread effective discussion about quality and standards in British universities.

The Reynolds Committee completed its work in 1986 and was followed by a further enquiry in 1988 by CVCP into the extent to which universities had implemented the recommendations of good practice contained in the earlier report. This revealed that most universities had adopted most of the recommendations, but left doubts in many minds as to the extent to which superficial compliance might be masking a less than wholehearted commitment to the assurance and monitoring of quality and standards. Rumbles of dissatisfaction (if not disbelief) continued to come from the Department of Education and Science. The Academic Standards Group was re-established by the CVCP in the autumn of 1988, under the chairmanship of Professor Stewart Sutherland, then Principal of King's College London, and produced in 1989 a further report on the implementation of the codes of practice. In the same year the Educational Reform Act of 1988 came into effect, with its establishment of the Universities Funding Council (UFC). That body, which was not so firmly rooted in the university world as had been its predecessor, the University Grants Committee (UGC), made it clear that if the universities did not begin to take action on the monitoring and improvement of quality and standards, it would be forced to do so itself. The Academic Standards Group subsequently recommended the creation of an Academic Audit Unit (AAU), to be 'owned' by the universities themselves, through CVCP, whose task would be to monitor the quality assurance mechanisms in place in the universities. CVCP accepted the recommendation, and steps were taken early in 1990 to set up a board of management, define the Unit's role, and decide its terms of reference and general method of working. The University of Birmingham was chosen as its location, and the Unit started work on 1 October 1990.

Scope

In deciding exactly what the Unit was to do and how it should do it, CVCP looked at a variety of models, such as the HMI inspection, and the CNAA's validation and accreditation activities. It chose not to adopt either of these styles of assessment, preferring to look to financial audit for a pattern which could be adapted for the purposes of academic quality assurance. So the Unit neither inspects courses or teaching, nor does it validate courses or accredit institutions. (The terms 'inspection', 'validation' and 'accreditation' are here given their commonly used British meanings.) Rather, it monitors and comments on the structures and mechanisms by which the institutions themselves assure the quality of the educational programmes they offer, in fulfilment of their formal responsibility to set and maintain their own academic standards. The Academic Audit Unit's full terms of reference are:

1   to consider and review the universities' mechanisms for monitoring and promoting the academic standards which are necessary for achieving their stated aims and objectives;
2   to comment on the extent to which procedures in place in individual universities reflect best practice in maintaining quality and are applied in practice;
3   to identify and commend to universities good practice in regard to the maintenance of academic standards at national level;
4   to keep under review nationally the role of the external examiner system;
5   to report to the CVCP via the Management Board.

The Unit's work is concerned only with programmes of study, not research, although postgraduate education (including doctoral and masters' research programmes) does fall within its scope. In deciding its working method, the Management Board focused the Unit's investigations, in the first instance, on four areas where quality assurance mechanisms are particularly important, and where universities might be expected, if they were discharging their responsibilities effectively, already to have systems in place. The Board drew up the following checklist, which the Unit now uses (in a more detailed form), to monitor universities' quality assurance mechanisms and structures. It does this by examining and commenting on the adequacy of:

1   universities' mechanisms for quality assurance in provision and design of courses and degree programmes: i.e. their systems for:

central planning of monitoring of courses and teaching;

scrutinizing new courses or degree programmes (or revision of them);

monitoring course design in relation to student intake and non-traditional entrance; and

monitoring validation by the university of courses in associated institutions.

2 universities' mechanisms for quality assurance in teaching and communication methods: i.e. their arrangements for:

monitoring existing courses and degree programmes including data collection, such as student numbers, dropout rates, classified degree results, etc.;

monitoring postgraduate training and research, including appeals procedures at postgraduate research degree level;

seeking external examiners' views;

monitoring and informing students of their progress and examination performance, including appeals procedures; and

promoting innovative practice in universities such as use of interactive video and expert systems.

3 universities' mechanisms for quality assurance in relation to academic staff: i.e. their provision for:

assessing and monitoring academic staff; and

provision for staff development.

4 universities' mechanisms for quality assurance in taking account of:

external examiners' reports;

students' views on courses; and

views of external bodies — professional accrediting bodies and employers, etc.

The checklist originated largely from the recommendations in the Reynolds report and subsequent Academic Standards Group reports, as well as other CVCP codes of practice.

Definitions

So far in this paper the words 'quality', 'quality assurance' and 'academic standards' have been used without definition. As all who work in the field will acknowledge, these words represent concepts which, while universally

acknowledged as being important, defy simple definition, and lend themselves to the sort of abstract speculation which is not particularly helpful if
one is trying to introduce measures designed to improve quality or standards.
If one cannot say what improvement means in this context, because one
cannot define quality or standards, then one is in danger of spluttering into
silence. Pirsig, in his *Zen and the Art of Motorcycle Maintenance*, which has
much of interest to say about quality and standards, expresses the problem
well:

> Quality ... you know what it is, yet you don't know what it is. But
> that's self-contradictory. But some things *are* better than others, that
> is, they have more quality. But when you try to say what the quality
> is, apart from the things that have it, it all goes *poof*! There's nothing
> to talk about. But if you can't say what Quality is, how do you
> know what it is, or how do you know that it even exists? If no one
> knows what it is, then for all practical purposes, it doesn't exist at all.
> But for all practical purposes it really *does* exist. What else are the
> grades based on? Why else would people pay fortunes for some
> things and throw others in the trash pile? Obviously some things are
> better than others ... but what's the 'betterness'? ... So round and
> round you go, spinning mental wheels, and nowhere finding any
> place to get traction. What the hell is Quality? What is it? (Pirsig,
> 1974)

For its part, the AAU does not attempt to define either quality or
standards in terms of a single, externally acknowledged, level of achievement
or activity. The variety of types of universities and the differences which exist
among them in terms of what they see themselves as being and doing, would
render such a single 'gold standard' approach entirely inappropriate. In
undertaking its audits, the Unit seeks to discover the extent to which the
universities' quality assurance systems are appropriate for the purposes they
are designed and used for, and that they work effectively. It is for the
universities themselves to say what they mean by quality and standards, and
to show how they are achieved. This may not seem an unreasonable or
unusual requirement, but the notion of a university, in its capacity as a
qualification-awarding institution, addressing formally, systematically and
rigorously, the question of what are its institutional standards and what is its
institutional view of the quality of its teaching is, in most respects, comparatively new.

It may be, as has sometimes been suggested, that good quality assurance
systems do not guarantee good teaching or learning, and that these,
conversely, can well exist without the hindrance of elaborate quality assurance systems. But good teaching and learning are more likely to flourish
when matters of quality are seen publicly to be an important concern to

an institution. If good quality teaching is formally acknowledged and out-standing quality rewarded (as is already the case in relation to research achievements), they will be seen to be worth the devotion of time and effort. A fully professional approach to their teaching responsibilities by university teachers (which is not as fully evolved as it might be at present) may then develop. When high quality teaching is found in an environment of institutional indifference, it is much more likely to be a patchy and spasmodic occurrence, the preserve of the few, and without much hope of dominating the prevailing local pedagogic culture. The AAU is committed to promoting the spread of just such a fully professional approach to their teaching by university academic staffs. Institutional awareness of the need for effective formal quality assurance mechanisms, which the existence of the Unit is accelerating, is a significant development in this direction.

Method

The Unit's first two terms of reference require it to consider and review the universities' mechanisms for monitoring and promoting the academic standards which are necessary for the achievement of their stated aims and objectives; and to comment on the extent to which procedures in place in individual universities reflect best practice in maintaining quality and are applied in practice. To do this it has developed a tripartite auditing process which involves the scrutiny of briefing documentation supplied by the university under review; a visit by a team of 'auditors' to examine the effectiveness of the quality assurance systems in situ; and the writing of a report. To assist the auditors, a guide to the audit process has been written, entitled *Notes for the Guidance of Auditors* (AAU, 1991), which not only outlines the basic concepts of the Unit's work, but also includes an extensive list of questions which audit team members are encouraged to use as triggers for their enquiries. It is an aide-memoire which indicates the possible range and scope of the audit. The *Notes*, although not formally published, are available on request from the Unit, and have already acquired the status of a guide to being audited, which nearly all universities have now asked for. This use of the *Notes* was foreseen and is welcomed by the Unit.

The Briefing Documents

The precise nature of the briefing material which universities submit is not prescribed by the Unit, but they are advised that the purpose of the documents is to ensure that the auditing team gets a clear view of the quality assurance systems in operation. An illustrative list suggests three sorts of documents as being likely to provide the team with the necessary infor-mation: formal publications (prospectuses, calendars, annual reports and the like); codes of practice, regulations, and internally circulated handbooks; and examples of the quality assurance mechanisms in action, such as external examiners' reports and follow-up papers, new course approval documents, relevant committee minutes, etc. In addition, the university is asked to supply a brief overview account of its systems and how they work. Theoretically, the production of the briefing material should not be onerous: a well-developed quality assurance system will already have produced for its own purposes a full range of documents describing the mechanisms and structures, and the papers showing them in action should be readily accessible. The ease with which a university can put together its briefing papers and the number of documents which need to be specially written for the audit are, in themselves, interesting informal indicators of the stage of development of its quality assurance systems.

On receiving the briefing material, the auditors, normally three to a team, have about three weeks to read and assimilate it. A briefing meeting is then held, at which a member of the Unit's directorate is present to offer guidance. At this meeting the auditors discuss the systems described, in order to ensure that they all share the same understandings, and decide on the programme for the audit visit. Typically the visit lasts three days, and consists of interview discussions with senior management members, representatives of the main quality assurance committees, and various groups of staff and students. As the primary purpose of the visit is to provide an opportunity for the audit team to test the mechanisms and structures described in the briefing papers, the programme for the visit needs to include meetings with those who have responsibility for administering the procedures, as well as those who are on the receiving end of them. Of necessity, a sampling system has to be employed. To examine some parts of the system in depth, the audit teams try to ensure that part of their visit is devoted to the pursuit of 'audit trails', extensive investigations of three or four particular examples, which the team selects, of the procedures described in the briefing papers. At the pre-visit briefing meeting appropriate trails are identified, as is any additional documentation which the team feels it needs for a full appreciation of the picture. Universities are typically given a month to provide the extra material and to arrange the visit programme.

The Visit

The visit itself is an intense and concentrated endeavour. During three days the audit team will talk to probably more than a hundred people in some twenty or so sessions, ranging from the Vice-Chancellor to first-year students. Each session will have a different purpose, but all will be informed by the team's need not only to satisfy itself that it understands what is supposed to happen, and the extent to which it actually does so, but also the extent to which the mechanisms and structures in place are adequate and appropriate to meet the quality assurance needs of the institution in terms of its own stated aims and objectives.

A typical audit visit will involve meetings with the Vice-Chancellor, Pro-Vice-Chancellor, members of teaching or academic standards committees, staff development committees, the staff development officer, representative groups of recently appointed academic staff, non-professorial members of Senate, deans, course organizers, heads of department, student representatives, postgraduates, and overseas and mature students. The audit trails which are followed may be thematic in character, examining in depth, for example, a particular new course approval, course evaluation, departmental review, or staff development activity, or following a representative number of external examiners' reports through the system. Alternatively, a team may choose two or three departments at random, and ask to follow a number of quality assurance processes and procedures within them. This small-sample testing method has its critics: it is said by some that large assertions and generalizations should not be made on the basis of small samples. But the essence of this kind of auditing, as of the financial audit, is the use of random sampling to determine whether there are any shortcomings in the operation of systems. If shortcomings are detected, it follows that the system is not watertight; that remains true whether or not the malfunction is occasional or frequent. Well-ordered quality control systems design quality in, so as to forestall the possibility of malfunction; and quality assurance systems should be able to spot any defects in the quality control process. The sampling method is valuable as one means of piercing the 'corporate façade', the impressive shop window which all institutions will offer in a natural desire to present the best possible impression to the Unit and the world. Apparently naïve questions are also proving to be an effective means of discovering how things really stand.

Following completion of the visit, the audit team prepares a draft report. How this is done depends upon the members themselves: some prefer to draft in committee; others seek a volunteer to write a first version, which is then subject to review and amendment by the other members; while a third method would see a section of the report being written by each member. The draft is submitted to the directorate, which edits it to ensure consistency with the general pattern of audits. The finished draft is then sent to the Vice-Chancellor of the university, who is invited only to correct errors of fact, or to indicate where particular comments or judgments may have resulted from a fundamental misconception of the facts of the matter. In the light of the Vice-Chancellor's comments, a final version is prepared and sent to the university.

The Audit Report

The audit report is intended to provide a full, accurate and fair account of an institution's quality assurance structures and mechanisms. In doing so, it draws attention to any examples of particularly good practice which the audit team has encountered, and which might be commended to others, as well as any evidence of defective or inadequate systems. To ensure consistency among the reports of different institutions by different audit teams, all reports have a broadly similar format, viz.:

> brief background information about the institution, its type, size, academic and environmental characteristics;
>
> a description of the audit procedures used;
>
> an account of the institution's formally stated aims, objectives, mission, purposes, etc., together with any specific strategic policies which have a bearing on its attitudes to matters of quality or academic standards;
>
> a summary of the formal procedures adopted by the institution in each of the areas listed in the outline checklist, together with an account of their effectiveness as perceived by the audit team. This may include a note on the extent to which they conform to, or vary from, the recommendations in the CVCP's relevant codes of practice. The section may also include a comment on any special circumstances affecting the institution, such as resource availability, stage of development and implementation of quality assurance programmes, institutional ethos, etc.;
>
> a view on the extent to which the institution's academic activity is underpinned by an active, effective and pervasive commitment to fulfilling its stated aims and objectives in matters of academic quality and standards;
>
> a list of practices worthy of commendation;
>
> a list of suggestions for improvement of quality assurance structures and mechanisms, for consideration by the institution.

No attempt is made in the reports to grade universities, or to use terms which might facilitate the creation of a quality assurance 'pecking order'. Each report addresses the university's systems on their own terms, and is written with the university in mind as its primary audience. That is not to say that the possibility of the report having outside readers is ignored: every effort is taken to ensure that adequate contextual information is included, and that explanations of mechanisms and structures are written in a clear way which does not require prior knowledge of the institution.

At present there are no plans for a formal follow-up programme of universities after a set period to see what action has been taken on the Unit's recommendations. The current expectation is that all institutions will be re-audited on a triennial basis, but if a university wishes the Unit to see what progress has been made in the intervening period, it may invite an informal visit. In such cases it is likely that one of the audit team or a member of the directorate will go to the university to discuss the changes, but it is not envisaged that any formal supplementary report will result.

Access to Universities and Publication of Reports

One of the distinctive features of the AAU's method of working, which was thought to be necessary to ensure general acceptance of the Unit by the universities, is that it has no right of entry to any institution. Audits are undertaken by invitation only. That is not to say that there is any university which intends to exempt itself from audit: already a schedule of visits has been agreed with every institution. Nor to invite the Unit would arouse intense speculation as to the reason, and would undoubtedly create a great deal of doubtful publicity.

A similar convention governs the publication of the reports. The AAU does not itself publish its audit reports, as these belong to the individual universities. The Unit does, however, retain the copyright, so as to dissuade institutions from seeking to quote selectively from their reports. It is for each university to decide what publicity it gives to its report, although there is little doubt that all will, in due course, see the light of day. Not only is it virtually impossible to keep secret the contents of a document which will need to be considered widely within an institution, but there will also be external requests (e.g. from the UFC and the press) for copies. The probable course of action in most cases will be for the report to find its way into the public domain, accompanied by a commentary prepared by the university. The conventions on both access to universities and publication of reports are likely to be changed as the result of proposed legislation on quality assurance by both major political parties (see below).

Logistics

The AAU is a small, cost-effective organization, which is consciously adopting a low overhead, high value approach to its work. The directorate consists at present of three full-time staff, the Director, Deputy Director and Administrative Secretary. The first two groups of auditors are all senior serving academics from British universities, selected from an extensive list of nominations submitted by vice-chancellors. They number twenty-three at present, all seconded on the basis of one-fifth of their time for two years, and are paid a modest daily fee for their work. They have been chosen on the basis of proven experience in quality assurance-related activities, geographical distribution (one of the ways of disseminating information about the Unit's work is by selecting the auditors from as many institutions as possible), and subject spread (although, as the audit activity is centred on institutions rather than disciplines, this is of secondary relevance).

The auditors undertake a three-part induction programme, lasting some six days in all. The first part introduces the ideas of quality assurance, quality control, audit inspection and validation, relates them to the Unit's work, and offers comparative experiences and perceptions in the form of contributions from representatives of CNAA, HMI and university administrations. There are also discussions about the Unit's own objectives and methods. The second part of the induction programme considers in detail the audit process, using actual briefing materials and simulated interviews. Report construction is also addressed. The final part of the programme, which takes place after the auditor's first 'live' experience of an audit visit, consists of a debriefing session, with an opportunity to talk about the experience with a view to improving personal performance and the process as a whole. Regular 'reunion' meetings are also planned, to allow the auditors to meet as a full group and to receive new ideas or information about the Unit and its work. The induction programme has been devised and implemented with the help and close cooperation of the Universities' Staff Development and Training Unit (USDTU), another CVCP enterprise, based in Sheffield. Auditors can expect to have visited eight to ten institutions during the course of their period of secondment.

The universities fund the AAU through earmarked subscriptions to CVCP, and are charged pro rata according to their student numbers. The budget for 1991–92 is around £450,000, although this does not include the cost to each institution of its being audited (or, of course, of setting up and maintaining quality assurance systems). The Unit is managed by a Board comprising eight vice-chancellors, four independent members from the non-university world, and the Secretary of CVCP. A consultative committee, with membership from a large range of interested organizations (e.g. CNAA, HMI, UFC, National Union of Students, Association of University Teachers, Committee of Directors of Polytechnics, USDTU, and the Enterprise in Higher Education project), provides help and advice to the Unit and the Management Board. The Chairman of both the Board and the Consultative Committee is Professor Stewart Sutherland, Vice-Chancellor of the University of London.

The Pilot Audits

In the course of the discussions which led to the establishment of the AAU, it was agreed that there should be a short series of experimental 'pilot' audits, prior to the start of the main exercise. The object of these would be to test the method which had been devised, and to identify any unforeseen difficulties which might come to light in practice. The pilot audits would also allow some variations in approach to be tried. Five willing volunteer institutions were identified, representing a variety of types and traditions (the Universities of Aberdeen, East Anglia, Loughborough, and Southampton and the University College of Wales, Aberystwyth); the procedures described earlier were followed closely, and the visits ran remarkably smoothly. The audit teams expressed confidence after the visits that three days had been long enough to get a proper appreciation of the structures and mechanisms in place, to discover whether these were operating effectively, and to determine where there were significant shortcomings either in practice or in the system itself.

The draft reports which the directorate received from the teams differed markedly in form and quality, as was to be expected. In the absence of any model examples to follow, teams had to decide for themselves the extent to which they should write narratives of their visits or more schematized accounts; whether to couch criticisms in a tentative, coded style, or to adopt a more vigorous and overt approach; and how much weight to place on the evidence of particular individuals or interest groups. In coordinating these drafts, the directorate needed to ensure that there was a proper degree of consistency of form among the reports, while not extinguishing the individuality of approach of the teams. In the end, only such editorial work was undertaken on each draft as proved necessary for it to conform in broad terms with the basic report format. In two cases this involved substantial re-ordering of the draft, and in one of these a significant amount of re-writing. By the time the drafts were submitted to the relevant vice-chancellors, the directorate was satisfied that they represented a fair account of the five institutions' quality assurance systems and their effectiveness in operation.

The responses of the institutions on receipt of their draft reports provided the most interesting aspect of the pilot audit procedure. Two institutions offered no more than straightforward corrections of errors of fact, as they had been invited to do. A third added a comment on the tone of the report, couched in constructive and supportive terms. A fourth expressed, informally, severe misgivings about its draft, based again on an evident dislike of the tone adopted, which it considered to be condescending, as well as a belief that the auditors had made naïve errors of judgment as a result of taking too much notice of the views of representatives of a disaffected minority of the academic staff, whom it had happened to encounter on its visit. A fifth institution protested in even more robust terms about its draft report: it claimed that there were large numbers of factual errors in the text and complained about generalizations based on limited evidence, the superficiality of the method, and the insupportability of the (not inconsiderable) range of criticisms made by the audit team.

The number of factual errors in the reports, given the complexity of universities and the variety of their administrative arrangements, was actually very small. For the most part they consisted of errors of nomenclature or minor local usage lapses of little consequence. The criticisms of tone were more substantial and readily addressed: after weighing the relative merits of different approaches, it was agreed to move to a generally less vigorous and categorical style of description and recommendation. In so doing, the pattern for future reports was set, and the adoption of slightly more veiled language, in which nuance assumes more significance, determined upon. Claims of errors of judgment were more difficult to agree, the audit teams standing firmly by their views. It is possible that some of these criticisms were made in an attempt to repair the corporate façade which the auditors had effectively pierced, or because the report could not be used as a management lever in quite the way which had been expected. Whatever the reason, one or two institutions may not have received the report they had been expecting.

The final reports took all the comments into account. Some differed substantially in detail and tone from their draft form, but the findings and recommendations remained largely unaltered. The Management Board, in reviewing the pilot audit series, expressed its general satisfaction with the outcome, while proposing some changes to the report format to ensure a more uniform style and coverage of the checklist's main points. Some small procedural changes were also recommended.

The pilot series was a success. It achieved its main object of testing and proving the validity of the audit method and of revealing ways of making it more effective. Lessons were learnt, particularly in relation to the design of the visit programme, methods of interview and the content and form of the report. It also provided the first auditors with an initial opportunity to learn their art and to mark the path for others to follow.

Having successfully tested the audit process, the Unit has drawn up a schedule which will involve all UK universities being audited by June 1993. It is probable, whatever the outcome of the political initiatives at present being considered, that this round will be completed, and that it will produce a full set of audit reports which will provide a map of the quality assurance scene not hitherto available.

Dissemination of Good Practice

The AAU's third term of reference requires it to 'identify and commend to universities good practice in regard to the maintenance of academic standards at national level.' The primary method of doing this will be through the Director's Annual Report to the Management Board, which will include descriptions of some of the most interesting and potentially valuable quality assurance procedures and practices which have been encountered during the course of the year's auditing. The report will also comment on matters of system-wide importance, such as the development of modular courses, or the extension of the role of external examiners, or the cost of quality. The hope is that the annual report will become a useful reference tool for all those seeking to improve their own institutions' quality assurance.

The Present Scene

It is too early for the Academic Audit Unit to claim many achievements for itself, other than its establishment and the successful development of the pilot stage of its work. Nevertheless, its mere existence, and the knowledge that all universities are to be scrutinized by it, have already had a remarkable effect. It is no exaggeration to say that the question of quality has burst onto the university scene in a way which few would have predicted five years ago. Few institutions are now without their academic standards or teaching committees; most are reviewing their procedures in the light of the *Notes for the Guidance of Auditors* and CVCP codes of practice; responsibilities are being apportioned; students are being asked for their views. Although it would be gratifying to believe that this activity reflects a pervasive, if sudden, conversion to a deep-rooted commitment to teaching quality, it is more likely that the real motivating force behind it is the expectation that questions of quality will begin to inform the funding decisions made by the UFC and its successor bodies. This is already the case in the 'public sector', where the Polytechnic and Colleges Funding Council (PCFC) has used HMI's judgments on course quality as a factor in its grant distribution processes. The extent to which all these animated endeavours are directed towards, and will lead to, an enhanced experience of higher education for students, however, it is not yet clear. But consideration of matters related to quality and standards is unlikely to diminish in public importance; the main question now at issue is whether the forthcoming political initiatives in the area will enhance or diminish the beneficial effect of these developments.

The Future of Quality Assurance

In November 1991, following publication of a White Paper (DES, 1991), the British Government presented a Bill to Parliament on higher and further education in England and Wales, which will bring about widespread structural changes in the system. A similar Bill is to be introduced in respect of Scotland. The main effects of the legislation will be the abolition of the binary line and the establishment of geographical, rather than sectoral, funding boundaries. There will in future be no distinction between universities and polytechnics, which will be able to designate themselves as universities if they so wish. Three new higher education funding councils will distribute money in England, Scotland and Wales. All polytechnics will be granted degree awarding powers, and the CNAA will be wound up.

So far as quality assurance is concerned, there will be a three-level system. Quality control systems will continue to be operated within and by each institution. A new term, 'quality audit', has been introduced to describe the work of a new 'quality audit unit', whose mode of operation will mirror closely that of the AAU, and which might well develop out of it, but whose scope will be extended to cover all higher education institutions across the whole of the United Kingdom. The quality audit unit will be essentially owned and operated by the institutions, although its terms of reference will require publication of reports and a greater involvement of outside interests in its management. The Bill gives the Secretary of State reserve powers to instruct the funding councils to establish their own quality audit function, presumably in the event of his being dissatisfied with the institutions' own unit. The third level of quality assurance is to consist of 'quality assessment committees' attached to and owned by the funding councils, operating by means of 'quality assessment units' consisting of a combination of ex-HMIs, ad hoc groups of serving academics, and representatives from outside the higher education world. These units are to be given the task of inspecting the quality of what is actually provided in individual institutions, with a view to their judgments (in the words of the White Paper) 'informing the funding decisions of the new Funding Councils'. Their opinions will be taken in conjunction with 'quantifiable outcomes', i.e. 'performance indicators and calculations of value added', to reward (presumably) some institutions at the expense of others. The assessment units are to provide 'external judgments on the basis of direct observation of what is provided. 'This includes the quality of teaching and learning, its management and organisation, accommodation and equipment.' A quality assessment scheme, which will examine the standard of teaching and learning provision within grouped disciplines, is at present (November 1991) under development by a working party consisting of representatives of the UFC, PCFC, HMI, the Scottish Education Department, universities and polytechnics. Their intention is to develop a credible methodology, recruit and train staff, undertake eight pilot studies in the fields of engineering and science (for England and Wales) and engineering and business studies (for Scotland) and then to complete a comprehensive inspection of all provision in those fields in all higher education institutions in Great Britain by the end of 1992. This programme is to be followed by similar sequences of inspections covering all other disciplines. Whether such an ambitious programme can be completed in other than a very superficial manner, given the very tight schedule, remains to be seen. If it cannot, bearing in mind that the reports of the assessment units are to inform competitive funding decisions, then the validity of the quality assessment exercise is certain to be seriously challenged.

In their proposals concerning quality assurance, both the White Paper and the subsequent Bill leave many fundamental questions unaddressed. For example, not only are there no working definitions of what the Government or DES understands by quality or standards, but the intention — explicitly stated in the White Paper — that the quality assessment units will provide relative and comparative quality judgments on courses, for use by prospective students and employers, seems to imply an annual update on the quality of the 25,000 or so higher education courses currently on offer in the UK. It is doubtful whether that aim could ever be achieved without very considerable resources being devoted to it. The Government has brought forward its original timetable for the higher education legislation by including it in a Bill which contains equally radical proposals for further education; the intention now is that the combined Act should become law before the general election, which is due by May 1992. Whether the Government succeeds in its aim may depend upon the resolution of contentious questions concerning the further education elements of the Bill.

Earlier in 1991 the Labour Party published a consultative document on its own intentions for quality assurance in higher education. This envisaged the establishment of an Academic Standards Council with responsibility for quality assurance across the whole of higher education. It left vague how it would operate, although it envisaged a membership comprising representatives of a very wide variety of interests. There was to be a strong inspectorial element, and the Council was to have reserve powers to close courses or even institutions. This document was followed, in mid-July 1991, by a policy statement which showed a number of significant changes from the earlier draft. As it now stands, the Labour Party's policy proposes the creation of a Higher Education Standards Council, independent of any controlling interest, but with representatives of the major participants in higher education. The Council would 'bring together many of the functions of CVCP quality assurance unit, the CNAA, and the section of Her Majesty's Inspectorate dealing with higher education.' Its overall responsibility would be to 'monitor quality in higher education, and to advise institutions, the funding council, the public and the government accordingly.' The detailed terms of reference bear a surprising resemblance to those of the AAU. Its work would involve monitoring, reviewing and advising on:

institutions' quality assurance mechanisms;

the external examiner system;

the development of credit accumulation and transfer schemes;

student evaluation of courses, spreading the best practice already operating in a number of institutions;

staff appraisal and career development, including practical help with teaching techniques.

There is little direct reference to inspection of individual courses. The Council would, however, be granted powers to close, *in extremis*, courses or even institutions, although these are envisaged as being necessary only to ensure their rare use. The Labour Party's proposals also include a statement of intent to amend any legislation already passed by an outgoing Conservative Government. The assurance of quality in Scottish higher education would rest with a new Scottish Parliament. There is no mention in the document of Wales or Northern Ireland which, presumably, would be subject to the provisions of the main proposals.

If implemented, either of these two sets of proposals would represent a fundamental change in the nature of university autonomy in the United Kingdom.

The Future of Quality

The future of quality in the universities will now depend on the result of the next general election. Whichever party wins, British higher education would appear to be faced with an increasingly invasive and demanding quality assurance policy, although this will be less of a shock to the former polytechnics, which have experienced something similar through the HMI and CNAA inspection and validation systems. Under the Conservative plans, funding will be linked to quality. It seems inevitable that, in consequence, a compliance culture will develop, the aim of which will be to meet, or appear to meet, the criteria and standards laid down by the assessment units, irrespective of whether those are appropriate or desirable in the context of specific institutions. That the resulting quality of provision will be as high as before is not clear: if standards are to be common to the whole spectrum of higher education institutions, they may well end up as lowest common denominator threshold standards. Some institutions, pressed financially, and wishing to increase their student numbers significantly, may consciously decide to level their quality down, while still staying above the threshold. Paradoxically, under the politicians' externally controlled quality assurance models, there may well be little incentive or opportunity actually to improve quality.

In the face of the Government's belt and braces approach, what is the future for the Academic Audit Unit and its methods? The White Paper seems to have accepted its worth and the Government to have embedded it in its strategy. As its reports are more widely circulated, the quality of the auditors' work is being increasingly remarked. Whether or not the CVCP Unit will emerge as the Quality Audit Unit for higher education as a whole will depend on a variety of factors, some of which are related to the ways in which the representative bodies of the present two sectors of higher education come to terms with each other and ultimately coalesce. But whatever happens, the opportunity which the Unit is already offering universities, by acting as a stimulus for them to define and defend their own standards and quality, in promoting self-reflection and self-criticism, and (hopefully) in encouraging a much needed development of a sense of professionalism in university teachers (as opposed to researchers), much not be put at risk.

References

CVCP ACADEMIC AUDIT UNIT (1991) *Notes for the Guidance of Auditors*, Birmingham, CVCP Academic Audit Unit.

DEPARTMENT OF EDUCATION AND SCIENCE (1991) *Higher Education: A New Framework*, London, HMSO, Cmnd 1541.

JARRATT, A. (1985) *Report of the Steering Committee for Efficiency Studies in Universities*, London, CVCP.

LABOUR PARTY (1991) *Quality Assured: A Consultative Document on Labour's Proposals for Quality Assurance in Higher Education*, London, The Labour Party.

PIRSIG, R.A. (1974) *Zen and the Art of Motorcycle Maintenance: An Inquiry into Values*, New York, Morrow.

REYNOLDS, P.A. (Chairman) (1986) *Academic Standards in Universities*, London, CVCP.

SMITH, ANDREW (1991) *Quality Assured: Labour's Proposals for Safeguarding and Enhancing Quality in Higher Education*, London, The Labour Party.

11 The US Accreditation System

Marjorie Peace Lenn

Accreditation in the United States is a communal process of assessing educational quality and promoting improvement in post-secondary education. Approximately 100 non-governmental institutional and professional bodies accredit institutions or programmes using agreed standards, in-depth self-studies, and site visits by a team of peers. The value of accreditation for students, funding agencies, professions and employers and for the institutions themselves is reviewed. The meaning of accredited status, and the role of the American Council on Postsecondary Accreditation (COPA) in 'accrediting the accreditors' are explained.

Unlike most countries, the United States has no ministry of education to authorize the offering of education programmes, set educational standards and establish regulations for enforcing standards. The United States constitution reserves to the states and local governments the primary responsibility for education, including higher education. In interpreting and exercising that responsibility, however, the states often differ radically, and the unevenness and lack of uniformity of educational standards and practices that can result led in the late nineteenth century to the beginnings of a system of regulation called accreditation.

This accreditation is based on peer review and is essentially a non-governmental, voluntary, and self-regulatory approach to quality assessment and enhancement which clearly reflects the divergent, semi-autonomous character of American higher education. Academic institutions in many other countries look to an external, often governmental, entity for evaluation. Accreditation in the US, on the other hand, operates on a communal concept — an internalized activity which is a direct creation of the academic and professional educational communities. Quality is not decided by the external 'they', but by the internal 'we'.

Thus American accrediting bodies are voluntary, non-governmental associations of institutions involved as a community in fulfilling two fundamental purposes: quality assessment — evaluating an institution or programme to determine whether it meets or exceeds stated criteria of quality; and quality enhancement — assisting an institution or programme in continuing to improve itself. Funding for the evaluation process comes from the accredited institutions, programmes and professional associations, and there is no dependency on governmental funding. Recognition for accrediting bodies derives from the Council on Postsecondary Accreditation (COPA), a primary function of which is periodically to review the standards set and processes used by the various institutional and specialized accrediting bodies.

Types of Accreditation

The meaning of accredited status depends on the type of accreditation involved. *Institutional accreditation* is granted by regional and national accrediting bodies which collectively serve most of the institutions, currently about 6000, chartered or licensed in the United States and its possessions. The evaluation focuses on the institution as a whole, giving attention not only to the overall educational programme but to such areas as effective management, student personnel services, financial and physical resources, and administrative strength. The standards expected relate to the achievement of the institutional mission and objectives as determined by the academic community. Degree programmes, however specialized, must rest upon a base of liberal or general studies as a requirement for all or most students. The institutional accrediting bodies recognized by COPA include nine regional and six national organizations which accredit total operating units only.

The criteria of an institutional accrediting body are broad, as is demanded by the focus on the whole institution and by the presence in the United States of post-secondary institutions of widely different purposes and scopes. Such criteria also provide encouragement to institutions to try innovative curricula and procedures, and to adopt them when they prove successful.

Specialized accrediting bodies accredit programmes or single-purpose institutions that prepare professionals, technicians, or members of special occupations. *Specialized accreditation* usually applies to fields in which there is a recognized first professional degree and where health, welfare, safety, and professional competence are matters of academic, professional, and public concern. Each specialized accrediting body has its own distinctive definitions of eligibility, criteria or standards for accreditation, and operating procedures. These have been developed through the cooperation of educators and practitioners and with other interested parties such as educational institutions, employers, and public agencies. What is sought are reasonable conditions for achieving the objectives of satisfactory quality. (See Chapter 12 for an account of engineering accreditation in the US which is undertaken by the Accreditation Board for Engineering and Technology (ABET), a major specialized accreditation agency.)

The crucial dimension of quality in specialized accreditation is the adequacy of the educational programme as it relates to professional expectations and requirements for entry and practice in the field, including certification and licensure. During the review process, among other duties, a site-visit team may review the relationship of the programme to the larger unit and the adequacy of the organization and resources of the institution for programme maintenance and development. At the present time COPA recognizes approximately forty specialized accrediting bodies in such fields as business, engineering, teaching, law, and medicine. These include some which serve as umbrella agencies for an additional thirty review committees, bringing the grand total of institutional and specialized accrediting bodies to approximately 100.

The Accreditation Process

The accrediting process has evolved from quantitative to qualitative measures, from the early days of simple checklists to an increasing emphasis on measuring the outcomes of educational experiences. A common pattern used by both institutional and specialized accrediting bodies includes (1) a rigorous and candid self-study by the institution or programme, examining and evaluating objectives, activities, and achievements; (2) an on-site visit by a team of peers who provide expert evaluation and offer suggestions for improvement; and (3) a subsequent review and decision by a central governing commission or board.

The process begins with the institutional or programmatic self-study, a comprehensive effort to measure progress according to previously accepted objectives against the standards of the accrediting body. The self-study considers the interests of the constituencies — students, faculty, administrators, alumni, trustees, and the community — and results in a written report.

This report serves as the basis for evaluation by a site-visit team from the accrediting body. The site-visit team normally consists of professional educators, specialists selected according to the nature of the institution or programme, and members representing specific public interests. The visiting team assesses the institution or programme in the light of its objectives and provides judgments based on its own expertise and its external perspective on the degree to which standards are met. The team prepares an evaluation report which is reviewed by the institution or programme for factual accuracy.

Subsequently, the original self-study, the team report, and the institutional or programme response are forwarded to the accrediting body's governing board as the basis for a decision about the accreditation status of the institution or programme. Negative decisions may be appealed according to established procedures of the accrediting body.

Generally, institutions are reviewed every five or ten years, but accrediting bodies reserve the right to review member institutions or programmes at any time. They also reserve the right to review any substantive change such as an expansion from undergraduate to graduate programmes or an expansion of off-campus offerings. Such changes may require prior approval or review upon implementation. In this way, accrediting bodies hold their member institutions and programmes continually responsible to their education peers, to the constituents they serve, and to the public.

Values and Uses of Accreditation

Accreditation is used by several constituencies in a variety of ways. It is used by institutions and programmes primarily as a stimulus for self-evaluation and self-directed improvement. It provides an assurance of the relevance of preparation for effective contemporary practice, and it facilitates inter-institutional cooperation in diverse ways including the admission of students to graduate programmes and the transfer of credit.

The reputation of an institution or programme is enhanced because of public regard for accreditation. For the public, accreditation provides an assurance of acceptable quality as determined through external evaluation, a commitment to quality enhancement by the institution or programme, and some guarantee of conformity to general expectations in post-secondary education. It also assures improved professional services to the public since accredited programmes are expected to modify their requirements to reflect changes in knowledge and practice generally accepted in the field.

Accreditation serves the professions by providing a means for the participation of practitioners in setting the requirements for preparation to enter the professions. It contributes to the unity of the professions by bringing together practitioners, educators, and students in an activity directed at improving professional preparation and professional practice.

Accreditation is used by the federal and state governments too. It is one means by which an institution can establish eligibility for participation in federally funded programmes and for student financial aid. There is a decreased need for state intervention in the operation of educational institutions because through accreditation the institutions are providing privately for the maintenance and enhancement of educational quality. In many states accreditation serves as a vehicle for consumer protection, where the authorization of institutions to operate and grant degrees is dependent upon the institution's achieving and maintaining accredited status. In a number of professions, completion of an accredited programme is a prerequisite for state licensure and entry to professional practice.

Businesses and industries look to accreditation for quality assurance when financing educational programmes for employees, contributing to scholarship programmes, supporting foundations or awarding grants to individual students or institutions. Accreditation is also usually relied upon by private foundations as a highly desirable indicator of institutional and programme quality.

At an international level, institutional accreditation is an important marker for the many American programmes currently operating abroad; specialized accreditation is only recently considering such overseas activity.

Accredited Status

What does it mean to say that an institution has been awarded accredited status? In general, it means that the characteristics of the total institution have been considered and that the total pattern the institution provides of strengths and weaknesses has been weighed. The institution has been found to:

1 have educationally appropriate objectives as defined over time by the American higher education community;
2 have the financial, human and physical resources necessary to achieve these objectives;
3 have demonstrated that it is in fact achieving these objectives now; and
4 have provided sufficient evidence to support the belief that it will continue to achieve its objectives over a reasonable future.

Critical to understanding US institutional accreditation and its uses domestically and abroad is knowing what its status can and cannot do. A summary point-counterpoint follows:

Accreditation can attest to the general quality of an educational institution when reviewed as a whole. Institutional accrediting standards apply to such critical matters as mission, governance, academic programme, faculty, student services, financial resources, library and buildings.

Accreditation cannot attest to the quality of individual programmes or courses within an institution. In the case of professional programmes, students are advised to choose among those which have specialized accreditation. In some professions, having attended an accredited programme is imperative for licensure (e.g. medicine, law).

Accreditation can assure the student that the educational activities of an accredited institution have undergone external evaluation and are found to be in conformity with expectations of quality in US higher education as reflected in the institutional accrediting standards mentioned above.

Accreditation cannot guarantee that a student will either be admitted or will graduate from an institution, nor can it guarantee the quality of individual graduates. Admissions is the prerogative of the institution and graduation is the responsibility of the individual student.

Accreditation can help a student transfer academic credits from one US institution to another and can help in the admission of a student to an advanced degree programme, provided the performance of the student has been satisfactory and the credits to be transferred are appropriate to the receiving institution.

Accreditation cannot guarantee the transfer of academic credits from one US institution to another or the admission of students to advanced degrees, because, again, admission requirements are the prerogative of each institution or programme.

Accreditation can benefit US institutions and programmes by providing a stimulus for self-evaluation and improvement.

Accreditation cannot provide a ranking of US institutions or programmes, often requested by international audiences. The academic reputation of institutions and the stature and success of programmes in the professions is information generally understood within a discipline or profession but is not information officially published.

Accreditation can attest to the educational quality of an institution or programme for a reasonable period into the future. (Most accrediting periods range between five and ten years with interim evaluations as needed.)

Accreditation cannot have indefinite duration. If the institution or programme changes in any substantive way, the accrediting body re-evaluates its status.

Accreditation can enable an institution to become eligible for certain programmes of governmental funding. An institution must be accredited before it can apply for governmental funding for such endeavours as research. Also, students who apply to and attend accredited institutions are eligible for governmental student loans. Private foundations also rely on the accredited status of an institution to allocate their funds.

Accreditation cannot gain access for foreign nationals to US governmental student loans.

Caveat Emptor

It is possible in the United States to start your own institution and your own accrediting body without external validation. Some of these institutions, often called 'diploma mills', come from states which do not have an authorization agency for post-secondary education (the initial step taken by institutions prior to seeking accreditation). These diploma mills dot the globe, feeding off the unwary in credential-crazed environments. In addition, at least one state has offered an alternative to accreditation for those institutions unable to receive accreditation. These 'state approved' institutions have also appeared around the globe falsely claiming that state approval and accreditation are equivalent in status in the American post-secondary community.

Accreditation and the Federal Government

The federal government has provided financial support to students and educational institutions through a wide variety of programmes aimed at improving the welfare of society. With this financing has come a legitimate federal interest in determining which institutions and programmes are educationally sound. Because there is an effective non-governmental process for making such determinations, and because the federal government is restricted in its jurisdiction over education, a relationship has been established between accreditation and the determination of eligibility for federal funds.

Through accreditation the US Department of Education is provided with reasonable assurance of the quality and integrity of institutions and programmes, and the Secretary for Education publishes a list of accrediting bodies which are recognized as reliable authorities of educational quality. In carrying out this recognition function, the Department of Education establishes criteria and periodically reviews institutional and specialized accrediting bodies to ensure that they are in fact functioning as appropriate indicators of quality. Thus the federal government provides for an appropriate use of accreditation while also adhering to the principle of separation of governmental from non-governmental functions.

The Council on Postsecondary Accreditation (COPA)

COPA also grants recognition to the accrediting agencies and is the national non-governmental organization that works to foster and facilitate the role of accrediting bodies in promoting the quality and diversity of American post-secondary education. The accrediting bodies, while established and supported by their membership, are intended to serve the broader interests of society as well. To promote these ends, COPA recognizes, coordinates, and periodically reviews the work of its member accrediting bodies, and it evaluates the appropriateness of existing or proposed accrediting bodies and their activities. It is thus an integral part of the self-regulatory process of American accreditation. COPA's membership includes institutional accrediting bodies, specialized accrediting bodies, and the major higher education organizations all of which endorse COPA as the lead organization for establishing policies and practices in post-secondary accreditation.

COPA 'accredits the accreditors' through the granting of recognition to those bodies which meet its criteria on organizational structure and scope, public responsibility, evaluative practices and procedures, educational philosophy and related procedures. To be recognized, an accrediting body must be a non-governmental agency, and must require as an integral part of its evaluative process a self-analysis of the programme or institution, and an on-site review by a visiting team.

COPA conducts its business and offers professional development sessions on issues in accreditation at least twice a year. These meetings are open, and the international accrediting community is often found among the participants. Current issues include the accreditation of distance education and international links, the assessment of educational outcomes, and the further development of the communal process of peer review in evaluating the educational quality of American higher education.

In the late twentieth century the self-regulatory accrediting process of American higher education celebrates a 100-year history. During this period major changes have occurred relative to both the standards and process of accreditation. It is expected that this dynamic characteristic will continue into the future in evaluating educational quality throughout American higher education.

12 Engineering Accreditation in the United States

Leslie Benmark

Chapter 11 offered an overview of institutional and specialized accreditation in the United States. Here quality assurance in engineering education is described as an example of the latter. The Accreditation Board for Engineering and Technology (ABET) monitors, evaluates and certifies the quality of engineering and engineering technology education. ABET's accreditation role, policy guidelines, procedures and criteria are outlined. With increasing global mobility, the importance of establishing the equivalence of engineering programmes is emphasized, and international developments in the mutual recognition of engineering credentials are also reviewed.

Introduction

How do we assure that the graduates of engineering, engineering technology and engineering-related (engineering spectrum) programmes receive the best education possible? One proven method in the United States is through accreditation of engineering programmes by the Accreditation Board for Engineering and Technology (ABET).

The Role of ABET

ABET (formed in 1932 as the Engineers' Council for Professional Development, ECPD) is a federation of engineering and engineering-related societies (currently twenty-seven societies). It is recognized by the Department of Education and the Council on Postsecondary Accreditation (COPA) as the sole agency in the United States responsible for the accreditation of educational programmes leading to degrees in engineering, engineering technology and engineering-related areas.

Figure 1. *Accreditation Board for Engineering and Technology*

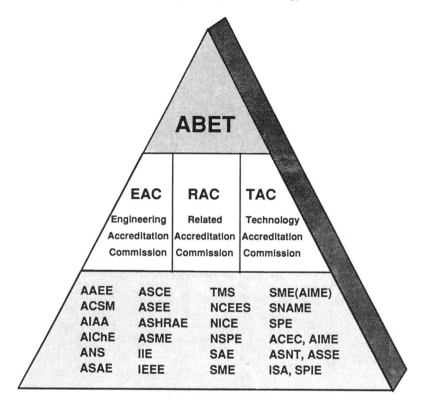

The accreditation is carried out by three ABET Commissions: the Engineering Accreditation Commission (EAC), the Technology Accreditation Commission (TAC) and the Related Accreditation Commission (RAC). These Commissions are made up of representatives of the participating bodies which constitute ABET in proportion to the number of programmes for which each is responsible (see Figure 1).

ABET provides leadership for the promotion and advancement of engineering spectrum education, and seeks to further public welfare through the development of better educated and qualified engineers, engineering technologists, engineering technicians and others engaged in engineering or engineering-related work.

ABET initiates, sponsors and co-sponsors educational forums, conferences, seminars and studies, and represents the engineering profession in education areas where appropriate. It provides technical assistance about accreditation to agencies having engineering-related regulatory authority, and it identifies engineering spectrum programmes which meet minimum accreditation requirements to potential employers, government agencies, state examining boards, parents, potential students and the public at large.

Through the efforts of over 2000 volunteers — educators, knowledgeable practitioners and practising professionals from all engineering disciplines — ABET is primarily responsible for monitoring, evaluating and certifying the quality of engineering education in colleges and universities in the United States. It also provides guidance for the improvement of existing programmes and the development of new ones.

ABET recognizes the value of experimentation in education and seeks to foster an environment conducive to innovation so that the curriculum will better prepare undergraduates for careers in the next century. Recently, it established an Award for Educational Innovation to recognize creative programmes in engineering education. This emphasizes ABET's interest in improving the quality of engineering and engineering technology education: the awards seek to recognize new approaches to meeting educational needs through non-traditional ways of resolving the problems that face education. It is hoped that they will help to dispel the commonly held belief that ABET is a barrier to educational innovation. Each year the members of the three ABET Commissions nominate for this award new and different programmes observed during accreditation reviews that represent excellence in programme quality. The awards are presented at the ABET Annual Meeting.

ABET and Quality Assurance

Firms using Total Quality Management (TQM) principles design quality into their product rather than inspect it in. Quality improvement relies on defect *prevention*: 'Do it right the first time.' Applying TQM principles to the engineering education process is a challenge. First, we must ascertain who are the customers of engineering education (employers, students, society, etc.). Next, we must determine how to obtain feedback from customers on the important characteristics for engineering graduates and use this feedback to improve the quality of engineering education. Finally, we must identify critical points within the educational process where monitoring will assure the quality of the education of engineering graduates.

ABET has established a Quality Assurance in Engineering Education Committee to investigate these important engineering and engineering technology education issues. The goal is to have an impact on and change engineering spectrum educational programmes nationally, and also the way ABET conducts the accreditation of these programmes. This suggests, perhaps, a developing role for ABET in helping institutions establish internal quality assurance processes for their engineering programmes.

Accreditation Guidelines

ABET policy is to accredit engineering and engineering technology programmes rather than institutions, departments or degrees, for it is well recognized that

Figure 2.   *Accreditation Guidelines*

Institution must request accreditation for a particular programme(s) in engineering, engineering technology or engineering-related field.

Programme must have graduates before an evaluation review can be made.

Avoid rigid requirements to prevent standardization of engineering education. Allow considerable latitude in choice and arrangement of curriculum subject matter as long as minimum criteria are met.

Programmes with interdisciplinary focus that prepare students to take advantage of as many different career opportunities as possible are encouraged.

Programmes accredited for specific period, usually three or six years.

General review of ALL engineering programmes at an institution at intervals not to exceed six years.

programmes of quite different quality may sometimes be found at the same institution. Institutions are expected to submit programmes for accreditation review without persuasion or pressure.

ABET encourages educational programmes with an interdisciplinary focus that prepare students to take advantage of as many different career opportunities as possible. It encourages innovation and strives to avoid rigid requirements as a basis for accreditation, in order to prevent standardization and ossification. Considerable latitude is allowed in the choice and arrangement of curriculum subject matter as long as the minimum criteria are met.

Programmes are accredited for a specific period, usually three or six years. A general review of *all* engineering spectrum programmes at an institution is carried out at intervals not exceeding six years. (Figure 2 sets out the accreditation guidelines.)

The Accreditation Process

After an institution requests an accreditation review for some or all of its engineering programmes, it prepares self-evaluation materials and submits these to ABET. An evaluation team is assembled for each institution consisting of a team leader and a programme evaluator for each programme being reviewed.

Team members are selected from lists of qualified evaluators furnished by the professional societies assigned curricular responsibility for specific engineering programmes. Ideally the evaluation team should have an equal mix of academics and practising professionals from industry, private practice and government.

A thorough review of the self-evaluation materials is undertaken by each of the team members. This is followed by an extensive on-campus visit by the full team, to evaluate each engineering programme, and the institution and engineering unit as a whole. This involves discussions with faculty, staff and students, review of course materials and student work, consideration of financial and resource matters, examination of engineering and related area facilities, observation of working conditions, evaluation of libraries, computer systems and other facilities, and interviews with the institution's central administration.

After the on-campus evaluation, a preliminary report of findings is prepared and reviewed at several levels within ABET to ensure consistency among all programmes. The institution has the opportunity to review the preliminary findings and submit information to correct errors of fact (referred to as the 'due process' step). Comments from the institution are studied and appropriate modifications are made to the preliminary report. The modified report and recommendations for accreditation action for all programmes are submitted for decision to the full Commission. After considerable deliberation at this meeting, the final report with accreditation action for each programme is sent to the institution.

There are six major areas that are examined during an accreditation review of engineering programmes: curriculum, faculty, administration, student body, institutional facilities and institutional commitment. Each of these areas is considered below, bearing in mind the general engineering criteria which must be met by all engineering programmes and specific engineering criteria for each engineering discipline. (Figure 3 summarizes the accreditation process.)

Curriculum

A significant measure of engineering education is the degree to which it has prepared the graduate to pursue a productive engineering career that is characterized by continued professional growth. The overall curriculum must provide an integrated experience, developing the ability to apply pertinent knowledge to the identification and solution of practical problems in the designated area of engineering specialization.

While ABET favours a flexible approach to the design of curricular content, it also recognizes the need for specific coverage in each curricular

Figure 3.   ABET Program Accreditation Process

After requesting that ABET evaluate engineering programme(s), the institution prepares self-study materials and submits to ABET for review

Group of professional peers from both industry and academia are selected as programme evaluators

Programme evaluators review self-study materials prior to campus visit

On-campus evaluation of programme(s) by team of programme evaluators

Preliminary report of evaluation team findings is prepared and sent to institution for review

Institution has opportunity to correct errors in fact or observation contained in preliminary report

Review, discussion and decision on accreditation action by full membership of Commission

area. Therefore, it is required that the curriculum content of each engineering programme includes the equivalent of at least three years of study in mathematics, basic sciences, engineering sciences, engineering design and the humanities and social sciences. Courses must include at least:

* one year of an appropriate combination of *mathematics and basic sciences*: studies in mathematics must emphasize mathematical concepts and principles rather than merely computation. The objective of the studies in basic sciences is to acquire fundamental knowledge about nature and its phenomena, including quantitative expression.

* one year of *engineering sciences*: the engineering sciences have their roots in mathematics and basic sciences but carry knowledge further toward creative application. These studies provide a bridge between mathematics/basic sciences and engineering practice.

* one-half year of *engineering design*: the engineering design component of a curriculum must include at least some of the following features: development of student creativity, use of open-ended problems, development

and use of design methodology, formulation of design problem statements and specifications, consideration of alternative solutions, feasibility considerations and detailed system descriptions. Further, it is essential to include a variety of realistic constraint factors such as safety, reliability, aesthetics, ethics and social impact. Some portion of this requirement must be satisfied by at least one course which is primarily design, preferably at the senior level, and draws upon previous coursework in the relevant discipline.

* one-half year of *humanities and social sciences*: studies in the humanities and social sciences serve not only to meet the objectives of the engineering profession for a broad education but also the institution's educational objectives. Studies in this area must provide both breadth and depth and not be limited to a selection of unrelated introductory courses.

Faculty

The heart of any educational programme is the faculty. Faculty must be large enough to cover, by experience and interest, all of the curricular areas of the discipline and to provide technical interaction and stimulation. Teaching loads must be compatible with the existing climate at the institution for research and professional development.

Administration

The attitude and policy of engineering administration towards teaching, research and scholarly production, and the quality of leadership at all levels of administration are critical to the success of each engineering programme. A capable faculty can perform its functions best in an atmosphere of good relations with the administration. Good communications between faculty members and administrators and a mutual concern with policies that affect the faculty are required.

Student Body

An important consideration in the evaluation of an engineering programme is the quality and performance of the students and graduates. When students are carefully selected at the time of admission and/or by appropriate retention standards, the level and pace of instruction can be high. Student performance is assessed through examining samples of homework problems, laboratory reports and design experiences.

Institutional Facilities

An engineering programme must be supported by adequate physical facilities including office and classroom space, laboratories and workshop facilities suitable for the scope of the programme's activities. The libraries in support of the engineering unit must be both technical and non-technical and include books, journals and other reference material for collateral reading in connection with the instructional and research programmes and professional work. Computing facilities available to the engineering faculty and students must be adequate to encourage the use of computers as a part of the institution's engineering educational experience. Laboratory facilities must reflect the requirements of each educational programme.

Institutional Commitment

The organizational structure of the institution should demonstrate a commitment, both financially and philosophically, to the engineering programme. ABET is specifically interested in the general status of the engineering unit, its programmes within the institution and the overall administration as it relates to the engineering unit and achievement of its educational objectives.

Accreditation Coverage

Over 1400 programmes in engineering at approximately 400 institutions in the United States are currently accredited by ABET. The largest number of accredited engineering programmes is in the electrical and bioengineering area, followed in size by civil, mechanical, chemical and industrial engineering programmes (see Figure 4).

Over 750 engineering technology programmes at approximately 225 institutions in the United States are currently accredited by ABET. Approximately 60 per cent of these are associate programmes, and the largest number is in the electrical engineering technology area. Mechanical and civil engineering technology programmes follow in magnitude (see Figure 5).

International Developments

With the increased global mobility of engineers, there is a need to understand educational credentials of engineers from other countries. In the light of this, ABET's commitment to quality engineering education goes beyond engineering accreditation in the United States to a role in international credentialling. This commitment is reflected in the ABET Vision Statement: 'ABET

Figure 4.   Engineering Programmes, November 1990

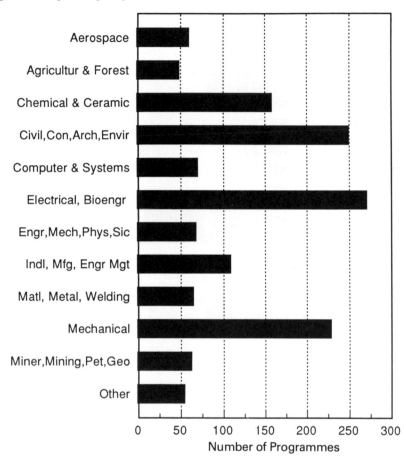

will help identify substantially equivalent educational programs from other countries and will assist agencies in other countries in the development of accreditation processes and systems.'

For over twenty-five years ABET has had a long standing agreement with the Canadian Council of Professional Engineers whereby each group recognizes the engineering education credentials of graduates of accredited engineering programmes of the other. Recently, the Washington Accord extended this agreement with the aim of including Australia, New Zealand, the United Kingdom and Ireland. A Secretariat, initially to be located at ABET headquarters, will serve as the central point for communications among the participants of this Accord.

In 1989 ABET entered into an agreement with the Fédération Européenne d'Associations Nationales d'Ingénieurs (FEANI) whose membership

Figure 5.   Engineering Technology Programmes, October 1990

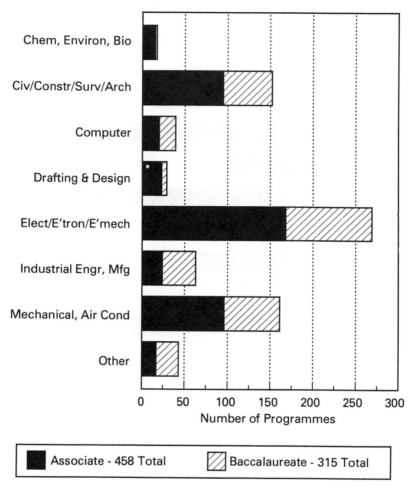

includes the leading European engineering registration bodies and a large portion of the engineering community in Europe. The FEANI Accord is based on the equivalency of education represented by attainment of FEANI Eur.Ing. Class I designation. Eur.Ing. Class I is granted to individuals who have graduated from a recognized engineering programme and are registered professional engineers in their country and who have obtained the highest degree of membership under their country's registration criteria. The FEANI agreement allows American engineers who are graduates from ABET accredited programmes and have successfully completed the Engineering Fundamentals examination of the National Council of Examiners for Engineering and Surveying (NCEES) the same 'rights and privileges' and professional courtesies as graduates from any of the FEANI Eur.Ing. Class I educational programmes.

To further understanding of the substantial equivalence of engineering education, the ABET Board of Directors has approved ABET's membership of the United States Council for International Engineering Practice (USCIEP). USCIEP is seeking to obtain a better global understanding of the requirements for the professional practice of engineering — in terms of education, experience and examination — to facilitate international mobility of engineers without undue constraints.

There are active discussions with leaders in the field of engineering education and the engineering profession in Mexico. A self-study process similar to that used in the United States was begun a few years ago. Now exploration is underway to determine how a comprehensive accreditation process can be implemented.

There is ongoing liaison with many other engineering organizations around the world such as the Union Panamericana de Asociaciones de Ingenieros (UPADI) and the World Federation of Engineering Organizations (WFEO).

ABET publishes annually a list of accredited programmes in the United States so that those which meet minimum criteria can be identified to the public, prospective students, educational institutions, professional societies, potential employers, governmental agencies and state boards of examiners. ABET will now supplement this with a list of engineering programmes offered outside the United States which have been determined to be substantially equivalent. This list will:

identify programmes which meet minimum standards;

provide information about engineering education systems and accreditation processes, policies, procedures and criteria; and

encourage quality enhancements to engineering education.

A preamble will describe the basis for substantial equivalence and the purpose and benefits being served by the list.

For the time being the list will be published in the ABET Accreditation Annual and will include programmes from Canada, Ireland, Australia and New Zealand. Efforts are currently underway to understand better the substantial equivalence of engineering programmes of the United Kingdom. As the number of programmes determined to be substantially equivalent increases and this list becomes unwieldy, then a separate publication will be used to share information about international programmes which meet minimum standards.

Since the professional practice of engineering is very much dependent on the output quality of the engineering education system, questions about mutual recognition naturally arise. International engineering practice will benefit from these developing methods of assessing the equivalence of various engineering education delivery and accreditation systems. ABET is keen to contribute constructively to this debate.

13   Mutual Recognition and Transfer of Credits: Developments in Europe

*Fritz Dalichow**

This chapter considers different approaches to promoting academic recognition between institutions and across national borders. It describes the European Credit Transfer System (ECTS) which is part of the European Community's ERASMUS Programme. ECTS is in the second year of a six-year pilot phase and covers eighty-six university departments or consortia in five subject areas. The promising evaluation results of the first year are noted. The extent of interest from outside Europe suggests good prospects for future international cooperation on the recognition of academic credit.

Introduction

When the European Community (EC) began its work on higher education cooperation in 1976, it saw clearly that one of the main barriers to student mobility between the member states was academic recognition. This has been the main focus of the EC's higher education policy, especially for the large-scale European Community Action Scheme for the Mobility of University Students (ERASMUS), which came into existence in 1987.

International student mobility is dramatically increasing as the twentieth century comes to an end. In the European Community the ERASMUS programme has given considerable impetus to this and is aiming at intra-EC student exchange of 10 per cent, which would mean well over 150,000 students per year. In 1988/89, 15,000 students were involved; by 1991/92, the figure was almost 60,000.

---

* Fritz Dalichow is assistant director of the ERASMUS Bureau in Brussels responsible for academic recognition and credit transfer matters. The views expressed here are those of the author and do not necessarily reflect the official position of the ERASMUS Bureau or the Commission of the European Communities.

How Can Academic Recognition Be Improved?

Normally, academic recognition occurs following individual evaluation after a study period in another institution, a posteriori. Unfortunately, this difficult and time-consuming evaluation of credentials on an individual basis fairly often leads to disappointment — partial or even non-recognition. With increasing mobility and organized student exchange, there is a growing need to ensure a priori academic recognition. How can this objective be reached?

The ERASMUS programme emphasizes four approaches:

1   *the individual approach*, where evaluators of academic credentials may be funded for study visits to improve their knowledge of foreign credentials. Since 1977 the European Community has assisted staff of universities and other organizations to make individual visits to improve their knowledge of academic recognition in other EC member states.

2   *the administrative approach*, where a central agency gathers information and offers advice on academic recognition. In 1984 the EC Network of National Academic Recognition Information Centres (NARICs) was created, which was later integrated into the ERASMUS programme.

3   *inter-university or inter-departmental cooperation*, as exemplified by the European Interuniversity Cooperation Programmes (ICPs) established by the ERASMUS programme. Here institutions or departments of EC member states enter into specific agreements, for instance to exchange third year students and provide for recognition of the first and second year of the home university at the host university and vice versa.

4   *the inter-university or inter-departmental super approach*, where a network for a priori recognition is formed. This is the basis of the European Credit Transfer System (ECTS) of the EC Commission, which is described in detail below.

From the Inter-university or Inter-departmental Approach to the Super Approach

One of the reasons for the success of the ERASMUS programme is that student mobility is only valid where there are academic recognition arrangements within the Interuniversity Cooperation Programme (ICP). These recognition arrangements are relatively easily established. An ICP normally unites similar departments in a limited number of institutions, and student mobility is generally restricted to a specific fixed period of time at a stage of the study course which is appropriate to student exchange. Recognition is feasible for one semester or one year at the host institution, and the major part of the study course is still completely governed by the home institutions.

The success of these ICP arrangements led ERASMUS to consider going much further — towards establishing a scheme involving different departments in a large number of institutions in all EC member states, where student mobility can take place at virtually any time during the study course, in which the students decide when to go, where, for how long, and where academic recognition is guaranteed a priori. The result was a decision to develop a European Community Course Credit Transfer System (ECTS). But before describing the ECTS pilot scheme, the meaning of academic credit and academic credit transfer should be clarified.

Academic Credit

The notion of academic credit was developed in the United States higher education system in the late nineteenth century. A typical four-year course for a bachelor's degree in the US requires 128 credits (thirty-two credits per year or sixteen credits per semester). One credit is given for a one-hour lecture together with two hours of preparation and study assignments per week per semester (or three laboratory hours per week per semester). Thus to accumulate sixteen credit points during a semester, the student's weekly timetable might consist of twelve hours of lectures (and accompanying study) (= twelve credits) and twelve hours of laboratory exercises (= four credits). A description of all courses taught and their credit value is published by the colleges and universities in their catalogues or calendars and is therefore known to all students and all other institutions. Each American student receives a 'transcript of records' which is a form indicating the student's consecutive performance — the courses followed, grades achieved and credits obtained.

Academic Credit Transfer

In a narrow sense, academic credit transfer is the transfer of specific credit points from one institution to another. The student asks for recognition of the credits gained in the first institution. The receiving institution examines the transcript of records and makes a decision based on the quality of the first institution and the comparability of the programmes involved. In other words, each one involves an *individual* recognition procedure.

The US higher education institutions have a well developed credit system, and many students do negotiate transfer of credits between institutions, but contrary to popular belief, there is no American credit transfer system. In contrast to individually negotiated credit transfer, a credit transfer *system* means the general a priori recognition by higher education institutions of courses, study periods and examinations which have been completed elsewhere. Such recognition can be based on national and international agreements between individual institutions themselves. It may also be the subject of multilateral, bilateral and unilateral arrangements at state level. The ERASMUS programme of the EC is pioneering a major initiative towards an international credit transfer system.

A Credit Transfer System for the European Community

In 1985 an ad hoc committee 'On a People's Europe' strongly recommended 'introducing a European system of academic credits transferable throughout the Community. This system would be implemented by means of bilateral agreements or on a voluntary basis by universities and higher education establishments which, by arrangements with one another, would determine the procedures for academic recognition of such credits.' These recommendations were approved by the European Council of June 1985 in Milan. Six months later the Commission reacted with the proposal for the ECTS scheme within the ERASMUS programme.

ECTS has borrowed a number of tools from the American credit system, including:

> *the credit itself*: participating institutions are required to give sixty credits to a full study year's academic programme and subdivide it appropriately to the courses given in the academic year;
>
> *the institutional calender or catalogue*: which gives exact information on the higher education institution, its rules and regulations and courses (including an outline of content and the number of credits for each course);
>
> *the transcript of records*: which in a very systematic way gives an overview of the courses the student has taken and the results and credits earned.

Going beyond the experience of the USA to develop a broad credit transfer *system*, it was decided to base ECTS on the principle of 'mutual trust and confidence'. The hypothesis was that higher education institutions are very different within the EC, but that their quality is far more comparable than the quality of institutions in similarly large geographical areas in other parts of the world. As a result, professors at EC higher education institutions should be willing to trust the course content and the academic judgment of their colleagues. It was therefore proposed to the EC higher education world that institutions should agree to automatic a priori recognition of credit.

More practically expressed, the central objective of the pilot scheme is to develop credit transfer as an effective currency of academic recognition. ECTS aims to provide universities admitting students from another

Community country with a quick and objective means of assessing incoming students' previous academic performance. In this way, they may be inserted at appropriate levels into host institution courses, even where there is no specific programme for student exchange with the foreign universities concerned.

The Development of ECTS

In 1987 and 1988 an ECTS brochure outlining a set of common rules was developed, discussed and agreed. This outline paper was sent to all EC higher education institutions in their respective languages in summer 1988, and they were invited to apply for participation. Late in 1988 eighty-one higher education institutions and three consortia were selected for participation, in the five subject areas business administration, chemistry, history, mechanical engineering and medicine. These institutions or consortia are all receiving a grant from the EC Commission to help implement the system, and their experiences with ECTS are being carefully monitored. These institutions form the 'Inner Circle' of the Pilot Scheme. The Commission tries to keep the many other institutions which have expressed interest in the scheme regularly informed about its development. These institutions are 'Outer Circle' participants. They receive no direct ERASMUS funding, and their experiences with ECTS are not being systematically evaluated by the Commission, but will be taken into account where this seems appropriate.

An ECTS student may go to an ECTS Inner Circle partner institution, study there and return to graduate at the home institution, graduate at the host institution or even go on to study in another institution of the same subject area group. Provided that the student participating in the ECTS pilot scheme complies with the legal, institutional and specific ECTS requirements of the home and host institution, she or he will receive full credit for all academic work carried out at these institutions. A certain number of ERASMUS student mobility grants are available.

More than 550 students participated in 1989/90 which was the first operational year of a six-year pilot phase. In 1990/91 more than 800 students were selected for participation, which is a controlled growth of almost 50 per cent.

First Results

The majority of the 553 students who participated in 1989/90 spent a full academic year at their respective host institution. Most of these students successfully completed their planned programme of study, gaining full credit from the host institution. Most of the students who returned to their home institutions received full credit transfer for this successfully completed ECTS programme. In three of the subject area groups there were students who gained awards at the ECTS partner institutions through the transfer of credits already achieved at their home institutions and the ECTS study period at the host institution. These awards ranged from diplomas to master's degrees. Some students stayed on at the ECTS partner institutions to complete their studies and a small number of students moved on to a third ECTS institution.

The pilot scheme has had a good start. With a few exceptions, the organizational arrangements have functioned appropriately. Students participating in ECTS received correct information on the study courses at the host institution, appropriate preparation for the study period at the host institution, and accommodation and necessary help from the host institution. Home institutions' credits were mostly completely recognized by the host institutions. Most students studied successfully at the host institution and many of the students received all the academic credits they had planned. For the most part, credit transfer back from the host to the home institution worked equally well.

International Reactions to ECTS

From its very beginning ECTS has generated enormous interest within and outside the European Community. In 1988 some 500 departments from all EC member states applied for participation of which only eighty-four could be selected. Hundreds of other departments decided to participate in the Outer Circle of the scheme, which is open to any subject area at any time. These Outer Circle activities are not eligible for direct financial support, but a number of departments have applied for and obtained ERASMUS grants for Interuniversity Cooperation Programmes. An international Outer Circle credit transfer consortium (Trans European Exchange and Credit Transfer (TEXT) Consortium), came into existence by private initiative and now links some forty EC higher education institutions.

Whole subject areas (e.g. sports science) are now thinking about organizing their study abroad according to ECTS rules. Some EC states have been trying to build on ECTS rules to organize total bilateral higher education cooperation. Additional institutions (including two from the new Länder of Germany) have recently been allowed to join in the five existing subject areas. This extension of the ECTS Inner Circle together with activities of the ECTS Outer Circle suggests a promising future for credit transfer within the EC.

There is also enormous interest in ECTS outside the EC. Many universities of the member states of the European Free Trade Association (EFTA) have been requesting access. During 1991 negotiations to include them in the ERASMUS programme were successfully concluded, and a number of these institutions will probably soon be allowed to participate in ECTS. During 1992/93 there will be a West European ECTS Inner Circle of twelve EC plus seven EFTA member states. ECTS Outer Circle activities will also be possible among nineteen West European states.

Central and Eastern European universities are disappointed that credit transfer is not part of the recently established EC TEMPUS Programme and are checking what ECTS Outer Circle cooperation possibilities they have. A number of them are considering joining the TEXT consortium. In the medium and long term Central and East European universities hope to develop partnerships with West European universities to participate in credit transfer cooperation.

Last but not least, individual American universities and also the US Department of Education are interested in cooperating with the ECTS scheme. American universities have a good deal of experience in international higher education cooperation. Globally, the most popular programme is still the 'junior year abroad'. This enables students, who have completed two years of higher education at their US home institution, to move to a partner institution abroad for a third study year under close supervision of the home institution, and then return to complete their final year at the home institution. This is more or less a home study year abroad with full home credit and no real credit transfer programme. Less frequent than the 'junior year abroad' are true bilateral or multilateral institutional exchange programmes; these are similar to the ERASMUS Interuniversity Cooperation Programmes with limited numbers of carefully pre-selected partner institutions. This mostly brings full credit transfer, because courses, which perfectly fit into the home institution's programme have been predetermined, and are per se transferable.

On a limited scale there are open-minded American institutions who trust their students and their overseas partner institutions rather more than this. They are convinced that their international partners are doing an equally good job in educating students, and they give more choice to their students as to when they want to go abroad and what courses they select. The equivalence concept of these institutions approaches the idea of mutual trust and confidence which is the leading modern EC principle both for professional and for academic recognition. It is exactly this kind of American institution which requests participation in the ECTS Pilot Scheme.

Within the US Department of Education some leading officials are fascinated by the daring concept of ECTS, where the student decides at what stage she or he goes to which of the many partner institutions in any of the twelve EC member states, in which of the nine official languages she or he studies and for how long, and which courses of the partner institution she or he chooses, and where full a priori academic recognition/credit transfer is guaranteed in any direction.

If and when the EC and the American partners can come to an agreement on cooperation in real credit transfer, the structural differences of their higher education systems and the wide variety and the diverse levels of

Fritz Dalichow

American higher education institutions are among the factors which will need careful consideration. However, it should be possible for willing partners to find solutions. If successful, this has the potential to open an important new page of higher education cooperation, and will be a significant development in international recognition and transfer of academic credit.

Part 3

Quality Assurance in Hong Kong

14 The Experience of Validation at Hong Kong Polytechnic

Diana Mak and Austin Reid

This case study of Hong Kong Polytechnic describes the introduction of systematic course validation in a British type education system with staff who are predominantly Chinese. The authors offer an insider perspective, as they are both observers and participants. They examine how staff resistance was addressed, and the changes in the validation process as staff experience and confidence developed. The ways in which internal and external validation processes may hinder and support each other are reviewed. It is suggested that an interactive model, involving open academic dialogue between validators and validated, is appropriate for both internal and external validation.

The Hong Kong Polytechnic grew out of the Hong Kong Technical College, and began to award degrees in 1983. It now has 26,000 full-time and part-time students, and by 1994/95 will have 60 per cent of its work at degree level. This increase in scale and scope of degree courses has involved the polytechnic in extensive internal and external validation processes.

The polytechnic has always had to obtain planning approval from the government funding body before introducing a new course. However, the idea of academic validation of a course was a novelty. Initially it was seen purely as an external process; any preliminary internal procedures were solely to prepare for the real event.

The arrival of a new Director in 1985 led to the quality of courses being given a high priority. During 1985 and 1986 a comprehensive system of course validation, re-validation and annual course review covering all courses was introduced. The validation process followed what House (1978) describes as the accreditation model where there is presumed consensus on criteria and procedures, with a methodology of self-study and panel review. The concept of validation was only vaguely handled. The first guide book devoted most of its coverage to procedures, operational guidelines and format of submission documents, reflecting the perception of validation as a task and an achievement concept leading to a judgment of the courses under examination.

This is understandable in a society that carried no tradition in validation. As seen by management, the motivation was to have some control over the courses to ensure 'the maintenance of appropriate academic standards' (quality control) and 'to use the course validation process to inform its resource decisions' (value for money). Thus the polytechnic was to be seen to be accountable to the public as employer and as taxpayer.

The Implementation Hurdles

Initially validation was the experience of a limited few. The majority watched with dismay. During the mid-1980s a vocational and narrow perspective of education focusing on the application of skills still prevailed at the polytechnic. The departments were left very much to themselves, enjoying 'autonomy' or, rather, non-interference from the central polytechnic administration apart from fiscal support and the occasional administrative intervention. Consequently, the departments had nurtured the ethos that as centres of higher education, they should control their own destiny.

> 'My course has been running for ten years, it is running well, it is popular, all the graduates are snapped up by employers, why all this analysis? I know it is running well.'

> 'One can understand (though difficult to accept) that our proposed degree courses require CNAA scrutiny, but it baffles me why the approach is extended to non-degree level courses.'

> 'It is unnecessary and self-inflicted work.'

Thus the need to establish some system of monitoring, internally and/or externally, bewildered the staff. The concept of validation was a novelty; the submission of degrees for internal then external scrutiny was certainly not a vision shared.

The new director, apart from introducing validation, also led the implementation of an institutional review which involved basic structural, programmatic, procedural and staffing changes. The breadth, scope and speed of such changes left the Hong Kong Polytechnic staff confused and further dismayed. In retrospect, however, validation may have fulfilled an unexpected function in absorbing much of the stress and strain sparked off by these other major changes.

The Validation Concept and Model

By 1988, the concept of validation was defined in a *Course Leaders' Handbook* as follows:

Validation ... an umbrella term to include the processes of initial validation, revalidation and review, and of the decision of approval. To be more precise, initial validation is the process whereby a judgement is reached on whether a new course meets the appropriate requirements for the award in question, this is basically an appraisal of intent; revalidation is a similar process on an existing course with the difference that evidence of the performance as well as of intent is available; review is the process whereby the progress of an existing course is appraised and any plans for change are considered; approval is the formal outcome of the validation process permitting the course to operate (or not to operate in the case of non-approval).

The definition falls in well with Alexander and Gent's (1983) observation that three main elements are commonly found in the definitions on validation: '... firstly a *judgement* as to the adequacy of an educational proposal; secondly, a *decision* to sanction the translation of proposal into action ... and thirdly the innovation and application of *authority* to legitimate both judgement and decision.' Its nature was further spelt out in the *Handbook* which stated that 'critical appraisal (of the course) is the central importance of the review process.' This process was described as

(i) formal, making explicit the information and the values used in arriving at a judgement;
(ii) open and public, as the Polytechnic believes that educators have to be accountable for the decisions they make in planning and implementing a course; and
(iii) recognising the collective responsibility and participation of the course committee as a group.

The 1988 *Handbook* also articulates more clearly the purposes of validation, and declares that the major aspects of a course to be considered in validation are its aims, contents, teaching and learning strategies, assessment arrangements, staff quality, facilities and resources, and management. Ongoing course evaluation and follow-up action were stressed, and validation was very much seen as a process 'of change and renewal'.

Responses to the Introduction of Validation

The introduction of a comprehensive system of validation provoked reactions from staff, some favourable, others negative.

Chinese Cultural Tradition

'It is not in the Chinese tradition to require a teacher to justify himself or his work.'

'Is this just an administrative game imposed by the British to justify their existence?'

'Although struggle sessions and self-criticism have been practised for some years in China, they are not part of true Chinese tradition.'

Staff reactions were complicated by the distinct sub-cultures exhibited by the local Chinese and the expatriate staff. The majority of the staff in the polytechnic are Chinese. Most of them have been exposed to Western cultures and have apparently adopted Western ways of life. Many have undertaken further studies in the 'Western' university system, but their value base and consequently their views and their ways of handling issues should not be taken for granted as being similar to those of their colleagues from the West. Studies have argued the persistence of the deep structure of the Chinese culture that lies beneath the manifestation of their behaviour (Sun, 1983).

The philosophies professed by the validation exercise — public accountability, open communication and self-criticism — are contrary to the views and values of traditional Chinese culture. As this, in varying extent, affects the way the local Chinese perceive validation, this is discussed briefly here.

Western culture generally views 'change' positively, assuming that this will bring improvement. Chinese culture basically values *stability* as it signifies *harmony*. 'Change' is often associated with 'confusion' ('Tung-luen' 動亂), something to be frowned on. Thus, in the Hong Kong way of life, it is common belief that 'harmony in the family generates prosperity' (家和萬事興); in business, harmonious relationship between employer and employees produces wealth (和氣生財); when ruling a country, the ruler aims at harmony and stability (國泰民安), and, consequently, stability gives rise to prosperity (安定繁榮).

Tolerance ('ren' 忍) of irregularities is revered as a virtue. This is derived from the Chinese view that man's existence is defined by his relationship with another man; thus, unlike the West, man is seen neither as a discrete individual with his own rights nor as responsible for his own actions. Man acts in accordance with what is expected of him, and to 'win the hearts of other men' ('de ren sin' 得人心) is something worth striving for. Hence, avoidance of being critical of others, tolerance of difference of opinion to maintain harmony and stability within a group relationship results.

The Chinese are much affected by Confucian philosophy. The often quoted five role-sets, namely, emperor-servant, father-son, husband-wife, brother-brother, friend-friend, still have much impact to guide the behaviour of the Chinese today. This provides the guidelines to how one should behave in each of the above role-sets, including paying respect to one's elders and complying with the wishes of one's seniors. Thus the structure of interpersonal relationships provides the basic frame of reference for Chinese behaviour.

In Chinese culture one man's relationship with another is sustained through 'heart-to-heart' exchange. Thus cordial *'personal relationship'* ('ren-tsing' 人情) becomes a priority in the maintenance of relationship with another person. Consequently, it is not surprising that affections and emotions intervene in decision-making, and giving 'face' to the other party is quite legitimate. Such a phenomenon often poses a dilemma for the Chinese professional exposed to a Western style of training when he/she tries to be 'objective' in drawing reasoned conclusions and making informed decisions. It follows that mutual *harmony* is valued.

'Why should we criticize our colleagues, let CNAA do it and so we rest in harmony one with another.' This was a response by members of staff asked to serve on validation panels. As validation was originally envisaged as preparation for a next stage, this was an entirely understandable approach.

In the Hong Kong situation such culture is further complicated by the exposure to Western culture — the two are not always compatible. In times of conflict a *pragmatic* approach is often the adopted solution. Such an approach is much supported by the unique local culture which stresses efficiency and quick, short-term returns.

The above has depicted Chinese staff exhibiting tolerance and passive compliance, with non-critical and pragmatic problem-solving attitudes. However, this should not be taken as representative of every individual. Scattered within the Chinese staff community were individuals who seemed to have adopted a critical and assertive approach to issues. They tend to be those staff who have resolved for themselves some of the dilemmas of Eastern and Western values. They have internalized some of the Western values and are more accepting of the beliefs and values that validation represents.

This latter group, in step with the change, would accept the challenge in validation while recognizing and acknowledging their basic cultural roots to be Chinese. For the others, one manageable aim was to look for a working agreement and re-orient thinking to reframe the problem so as to improve realistically on course provision.

A phenomenon which must not pass unnoticed was the relationship between the two groups. 'Racial discrimination' would be an exaggeration and an overstatement: *a sensitive and sensible co-existence* of the two groups is probably the appropriate description. In the context described, it was only sensible to maintain such co-existence and to avoid confrontation which might tip the balance.

Academic Autonomy

'I am the teacher of this subject, no one else has the right to tell me how it should be taught.'

'This is what academic freedom is about.'

Validation enquired into areas of academic staff activity which previously had not been under scrutiny. Understandably, some staff reacted by using the concept of academic autonomy as a shield against the intervention.

The most persuasive counterargument has been that the validation system is a peer review exercise of *mutual benefit*: that the challenge to the course team's values and practice can stimulate them to improve their course; and their acquired experience can later serve to challenge and stimulate colleagues in other departments in return.

The Amount of Work

The comprehensive scope of validation relating to course aims and how they are to be realized through course components, subjects, teaching methodology and assessment, demanded a lot of effort and time from the course committee. Frequently, it did not come through as a rewarding exercise. The course committees' submissions, usually thickly documented, were critically commented on by validation panels.

Frequently, follow-up work would lead to further frustrations, particularly so when course committees felt that their preparatory efforts had not been duly recognized. When the course was approved for implementation or continuation, neither the validation panel nor the course committee was ever really sure if subsequent changes would really lead to better results. Even if clear targets of change were identified for action (e.g. the poor teaching/learning environment of the outlying centres), improvements seemed so slow that one wondered if validation could really bring forth fruit.

In the area of allocation of staff time, expertise and leadership, the validation exercise was so demanding that it competed keenly with other (more satisfying and rewarding) important functions such as research and staff development, and was often held in abeyance unless course committees were pressed for action.

The extent of the documentation required was daunting, especially for staff unused to the formal expression of aims and philosophies, of teaching strategies, of carefully articulated syllabuses. The reaction against the required intellectual discipline of thinking through the academic design and structure of the course vented itself in frustration at the extent of the documentation.

Validation as a Threat

In addition to its dubious existence, the very nature of the validation exercise posed a threat to the staff. The philosophies it professed (public accountability, open communication, self-criticism) and the issues it addressed demanded of the staff a new attitude and approach to course monitoring for which they had not been prepared.

The confrontational aspect of the exercise in which one party proposed a thesis and defended it against questioning was seen as foreign, unnecessary and very anxiety-provoking. It was but natural that the validation panel meetings were viewed with anxiety and dislike.

Coping with Resistance

Thus the validation exercise was launched in an atmosphere of major change, frustration and low trust. The philosophies of the exercise, an outgrowth of Western ideologies, found only some sympathetic supporters among the staff. Others followed with passive compliance. For the exercise to have an impact on course improvement, validation had to be seen as a change agent with its own dynamics, operating in an environment with constraints. The interaction between these systems and sub-systems in the organization needed to be analyzed, and the way in which the whole issue had evolved within the organization had also to be considered. Resistance of the staff towards validation was a natural response. Understanding the *sources* of resistance was important to facilitate decisions for future action. Such sources roughly fell into the following categories.

1 resistance mainly due to *lack of understanding*. Hence improved communication through guidance sessions, training, information dissemination would help.

2 resistance mainly due to validation being a *threat to self-interest* (e.g. the approval or disappproval of a course being equated with the threat to a department's status, 'face' or power). Negotiations based on persuasion might lead to mutually acceptable agreements.

3 resistance mainly due to *different ideological convictions* (i.e. that validation not be used for course monitoring). In such instances compromises were hard to come by. In most cases acceptance and understanding was one possible compromise and establishing a working relationship was another.

4 resistance arising from scepticism coloured by *racial* issues such as 'this is a game that the British employ to justify their existence.' Again this posed the case of a 'no-win' situation. The use of power could easily be interpreted as an instrument of oppression! Hence, such situations were left quietly untouched.

A reliable assessment of sources of resistance from staff was difficult. Resistance due to opposing ideological and political convictions was often screened behind or disguised under that of self-interest and lack of understanding. As indicators for action, the latter two points were always kept in mind while the former two were addressed.

The Hidden Reality

There is a danger that the validation process may itself hide the reality. Escher's lithograph of the 'Three Worlds' illustrates three simultaneous views of reality. On the surface of the pond some dried leaves can be observed drifting in the slight wind. Somewhat distorted by the rippled surface of the water, the reflection of some large and sturdy trees can be seen; these form a second world. The third world can be glimpsed with much greater difficulty in the form of a large fish in the deep and dark waters of the pond. Similarly, there may be three alternative views of reality (or are some of them illusory?) in the validation of a course.

The first reality is the course proposal, into which so many months of hard work have gone to get it through hurdles. There it is, the laundered, trimmed, bound, sacrosanct, approved volume, the culmination of so much work.

The second reality which we can see, if we look past the sacred volume, are the procedures which have brought about the course document. These include the careful and painstaking frequent *monitoring* of the course operation by the staff closely associated with it. They include the regular, albeit infrequent, formal *evaluation* of the course operation by the staff, maybe including staff from other departments, students, employers and the validation panel. These form our second view of reality, our second world.

The third world is the most difficult to see. Administrators, accrediting agency staff and principals may never see it and even doubt its reality. It is the world where a member of staff teaches and a student learns. It is where that most precious commodity of all, education, is nourished.

All these three worlds exist interrelated, and cannot be isolated. When a validating panel looks at the first world of the document, it must pay attention to the world of evaluation, responsibility and accountability which has produced the course review document. The validators who are in the throes of living in that second world must also not forget the reality of that third world, and must be conscious of the links between that world of student learning and the world of validation.

The Multi-Dimensional Response

Based on these understandings, the polytechnic devised a plan of action involving different levels and sectors of the institution. Sole reliance on persuading individuals to change their attitude was not favoured.

The first move was to change the relationship between the validators and the validated. Closer interaction between the panel and the course team was fostered by informing the course leader of the membership of the panel at an early stage, by encouraging the panel chairman and course leader to meet, and prior to any meeting with the panel by informing the course team of the major issues to be discussed. The next step was to discourage the confrontational style of interaction and to encourage the development of a more facilitating atmosphere, congenial to open discussion. Here the style and skill of the chairman were important.

At the policy level, validation received stronger support. Internally, the polytechnic Director was seen to endorse the process. Externally, the Hong Kong Council for Academic Accreditation (HKCAA) was established as a local body responsible for validation. The fact that some of the polytechnic's own policy positions (e.g. on the aims of validation) were adopted by the HKCAA helped to legitimize the system within the polytechnic.

The validation operation was systematized and clarified, and all the procedures were clearly set down in writing in the *Course Leaders' Handbook* distributed to all staff. Criteria were elaborated as far as possible given the nature of the process, and topics which needed to be addressed by staff in the design, operation and analysis of courses were listed. This eased the anxiety of those whose resistance sprang from lack of understanding. Moreover an appeal system was introduced to ensure fair treatment and to protect the rights of the validated.

Frequent workshops stressing staff participation were held. The sharing of anxieties and exercises on validation procedures lowered staff fear and increased their understanding and commitment to the process. This, together with greater familiarity with the process, institutionalized validation.

The importance of course management, course leadership and the care of a course was enhanced by giving a specific allocation of staff for course management purposes (although the overall staff establishment within the polytechnic did not change significantly).

Specific support was given by the polytechnic to the funding of educational research and development projects. Successful proposals ranged from funding week-long workshops and the development of multi-media learning packages, to research into the learning patterns of students. The intention here was to support curriculum development and course implementation, as a parallel to the validation system which identified what needed to be done.

As the process of validation became institutionalized, the membership of internal panels was deliberately constructed to include staff experienced in course development as well as staff who were newly appointed course leaders. The chairmanship was also spread so that about fifteen persons, including Chinese and expatriates, were involved, and they met occasionally to review their experience.

At the same time Chinese became accepted as a language of validation. The re-validation, including the formal documentation but excluding the validation report, of a course could take place in Chinese. This indicated the ability of the process to be localized, at least in language.

Care was taken not to establish the idea of validation as a process in its own right but rather as an effective way for improving the educational work of the institution. Mindful of the reactions of the staff, an interactive model which stressed increased communication between the panel and the course team was explored (see below).

As well as specific responses to the problems raised by validation, the institution as a whole started to address the issue of quality in a more broad ranging fashion. One of the strengths of a course-based validation system, whether internal or external, is that it focuses on the *course* as a basic functional unit for analysis to which the other aspects of the institution contribute. This is healthy as this is what the *students* experience during their higher education experience; and facilitating students' learning is what the institution is primarily about.

However, an overconcentration on course-based validation may lead to neglect of other perspectives which are crucial to the quality of work of an institution and to the courses it offers, but which are not directly related to individual courses. These issues often arise from individual course validations but need to be addressed within an institution on a more systematic and broader basis. Thus the institution, in addition to its course validation activities, sought to establish a view on the nature of the education provided to its students, student and staff quality, academic and intellectual ethos, and physical environment.

From Internal Validation to Its External Counterpart

Observed Features of Validation

In the polytechnic's experience of the internal and external process, two interesting phenomena were observed. The first was '*tribal affiliation*', when panel members were drawn from the same subject, discipline and professional background as the course team. This was often the case in the external validation system, where there was a common language, a common context and a common understanding between panel and course team, and an emphasis on those aspects which they shared, i.e. the subject matter. The interaction could become cosy, especially in disciplines which felt that they were somewhat out of the mainstream, with both the panel and the course team facing an external common threat which drew them together in mutual support.

However, for internal validation, the panel members were likely to be drawn from different subject, disciplinary and professional backgrounds. The panel was likely to ask 'ignorant' or 'obvious' questions on the conventions, paradigms and presuppositions of that discipline, and might have different

and possibly higher expectations of staff development and student performance than were traditionally characteristic of that discipline. There tended
to be an emphasis on general educational aspects of institutional matters
(e.g. staff development strategies), on organizational aspects, regulations and
assessment, rather than on subject matter. The lack of a common heritage
could lead to a less congenial discussion, less sharing and a sharper exchange.

A second interesting phenomenon was *'sibling rivalry'*. Some course team
members were anxious about the appointment of local members from closely
related departments within the same institution or drawn from their
counterparts from sister institutions. Critical comments might be suspected
as attempts to denigrate a competitor for resources or status. Another was
that good ideas might be borrowed without the courtesy of acknowledgment
especially by institutions whose courses are not subjected to scrutiny.

Thus members drawn from too near home could give rise to rivalry, to
the detriment of a useful academic interchange. On the other hand, they
could have greater inside knowledge about the underlying issues which gave
rise to the characteristics exhibited in the course. For example, they might be
better able to identify problems of management and resource allocation, yet
they might be less able to address those issues since they themselves might be
part of the system.

Characteristics of Validation

The primary characteristic of an external validation system is that it is an
intermittent activity carried out by persons without day-to-day responsibility
for the course. This allows it to make disinterested decisions, *uninfluenced* by
the institutions's internal political and managerial system. It also allows it to
make decisions *uninformed* by the institution's internal system.

An internal validation is set within the context of the institution itself.
The strength of this is that decisions and deliberations of the internal
validation can be focused to make the most effective intervention possible.
The weakness is that it is likely to operate within the constraints of the
existing system without challenging that system and without an independent
perspective.

The relationship between the two systems at the polytechnic necessarily
developed over time. Initially the internal system was a process of 'vetting' a
proposal before forwarding it in its polished form to the external. Thus quite
a lot of stress was placed on the documentation of the submission. But as
validation developed, the role of the internal validation became a preparation
of the course team for the external event, testing its proposal and its
philosophies (not just 'vetting' the documentation) against the polytechnic's
own standards.

Mutually Supportive Processes?

An external course-based validation system can support an institution's own system of quality assurance in the following ways.

1   Through its existence, the presence of an external course-based validation system does act as a sanction and reinforcer of the internal processes.
2   Where the external validation panel identifies issues which need to be addressed, but then leaves it to the internal system to carry out the monitoring of conditions and recommendations, it is most supportive. This is a particularly constructive approach in that it reinforces the authority of the internal system and ensures that the internal system itself is active in pursuing the improvement of the course.
3   An external panel in the present pattern has stronger subject expertise than does an internal panel and because of that can suggest remedies as well as identify weaknesses.

But the external system can also undermine the institution's internal quality assurance system.

1   The very existence of an external system which repeats the internal processes calls into question the need for an internal system.
2   Where the external validation system holds values different from those of the institution, questions arise. For example, if the institution emphasizes general education or the need for all students to be aware of the social context of Hong Kong, the subject panel can undermine that emphasis, even by its attitude. If standards expected by the external panel are lower than demanded by the institution of its own courses, or if the external panel is less penetrating, thorough or stimulating than the internal panel, the question arises — is the external necessary?
3   Course-based validation panels *can* concentrate on the subject of the course, giving less emphasis to those issues which to the institution are of greater underlying importance such as staff development, or the institutional support for research.

How then are we to ensure that the relationship between the two processes supports quality assurance?

Merging of the Two Systems

One way is to work toward a gradual merger of the two systems. Three stages are illustrated in Figure 1. This describes the merging of external with internal course validation as it is expected to develop in Hong Kong.

Figure 1. The Merging of the Internal-External Validation System

Stage A	Two 'separate' consecutive processes, owned respectively by the institution (internal) and the validating agency (external), with the internal validation including external members but not vice versa.
Stages B and C	Still two separate internal and external events but some internal members on externally owned events and more external members on internal events.
Stage D	The position planned for the future when the institution is accredited is where the formal responsibility for and ownership of *course* validation rests with the institution but more external membership is used.

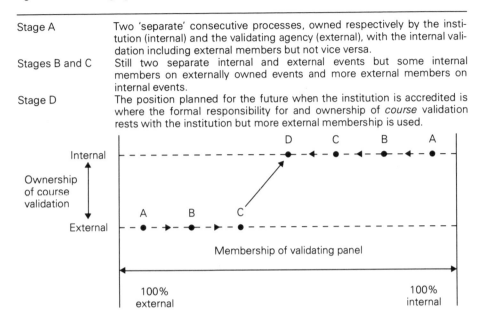

An Interactive Model of Validation Explored

Barnett (1983) suggests that it is the duty of validation to generate a systematic and critical reflection on the curriculum as a whole. He advocates that a frank and open dialogue between the two parties should be sought, undominated by any member. In this way both parties participate as equals, questioning each other, examining one another's assumptions and values, critically discussing different aspects of the course, and valuing this experience as 'genuine peer review'. Having considered suggestions, improvements will be made and the course team assumes responsibility to monitor the development, feeling that it 'owns' the course.

> The validators are not 'guardians', there is no need to guard, for they are not imposing their authority: they are essentially asking critical questions. If they provide a counter set of claims, values, these, in turn, are submitted to the forum for debate ... it is potentially subject to scrutiny. Validation is thus essentially an *interactive* process. (Barnett, 1983, p. 158)

When staff appreciate the intrinsic values of validation, the structure, the form, the standard and the judgment will no longer be the main concerns of the participants. Their foremost interest will be excitement in the exploration and exchange on issues of common concern, and they are as partners searching for ways to improve the course. In such a discourse the ownership of the course has been transferred; the responsibility belongs truly to the course team that takes care of the course. This genuine interaction can be termed 'an interactive model of validation', where validation is a peer discussion between equals.

Conclusion

The Hong Kong Polytechnic's experience of validation, both internal and external, gives rise to our view that the two most significant issues in the exercise of course validation are the concept and function of validation, and the relationship between the validated and the validators.

Concept and Function

For validation to improve the quality of the education offered to students, it must be organically related to the operation of the course and be supportive of its development; it needs to be a process intrinsic to the nature of the education, a development process owned by the course team and not just a control measure externally imposed.

This idea is often referred to, borrowing a concept from industry, as quality assurance, distinguishing it from quality control. Quality control is where the quality of a product is assessed at the output. A quality assurance system assures the quality of the product by ensuring that all the persons involved in the enterprise learn to collaborate and accept personal responsibility for the quality of the product (the students' education in our case); where the concept of quality affects every activity in the enterprise. This, as compared to quality control, is a more normative and developmental approach.

Relationships

A consequence of the move in validation from control to assurance and from a management dictated activity to a lecturer participation activity is that the relationship between the validated and the validators must approximate more closely to the ideal of a *peer* relationship.

Where course teams are inexperienced in the analysis of an educational process, and in pedagogical enquiry, it may be inevitable that a panel, whether internal or external, will have much greater experience, competence, and self-confidence than the course team offering the course. This can lead to expertise, both subject-based and educational, being seen to be vested in the membership of the validating panel and to that panel feeling it necessary to exercise the authority appropriate to their expertise and to tell the course team what to do.

However, as staff become more competent in educational issues relating to curriculum design and the teaching of students in higher education; and as they become more familiar with the intrinsic concepts of validation, they become more able to take increasing responsibility for their own courses and for their operation. This is an ongoing process.

If the function of higher education is *emancipatory*, i.e. if it is to provide a broad education for students as citizens, if it is to allow them to overcome constraints, and to formulate alternatives, then the function of validation which provides for a self-analysis of higher education must be to liberalize the experience of the staff: it must be emancipatory for the staff as well.

How can validation achieve this? Does it mean that the institution or the accrediting agency loses all authority, does it delegate it all to the staff offering the course? Rather the way forward is through *rigorous, critical, open academic dialogue*, between the staff offering the course and the panel, whether set up by the institution or outside agency, to validate the course; but for the dialogue to be effective, each side must be prepared to change its own philosophy in the light of reasoned discourse.

References

AINSWORTH, M. (1989) 'Monitoring, Evaluation and Validation of Courses: A Case Study', *International Journal of Educational Management*, 2, 1.

ALEXANDER, R. and GENT, B. (1983) 'A Case for Internal Validation', in CHURCH, C. H. (Ed.), *Practice and Perspective in Validation*, Guilford, SRHE.

BARNETT, R. (1983) 'The Legitimation of Validation', in CHURCH, C.H. (Ed.), *Practice and Perspective in Validation*, Guilford, SRHE.

BARNETT, R. (1990) *The Idea of Higher Education*, Guilford, SRHE.

BILLING, D. (1983) 'Practice and Criteria of Validation under the CNAA', in CHURCH, C.H. (Ed.) *Practice and Perspective in Validation*, Guilford, SRHE.

CHURCH, C.H. and MURRAY, R. (1983) 'Of Definitions, Debates and Dimensions', in CHURCH, C.H. (Ed.), *Practice and Perspective in Validation*, Guilford, SRHE.

COOK, C.M. (1988) 'Internal and External Evaluation: Reflections on the American Experience', Paper presented at International Conference on Quality Assessment in Higher Education, the Netherlands.

DAVIES, M. (1980) 'The CNAA as a Validating Agency', in BILLING, D.A. (Ed.), *Indicators of Performance*, Guilford, SRHE.

HONG KONG POLYTECHNIC (1988) *Course Leaders' Handbook*, Hong Kong, Hong Kong Polytechnic.

HOUSE, E.R. (1978) 'Assumptions Underlying Evaluation Models', *Educational Researcher*, AERA, March 1978, pp. 4–12.

KOGAN, M. (1986) *Education Accountability: An Analytic Overview*, London, Hutchison Press.

ROBBINS, L. (1963) *Higher Education*, Report of a Committee under the Chairmanship of Lord Robbins, London, HMSO, Cmnd 2154, pp. 107–125.

SUN, L.K. (1983) *The Deep Structure of Chinese Culture*, Hong Kong.

15 Quality Assurance at the Open Learning Institute

Gajaraj Dhanarajan and Andrea Hope

Part I of this chapter considers the particular characteristics of distance education, where the students and modes of delivery are very different from those in conventional higher education institutions. It sets out some of the criteria for measuring the quality of distance and open education, including its materials, exit standards, cost, and contribution to scholarship. Part II describes quality assurance procedures at the Open Learning Institute (OLI) of Hong Kong. External peer advisory groups, external assessors and external examiners provide regular monitoring. Elaborate internal validation and review structures, detailed monitoring of tutorial support, careful development and evaluation of course materials, and systematic feedback from students are all part of the OLI's efforts to achieve a high quality product at a price its customers can afford.

PART I: QUALITY ASSURANCE IN DISTANCE AND OPEN LEARNING

Introduction

The practice of education by distance and open learning methods continues to develop rapidly world-wide. It has been estimated recently that some 600 or so institutions offer one form or another of open and distance learning (Dhanarajan and Brahmawong, 1990), and of these a third are located in Asia. In Hong Kong alone there are around twenty-three providers (Castro, 1990), and in 1984 it was estimated that at least ten million adults participated in this educational innovation world-wide (Daniel, 1984). These students perhaps share one major characteristic in that they are usually *not* the educational élite of their respective societies, and do not necessarily have a common background of social status and education.

The emergence of this global phenomenon, basically in response to the numbers and the circumstances of the students to be served, seems to have developed in tandem with the development of good communication technologies. Some authors have ascribed the great attention of the public to distance education to its use of high tech media from radio and audio to television and interactive video (Granger, 1986). Not as visible, but equally important for the success of distance education, has been the effort made by distance educators to improve the effectiveness of their courses and programmes — in inculcating skills, competences and adding value to students' education. Distance and open education practices can contribute to these quality concerns — both to increase their own effectiveness and to serve as a model for conventional programmes.

Whether one considers quality in education in its conventional or distance form, there is a wide range of issues to be considered. Attention focuses not only on the 'quality of the educational process — how well students learn, but also on the coherence and purpose of education — what does it mean to be educated and why is it important within any culture?' (Granger, 1986). Concern about a decline in the quality of higher education across the globe has been related to phenomena such as increase in attrition rates, institutions becoming excessively vocational, irrelevant or fragmented curricula and non-achievement of programme objectives by learners. In its response to this state of affairs, a 1984 report by the National Institute of Education (USA) recommended that '*student involvement* is the key to learning, that learning is most effectively conducted as a joint enterprise, and that higher learning pays its greatest dividends when it serves to inform intelligent action in our society and economy' (Mortimer, 1984, as cited by Granger, 1988).

Student involvement was subsequently defined as the amount of time, energy and effort students devote to the learning process and the intensity of their engagement in the learning process. The direction suggested emphasizes a focus on students and their needs — both as students and as members of society — primarily because the majority of students no longer fit easily into the conventional categories which higher education has traditionally served. Distance education by definition and practice serves the unconventional student; its pedagogy therefore by design has to be student-centred. Materials containing knowledge are designed for independent study. The design in turn is expected to take into account the experience and knowledge students bring to learning; finally, knowledge itself is referenced to the context of the socio-cultural environment of the learner.

This student-centred approach to education inevitably leads to a rethinking of the role of faculty in the process. The traditional expectation of learning environments where the flow of knowledge is one way from teacher to student shifts in distance education. The intervention of (instructionally) well designed materials moves the teaching and learning activity from active teacher/passive learner to active learner/supportive tutor situation. Faculty role in this environment becomes secondary to the learning process. It is supportive at one end, i.e. tuition, laboratory and feedback, and managerial at the other, i.e. timetabling, training and monitoring tutors, scheduling practical work and supervising material development. Faculty does not provide instruction; students learn by active engagement with the course materials. It is in this student-centred, active learner situation that quality assurance is practised in open and distance learning.

Characteristics of Distance Education

Descriptions of distance education abound. Some that cover the field comprehensively include Kaye and Rumble (1981), Holmberg (1987), Mugridge and Kaufman (1986), Dhanarajan and Brahmawong (1990). Of the many characteristics that have an impact on the products and services provided by distance educators the following three are pertinent.

Nature of Learners

The obvious starting-point is the unconventionality of the learners. They are mostly part-time learners, older, generally possess fewer previous academic qualifications, and bring into learning experiential knowledge. In the OLI the typical student is male, between 25 and 30 years old, is in employment, and has the equivalent of one or two O-levels in terms of academic qualification. The learning environment we create has to address these characteristics if we truly believe in carrying out our mission.

Modes of Delivery

Clear differences in pedagogy and modes of delivery of instruction exist between distance and conventional forms of education. To begin with, in distance education systems, teachers and learners do not interact with each other as in campus classrooms. Second, it is difficult to ascribe a typical pedagogical approach followed by all distance educators. Some use only radio, others television, yet others electronic bulletin boards, while many use only print. Some systems use a mixture of media such as the Open University of UK and the OLI of Hongkong. What media are used for teaching depend on economics, facilities, ease of availability to institutions and learners and the purpose for which the media are employed. Organizations delivering distance education must make decisions on the medium or media used in their teaching functions within limits of practicality and purpose. In doing so, they must take account of the need for:

1   exposition which can be written (print, computer aided learning/ computer aided instruction), spoken (radio, audio cassette, tutorials), and visual (video, television);
2   self-learning, where the students must make knowledge presented to them their own by using it, working with it regularly and submitting formative and summative tests for assessment and feedback;
3   counselling for academic or social purposes to help the learner over-come temporary difficulties.

Student Motivation

Student motivation to pursue self-learning varies from culture to culture. The strategy adopted by the providers of open and distance learning to meet with student goals is an important criterion by which their performance is measured. In an investigation into why students chose to study at the Open Learning Institute of Hong Kong some 60 per cent of non-arts students and about 24 per cent of arts students indicated upward career mobility as a main reason (Kember *et al.*, 1990). This was not much different from a finding of McIntosh and Calder (1975) of British Open University students. On the other hand, North American studies by Egert (1975) of would-be adult distance learning students of the State University of Nebraska and the University of Mid-America seemed to indicate career-related agenda as a low priority, and reasons such as 'to improve self image', to 'simply learn', to 'attain specific skills' as higher needs. The design of curriculum and systems has to accommodate these wishes of clients which are subsequently subject to quality evaluations.

Assuring and Measuring Quality

The criteria used to measure the quality of distance education are by necessity multi-dimensional. Some of these are common to traditional systems (e.g. learner outcomes); others are specific to open learning. The following is a list of features most distance educators consider in assuring the quality of their activity.

Access

Supporters of open and distance learning will claim that their educational mission is to provide access and equality of opportunity for learning especially to individuals and groups who have been denied these before. However, as Gooler (1979) points out, success in providing access is not a sufficient condition for arguing greater opportunity — 'equality of opportunity is a matter of outcomes, not merely resource availability'; in other words, providing access is a starting-point, and equality of opportunity can only be achieved if the people provided with such opportunities are helped towards achieving their own goals. There is very little evidence in the literature to indicate whether such objectives have been achieved or even if these criteria are measurable.

Courses and Programmes

Distance educators invest a significant proportion of their resources and energy in ensuring that the quality of the products they offer for delivery is of a comparable standard to those of other systems. There are criteria available to measure the achievement of these quality intentions. The following four are crucial:

1 logic of products: the structure and content of courses, the level, sequence, relevance, currency, and sensitivity to social concerns are matters of academic importance. It is in this area that academic judgments relating to standards are made; it is also the area where knowledge and skills are conveyed.

2 development of products: the development process used to create the learning materials can reasonably be expected to mirror the concern for quality. Instructional design and product development procedures show quality control checkpoints in the system.

3 face value of products: this is concerned with the technical quality of the learning materials that are created for the individual learner whether they are print, audio, video, or computer aided learning packages. In some cases precise parameters can be applied to measure quality and in others judgments are made on 'feel' and 'impressions'. Badly packaged learning materials can have a negative impact on students.

4 delivery of products: the ability of the system to deliver the products to the intended learners is a measure of its success or failure. The question of delivery is an important consideration for any distance teaching institute whose clients are a heterogeneous mix. New technologies offer great opportunities to teach and learn only if staff and students accept their use.

Learner Outcomes

The measurement of learner outcomes or exit standards is another criterion applied by evaluators of quality in education. Distance education teaching in most environments provides clear statements of intentions for learners. Assessment strategies of courses are devised and applied to maximize goal achievements by learners and at the same time to provide security for the system. It is also important to determine the achievement of goals which learners set for themselves. Adult learners exercise their frustration with their feet and drop out of programmes that do not meet their personal objectives. The attrition rate can often signal dangers in the academic health of distance and open learning systems.

Economics

The cost efficiency and effectiveness of the system is an overriding concern of all distance educators. These factors have a major impact on the modus operandi of course development and delivery. Any measurement of quality of a distance education system will have to take costs and benefits into consideration.

Scholarship

Another important quality criterion for a distance learning institution is the contribution it makes towards knowledge about adult learning, the use of new technologies in delivering education and the impact of mass higher education on society. Studies relating to a better understanding of the problems, issues and practices in the field of educational opportunities and delivery should be a part of the scholarly pursuits of a distance and open learning institution (Gooler, 1979).

PART II: THE OLI MODEL

This case study reviews some of the procedures for assuring and measuring the quality of distance learning programmes at the Hong Kong Open Learning Institute.

Introduction

The Open Learning Institute was established in Hong Kong in early 1989. While its mode of delivery and entry requirements may differ radically, the objective of the OLI is to provide education of directly comparable academic quality to the other tertiary institutions in Hong Kong. Before any courses were offered to students, the UK Council for National Academic Awards (CNAA) visited Hong Kong to advise the Institute on its suitability to conduct work at degree level and the academic quality of the proposed degree programmes. In particular, the CNAA team examined the overall processes and arrangements for safeguarding academic standards.

The CNAA report strongly emphasized the need for the OLI to be seen at the outset to offer high quality education. Its recommendations were unequivocal. To ensure high academic standards OLI must:

1 take full responsibility for its own academic standards;
2 develop a system of internal quality assurance;
3 seek advice from appropriate discipline-based external peer groups on course selection, development and adaptation;
4 subject the revised courses and programmes to external peer group validation;
5 seek a further external audit in approximately twelve months' time.

Part I of this chapter has described the philosophy of quality assurance in open and distance learning. Part II indicates the steps taken by the OLI in its first two years to implement a fully integrated total quality management system. The model chosen integrates the contribution of external peers with the internal quality control procedures of the Institute at every stage, as described below.

The Contribution of External Peers

Advisory Peer Groups

From the outset each degree programme has an advisory peer group of up to nine people working in Hong Kong in related areas, drawn from the other tertiary institutions and from commerce or industry as appropriate. Working with the Institute academics, the aims of the programme are discussed and a set of courses to meet these aims is agreed. Where an existing course is identified for possible inclusion, the group advises on its suitability and any necessary adaptations for the Hong Kong context. Where no existing course is available, the group assists in preparing a syllabus so that a special course can be written. Once a programme has started, the advisory group continues to advise on course improvements and review.

External Assessors

If an existing course has not already had an external assessor, or where there are significant adaptations, and when a new course is being written, the OLI appoints a person of high standing in the appropriate discipline to review the proposed final version. This review assesses the course's structure, balance, relevance, content level, and pedagogy. The external assessor's report must be approved by the Academic Board before the course can be offered to students.

External Examiners

Experts from outside the OLI, usually from other institutions of higher education, are appointed as external examiners. Their task is to ensure the examinations are fairly set and marked. From their experience of degree level courses elsewhere they are able to judge if the quality of student performance ('the exit standard') is comparable to that in other institutions.

Programme Approval

In addition to this scrutiny of individual courses, the introduction and review of all degree programmes is subject to the overall approval of the OLI Programme Review and Validation Committee which includes three external peers with the power to co-opt additional specialists as required.

The Internal Committee Structure

The OLI Committee structure seeks to integrate external advice and assessment with its internal quality control mechanisms while preserving the integrity of each. The goal is to ensure that the production and delivery of courses and programmes, as well as the assessment and examination of all students are carried out in a controlled and uniform manner.

There are currently over 16,000 part-time students registered with the Institute on eighteen courses across the three Schools of Arts and Social Sciences, Business and Administration, and Science and Technology. It is expected to reach 'steady state' at approximately 30,000 students by 1993 when courses at all levels permitting students to graduate with the degree of BA, BSc, BBA, BSocSc and BGS (Bachelor of General Studies) will be offered. The achievement of uniform high quality across this breadth of provision to such a volume of students requires stringent control mechanisms.

Each proposed degree programme has a Programme Team working with the associated Advisory Peer Group (see above). Each individual course has a Course Review Committee of the academics involved in the course together with a representative from the Education Technology Centre. School Committees comprising all academics in each School consider the proposals for courses and programmes. Award Committees for each course recommend the award of results to students, and a Course Results Group at Directorate level maintains an overview of the award process on behalf of Academic Board.

Quality Tuition

As already indicated, one of the major differences between establishments of open and distance learning and conventional tertiary institutions is the role of faculty *vis-à-vis* the learner.

The Role of the Tutor

On registration to a course, each student is allocated to a suitably qualified and experienced part-time tutor. The tutor's role is to deliver both distance and face-to-face teaching to a group of thirty students. Tutors give written comments on compulsory marked assignments submitted by the students, and hold tutorials, attendance at which is optional for the students. Tutors in Hong Kong, like the students in these pioneering days for the Institute, sometimes have rather traditional ideas about appropriate delivery modes for higher education which may diverge from what was earlier described as the active engagement of the independent learner with the learning materials. Both distance teaching and learning are skills to be acquired, and the quality control mechanism of tutor monitoring and feedback is vital for the successful delivery of each presentation of each course.

The Role of the Course Coordinator

Course coordinators, high quality academic staff appointed to manage the delivery and development of a particular course or suite of courses, are responsible for monitoring tutor performance in both the marking of tutor marked assignments (TMAs) in conjunction with the external examiner appointed for each course, and in the delivery of face-to-face tutorials, dayschools or 'surgeries'.

The Role of the Education Technology Centre

The initial training and updating of tutors in both the philosophy and practices of open learning is crucial to the pursuit of quality; uniformity of approach is assured by the involvement of the Education Technology Centre, which provides tutor training material (including a distance learning package) for all new tutors.

The Quality Product

Imported Courses

Where courses have been bought in 'off the shelf' from other established providers and require only minor adaptations for delivery in Hong Kong, the quality of the material is guaranteed in advance. In its initial phase the OLI based its operations predominantly on the importation of externally produced course materials. This continues to be the case for courses in the School of Science and Technology, where the major source of courses is, and will remain, the UK Open University.

Courses Developed 'In-house'

In the School of Business and Administration and increasingly in the School of Arts and Social Sciences the overriding need to deliver courses totally relevant to the Hong Kong context (some of them to be delivered in Chinese) has dictated that more and more courses should be developed by or on behalf of the OLI. This development has put new pressures on the Institute to ensure the highest standards possible at the course design, development and production phases.

The Importance of Image

In the open learning context the face value of the products, and the use of design aspects of packaging to create the appropriate image of a high quality institution are very important. In this context the medium really is the message. 'By their works shall ye know them' seems particularly appropriate. The courses are in the public domain and must look good as well as being good.

Quality Course Development

Academic control mechanisms on the quality and appropriateness of the content are married with instructional design concerns, and the Education Technology Centre plays an important role here. A course developer is contracted initially to produce a blueprint of the course which is widely circulated and commented on throughout the Institute. If that is satisfactory, the developer is retained to produce the course in stages, each of which is closely monitored and critiqued to ensure that the finished product is of sufficiently high quality to be published under the OLI logo.

Course Evaluation

Course evaluation is a formal OLI requirement. This is a joint enterprise between course coordinators, who are responsible for collecting tutor evaluation material, and the Education Technology Centre, which designs and administers evaluation surveys sent to students, and ensures that the results are widely circulated. The Academic Board receives a report on each course no later than two months after the end of each presentation.

The Price of Quality

The tensions created in producing a high quality product at a price the customers can afford are huge, but the OLI is determined to continue to put quality first. To quote from the OLI mission statement published recently:

> The Open Learning Institute of Hong Kong dedicates itself to providing degree, non-degree, and postgraduate courses leading to awards and qualifications through a system of open access and distance education; thereby making higher education available to all those aspiring to it, regardless of previous qualification, gender, or race.

> The Institute through its Council and staff, in common with and through association with other institutions of higher education in the territory, commits itself to excellence in teaching, scholarship and public service.

> The Institute is further committed to achieving a balance of income and expenditure, in time, within the financial context of Hong Kong and to attaining this without sacrificing the level and quality of courses and support for its students. (OLI, 1991)

Quality Outcomes

Learner Outcomes

As noted earlier, dissatisfied students vote with their feet, and the local media have paid much attention since 1989 to 'dropout rates' in OLI. The students register for courses, not programmes, and are at liberty to rest for a semester or more before resuming study when work or domestic circumstances permit. But the OLI tends to be judged against the Hong Kong norm for conventional tertiary institutions, where with high entry requirements and a fixed two, three or four year programme, dropout and failure are relatively rare.

OLI examination statistics in the first three semesters reveal that while 72 per cent of examinees obtained a pass result, only 42 per cent of registered students presented themselves for examination. Work, health and family-related difficulties account for a relatively small proportion of those who defer or withdraw. For many, problems caused by attempting to study at undergraduate level through the medium of English, which is usually a second or even third language, are a major hidden cause of student dropout. Any open access system expects a high attrition rate at the end of the first course/year, and the pattern in OLI is no exception. However, whereas only 45 per cent of the initial intake (October 1989) enrolled on a course in the next semester (April 1990), 83 per cent of *that* group then proceeded to take a course in October 1990 and 75 per cent of those registered again in April 1991.

Increased resources and effort have been invested in improving counselling services to continuing students and new applicants. These include face-to-face sessions, a comprehensive computerized information line telephone service to supplement Registry hotlines, and presentation of a video about the OLI via the TV network.

Institute Outcomes

A second institutional review was conducted by the Hong Kong Council for Academic Accreditation during 1990, and reported that the OLI had made impressive and substantial progress towards the establishment of a suitable academic environment for the conduct of degree level studies. Recommendations made by the visiting panel on how to maintain and further improve quality are being addressed, and the Institute is now moving towards the accreditation of its individual degree programmes.

Conclusions

Distance and open education, like their conventional counterparts all over the world, have three responsibilities. These are, in the words of Bacchetti and Weiner (1991) who recently commented on accreditation in a diverse society:

Responsibility to individual students: the instruction we deliver is expected to help students understand fundamental areas of knowledge and to use this knowledge to be responsible citizens in a democratic and caring society.

Responsibility to society: we live in an interdependent world. Our societies expect us (colleges and universities) to deliver talented men and women to meet its needs. This is not only an economic necessity but also a democratic imperative.

Responsibility to support curiosity, creativity and culture: our universities and colleges are expected to support and nurture the creation of new knowledge. They are also expected to enhance our powers of creativity.

In setting up its quality assurance mechanisms, the OLI is aiming at the ideal so many espouse.

References

BACCHETTI, R.F. and WEINER, S.S. (1991) 'Diversity Is a Key Factor in Educational Quality and Hence in Accreditation', *The Chronicle of Higher Education*, 8 May.

CASTRO, A. (1990) 'A Digest of Tertiary Educational Developments in Hong Kong and Australia', Unpublished report, Hong Kong.

DANIEL, J. (1984) *The Future of Distance Teaching Universities in a World Wide Perspective*, Proceedings of the First International Symposium on the Role of Distance Teaching for the Development of Lifelong Education, Seoul.

DHANARAJAN, G. and BRAHMAWONG, C. (1990) *A Study of Training Needs in the Use of Media for Distance Education in Asia*, Singapore, Asian Mass Communication Research and Information Centre (AMIC).

EGERT, J. (1975) 'An Examination of Goals of Potential and Actual Learners', Working Paper No. 1, Lincoln, Neb., University of Mid-America.

GOOLER, D. (1979) 'Evaluating Distance Education Programmes', *Canadian Journal of University Continuing Education*, 6, 1, pp. 43–55.

GRANGER, D. (1986) 'Distance Education, A New Pedagogy Encourages a New View of Content', Conference on Distance Education, Open Learning Agency, Vancouver.

HOLMBERG, B. (1987) *Distance Education: A Survey and a Bibliography*, London, Croom Helm.

KAYE, A. and RUMBLE, G. (1981) *Distance Teaching for Higher and Adult Education*, London, Croom Helm.

KEMBER, D., MURPHY, D., SIAW, I. and YUEN, K.S. (1990) 'Report on the Open Learning Institute of Hong Kong: Quantitative Data from a Questionnaire Survey', Unpublished report, Hong Kong, Open Learning Institute.

McINTOSH, N. and CALDER, J. (1975) *A Degree of Difference: A Study of the First Year's Intake of Students to the Open University of Great Britain*, Milton Keynes, Open University.

MORTIMER, K. (1984) *Involvement in Learning*, Washington, D.C., National Institute of Education.

MUGRIDGE, I. and KAUFMAN, D. (1986) *Distance Education in Canada*, London, Croom Helm.

OPEN LEARNING INSTITUTE (1991) *Development Plan 1991–96*, OLI, Hong Kong.

16 External Examining at Hong Kong University

Leung Wai-sun and Shen Chun-ming

The use of external examiners to monitor the exit standard of degrees is a common practice in the United Kingdom. This chapter describes the external examiner system of Hong Kong University based on the UK model but modified to meet the special needs of Hong Kong. Some background information about the examiners is provided and their role explained. Some possible future changes to the system are considered.

Introduction

Quality assurance in many higher education institutions includes an external examiner system for quality control of student outcomes, and as a way of ensuring comparability with exit standards elsewhere. Hong Kong University uses external examiners for all its degree courses. Its system is modelled on United Kingdom practice and is similar to that at the Chinese University and the non-university degree awarding institutions in Hong Kong.

Hong Kong Characteristics

There are three major reasons for having external examiners in Hong Kong. First, Hong Kong degrees in the university sector do not have to be approved by an accreditation agency. In this situation the external examiner system provides some guarantee of standards for universities overseas when Hong Kong graduates apply to study higher degrees there. Second, through an external examiner system the academic standard of a Hong Kong qualification can acquire international recognition and reputation. Third, mutual visits between academic staff in Hong Kong and their counterparts elsewhere are limited by the relatively isolated location of Hong Kong; regular contact with external examiners enables Hong Kong not only to maintain the

Table 1.   Types of External Examiners

	Visiting	Overseas Non-visiting	Total	Local	Total
External examiners	60	45	105	11	116

Table 2.   External Examiners' Countries

UK	Aust	US	Canada	Singapore	Sweden	Japan	Germany	Taiwan	Denmark	Total
61	16	13	5	3	2	2	1	1	1	105

Note: Numbers include visiting and non-visiting.

standard of its degree examinations but also to keep abreast of higher education developments.

Hong Kong University appoints its external examiners from reputable overseas universities, and in this respect Hong Kong differs from the United Kingdom where they are mostly from other British universities. Furthermore, external examiners to British universities usually make annual visits lasting for a couple of days. In Hong Kong, by contrast, an overseas examiner normally visits once every three years (except for clinical disciplines) and the visit lasts for about one week. This lower frequency of visits is dictated by the need to keep travelling expenditure down, while the longer duration makes it possible for the external examiners to perform functions beyond just checking the standard of the examination results.

Facts and Figures

Some recent data on examiners currently working with Hong Kong University provide information about their numbers, country of origin and frequency of visits. Table 1 shows that they are almost all based overseas. Examiners for bachelor's degrees must visit the territory at least once every three years; master's and postgraduate diploma awards have non-visiting examiners. Table 2 shows that the majority of examiners are from the UK, although an increasing number come from other English-speaking countries and the Asian-Pacific region.

Tables 3 and 4 respectively indicate that most examiners are appointed for three years, and mostly visit Hong Kong once in that three years. Visits every two years are rare and for specific purposes only; in medicine, dentistry and architecture, the examiners visit every year. Table 5 shows the spread of external examiners in the nine faculties in the University.

Table 3.   Duration of Examinership

Duration of appointment	One year	Two years	Three years	Four years	Six years	Total
External examiners	9	13	89	4	1	116

Table 4.   Frequency of Visits

Frequency	Every year	Every two years	Every three years	Total
External examiners	11	2	47	60

Table 5.   Distribution of External Examiners in Faculties

Arts	Engineering	Science	Social sciences	Medicine	Dentistry	Architecture	Education	Law	Total
14	12	7	20	12	12	10	5	24	116

Note: Numbers include visiting and non-university.

Duties

The duties of external examiners vary from discipline to discipline. Their advice is sought on the curriculum of a degree course and for a science-based discipline also on laboratory equipment and experiments. Examination papers are sent to them for their scrutiny and approval. During a year when they do not visit the University, selected examination scripts and dissertation reports with borderline marks are sent to them for assessment and moderation. Those who visit the University annually usually take part in examining the students. Those who come only once every three years may conduct oral examinations and interviews with selected students on their visits. In addition, they attend examiners' meetings, staff meetings and student meetings. Many will be able to see students at work on their graduation projects in the laboratories, and they will frequently advise academic departments on general aspects of the course. Most external examiners pay particular attention to the input from students. In their reports to the University they are expected to comment on the standard of the examinations and make suggestions on how to improve the degree course as necessary.

Professional Degrees

Related to the external examiner system is the accreditation of professional degrees by relevant bodies in the United Kingdom. For instance, Hong Kong engineering degrees are accredited by the engineering institutions in the United Kingdom once every five years, and medical degrees are accredited by the British General Medical Council once every six to seven years. This accreditation process involves a visit by a team of British professional experts and is very thorough. External moderation is one of the requirements of the accreditation team. In other words, Hong Kong degrees are not accredited by the British professional bodies unless they are scrutinized by external examiners.

Some Strengths and Weaknesses

Draft examination papers have to be approved by the external examiners and the recommended results, sample examination scripts and dissertation reports are sent to them for comment before they can be finalized. The timetabling constraints are considerable for reviewing the papers and scripts. Another problem is a growing tendency to place more weight on the continuous assessment of coursework, as it is more difficult for external examiners to play a monitoring role in this aspect. Finally, an external examiner, in a non-visiting year, may have difficulty in resolving problematic cases without the benefit of talking to the students or examiners involved. More frequent visits would obviously be an improvement, but the financial implications are considerable.

Apart from participating in the assessment process, external examiners normally also comment on curriculum structure, course content and assessment arrangements. Their comments are especially valuable for newly established courses, and some staff believe they should have a greater advisory role in relation to course development and planning.

By and large, the external examiner system has served Hong Kong University well. It has helped to maintain the standard of degrees in the university and, more importantly, to gain international recognition for the degrees. On the debit side it does constitute a financial burden, although some twenty-seven air tickets annually to and from different parts of the world is still a relatively low price to pay for the return from the system.

Sceptics say that external examiners are no more than members of an old boys' club. While it cannot be denied that the system can be abused, the rule preventing consecutive appointments of the same examiners goes some way towards preventing this.

Conclusion

Although there is need for and merit in an external examiner system which relies heavily on the service of overseas external examiners in Hong Kong, we must now look to the future when (1) Hong Kong has its own accreditation authority for most of its degrees, (2) local professional bodies accredit the professional degrees, and (3) each of the nine local higher educational institutions has had sufficient experience in running degree courses. We envisage that there will still be a need for an external examiner system but that many of the overseas external examiners will be replaced by local academics from Hong Kong itself. That will be the day when higher education in Hong Kong has truly come of age.

References

CHAN, S.T.H. (1991) Private communication on deliberation of the University of Hong Kong Working Party on External Examiner System.

ESRC REPORT (1989) *The Role of External Examiners* (a summary report of the principal findings of a project on the role of external examiners in undergraduate courses in the United Kingdom during 1986), Economic and Social Research Council (ESRC), UK.

REYNOLDS REPORT (1986) *Academic Standards in University* (CVCP Code of Practice on the external examiner system) Committee of Vice-Chancellors and Principals (CVCP), UK.

WAI, H.W.K. (1989a) 'Academic Standards', position paper to University of Hong Kong Academic Development Committee, document 190/889.

WAI, H.W.K. (1989b) 'External Examiner System', position paper to University of Hong Kong General Purpose Committee, document 23/1189.

Part 4

Conclusion

17 Conclusion

David Bethel

In these closing remarks, Dr Bethel reflects on the growing consensus about the need for quality assurance in higher education, and notes that external appraisal by peers is increasingly favoured. He stresses the need for and value of continued international exchange of ideas and information on quality assurance issues.

Most industrialized countries world-wide recognize that to sustain and to develop the economy and to assure social stability, an ever-increasing pool of skilled people is required. The skills needed are changing more rapidly than ever before; in addition, the knowledge base of many academic disciplines, particularly in science and technology, is constantly expanding. These two factors put education in general, and higher education in particular, under great pressure.

This strain is exacerbated by the escalating costs of higher education due to the unprecedented increase in student places and the huge costs of sophisticated equipment and library provision. These costs are inescapable. Teaching, research and scholarship are interlinked. The system must produce the future teachers of higher education, leaders of industry and commerce, and sustain fundamental and applied research along with other activities if the skills needed by society now and in the future are to be met.

The management of institutions must be both effective and efficient — efficient in the use of human and material resources, and effective in providing the best framework in which the teaching staff, the support staff, and the students can operate to their full potential. Satisfying all these needs has become much more complex with changes in teaching method, curricular reform and the need for continuous staff development.

As the main providers and funders of higher education, governments face escalating education budgets (often in competition with other priorities) and need assurance that public money is well spent. The question of 'value for money' is both asked of and by government. How can the institutions best be helped to meet these new challenges? How can governments be persuaded that the taxpayers' money is being well spent? How can the public be assured of the quality of higher education? The diversity of higher education systems, which is to be valued, makes comparisons difficult. There is no one way for delivering quality higher education, and any evaluation must be handled with sensitivity.

A number of contributors to this symposium stress the link between institutional freedom and accountability. As Allan Sensicle comments, one of the operating principles of the Hong Kong Council for Academic Accreditation is that academic autonomy is a right which carries with it the responsibility for maintaining high standards of tertiary education. Professor Chandra notes that in India a highly centralized system has tended to dampen experimentation and innovation, but he adds that 'giving greater autonomy to the colleges ... and the working academics ... [must] be accompanied by a system of accountability.'

Professor Staropoli questions whether the traditional systems of quality assurance are adequate to allow for an increase of students by simple extrapolation; in other words, can the move towards mass higher education best be provided by the present arrangements? Are other modes required, and can the development of these be left to the institutions themselves? What kind of 'steer' is needed?

Many papers emphasize the need for some kind of external input into the evaluation of courses, teaching and research. As Malcolm Frazer suggests, this provides a mirror for the institution to see itself with a clear image. The process is one of self-improvement assisted by peers. Again there is no one way to arrange such evaluation if diversity is to be retained and quality encouraged. But peer review, the evaluation by informed, experienced persons, is strongly advocated: the cooperation of the institutions will not be readily available if the reviews are conducted by bureaucrats.

In her case study of internal and external validation procedures Ms Diana Mak describes how traditional Chinese sensitivities to criticism caused acute tensions when validation was first introduced to the Hong Kong Polytechnic, and 'the majority watched with dismay'. But it is fair to say that the same reactions to validation/accreditation procedures have been experienced in *all* countries. It takes time to develop any kind of quality assurance culture in institutions. Validation bodies of all kinds need to recognize this factor if their work is to be helpful to the institutions.

The two papers from the Netherlands clearly illustrate the tensions between state regulation and self-regulation. Perhaps what has become termed the 'ownership' of the method used is a key factor, one emphasized by Peter Williams of the UK (Universities) Academic Audit Unit. Professor Kwong Lee Dow takes up this theme in describing the Australian arrangements for course comparisons in all institutions, involving academic standards panels which are definitely not 'creatures of government'. But even this 'ownership' of the quality assurance system, whether by the institutions jointly or by an external body with members mainly drawn from the institutions, should not become standardized internationally.

Several countries mention the use of 'sectoral surveys', that is, looking at the same subject in all institutions to assess the health of the subject nation-wide. Gaps and gross overlap in provision can be identified, and one outcome can be that institutions are encouraged to develop the subject in particular ways which can result in centres of excellence.

Dr Marianne Bauer reminds us of the dangers of embarking on international comparisons, yet acknowledges that increased student mobility demands more internationally available information on systems, institutions and courses. Dr Dalichow's account of the European Commission's initiatives confirms that very many more students are crossing international boundaries to complete their higher education, and that such international collaboration must be based on mutual confidence in the academic standards of different higher education systems.

The papers and discussions at the international conference on which this book is based agree on the need to address formally and openly the question of quality assurance in higher education. There is an emerging consensus that effective mechanisms for this will depend on the history, traditions and culture of the country, state or territory concerned, and that whatever mode of quality assurance is adopted, an external element is needed to achieve a clear, objective and authoritative outcome.

There is no intention to develop an international system of quality assurance and little confidence in common criteria or performance indicators. But in the words of Dr Bauer, 'there is every reason to continue the interchange of experience on different procedures for strengthening the responsibilities of our universities and colleges.' The formation of an international association of agencies responsible for quality assurance will help take these discussions forward.

Appendix:
Abstracts of Additional Papers

Six additional papers were presented at the Conference. Copies of the full papers are available from the Hong Kong Council for Academic Accreditation or from the individual authors.

Professor Cha Chuan-sin of Wuhan University, PRC, sketched the system for approving degree courses in China. The State Council appoints an Academic Degree Committee (ADC) of senior academics and administrators. The ADC has specialist sub-groups which examine the curriculum structure, number and level of staff, and research activities to determine which disciplines in which institutions have the right to confer degrees.

Dr Eric Bitzer, deputy director of the Unit for Research into Higher Education at the Orange Free State University of South Africa, spoke about the proposal to introduce a system of accreditation for academic programmes and departments in universities, based on self-evaluation and peer review. He stressed that the fundamental goal of accreditation is twofold, namely to confirm publicly that the quality of work in an institution is acceptable, and to assist each institution to enhance the quality of its activities.

Dr Stephen Akangbou of the National Universities Commission in Nigeria described the arrangements for accreditation of undergraduate programmes at the thirty-one Nigerian universities. All courses are assessed against minimum academic standards, determined and published by the Commission for thirteen discipline areas. Assessment is based on self-study forms and a panel visit to the institution. 837 academic degree programmes were visited between March 1990 and May 1991; 20 per cent gained full accreditation but 70 per cent were granted only interim accreditation. These satisfied the academic content requirements, but had inadequate staff and/or facilities as a result of Nigeria's economic difficulties.

Dr Frederick Owako represented the Kenyan Commission for Higher Education which was established in 1985 to ensure that quality was maintained during a period of rapid expansion of higher education. One of the functions of the Commission is the accreditation and inspection of all the private universities; some of these were operating before the establishment of the Commission, with unknown and in some cases comparatively low standards. Public universities traditionally have autonomy, but with the recent major expansion of student numbers there is concern about the strength of their quality assurance measures. By harmonizing the Universities Act of 1985 with the Acts of individual universities, it is hoped to bring them within the ambit of accreditation by the Commission.

Ms Hilary Mar of the Education Technology Unit at Hong Kong Polytechnic spoke about course materials development in distance/open learning as an aspect of quality assurance. The separation of teacher and learner in distance education helps to focus more attention on how the learner learns. At the polytechnic distance learning courses for part-time students are offered as one of several modes of delivery. Mainstream staff participate in the design, development, production, implementation, user evaluation and revision of materials, and their involvement in this development process can enhance the general quality of their teaching.

Dr Diana Green spoke about feedback from students as an aspect of course monitoring and evaluation. The Student Satisfaction Project at Birmingham Polytechnic in the UK started in 1988 and focuses on students as consumers. The project is testing ways of measuring student satisfaction with the quality of their educational experience. A group feedback strategy and a polytechnic-wide questionnaire have been identified as useful methodologies. The goal is to enable senior management to enhance the quality of educational provision.

Notes on Contributors

Dr Marianne Bauer taught psychology at two Swedish universities before her appointment as Deputy Director of the Swedish National Board of Universities and Colleges. She is currently leading a project to develop an evaluation system for Swedish universities and colleges, and is a member of the OECD group on performance indicators.

Dr Leslie Benmark is an industrial and information (computer) engineer and also a qualified lawyer. She is President of the Accreditation Board for Engineering and Technology (ABET) in the US, the first woman to hold this position. She has been involved in national and international evaluations of industrial and computer engineering programmes.

Dr David Bethel is a member of Hong Kong's University and Polytechnic Grants Committee and founder Chairman of the Hong Kong Council for Academic Accreditation. He was Director of Leicester Polytechnic, UK for over fifteen years, and he has wide experience of higher education systems in Europe and elsewhere.

Professor Ashoka Chandra, a physicist, is currently Head of the Institute of Applied Manpower Research in India. As Technical Educational Adviser to the Indian government, he played a key role in formulating the 1986 National Policy on Education, and thereafter in establishing the All India Council for Technical Education and preparing for a National Board of Accreditation (NBA).

Alma Craft is a Registrar at the Hong Kong Council for Academic Accreditation. A sociologist, she has worked in higher education in England, Australia and Hong Kong. In the UK she was a member of the Schools Council Research and Evaluation Team, then a Professional Officer with the National Curriculum Council.

Dr Fritz Dalichow has studied in Germany, France, Ireland and Canada. In 1985 he became Secretary of the National Academic Recognition Information Centres (NARICs) in Brussels, and is now Assistant Director of the European Community ERASMUS Bureau responsible for academic recognition and credit transfer.

Dr Gajaraj Dhanarajan, originally a forest biologist, has been involved for the past fifteen years in setting up distance education systems in South and South-East Asia. In 1989 he came to the newly established Open Learning Institute in Hong Kong, and has recently been appointed to the Directorship of the Institute.

Dr Edgar Frackmann is a Head of Department at Hochschul-Informations-System (HIS), which is a publicly funded central research and service institution for German higher education. His work and publications focus on information systems development, higher education policy and management, and evaluation and performance indicators in higher education.

Dr Malcolm Frazer has had more than thirty years' experience in higher education. In 1986 he became Chief Executive of the UK Council for National Academic Awards (CNAA), which is the degree awarding body and quality assurance (accrediting) agency for the polytechnics and colleges in the UK. He is a member of the Hong Kong Council for Academic Accreditation.

Ms Andrea Hope is Registrar at the Open Learning Institute of Hong Kong, working there on secondment from the UK Open University. She is a linguist by background and has worked as an administrator in higher education in Britain since 1979. She came to Hong Kong in 1990.

Dr Jan Kalkwijk was a professor of hydraulic engineering at the Delft University of Technology, the Netherlands, until 1988 when he was appointed to the Inspectorate of Higher Education. The Inspectorate reports to the Minister of Education and Science with regard to education and research at Dutch universities.

Professor Kwong Lee Dow is Dean of Education at Melbourne University, Australia. From 1985 to 1986 he chaired a committee which recommended the establishment of Academic Standards Panels. He is a member of the Higher Education Council which advises government on quality assurance measures in Australian higher education.

Dr Marjorie Peace Lenn is Vice-President of the American Council on Postsecondary Education (COPA), and is also a member of the Hong Kong Council for Academic Accreditation. Her active career in higher education has included a division headship at the University of Massachusetts, and books, articles and international conference presentations on accreditation.

Professor Leung Wai-Sun is Dean of Engineering and Head of the Electrical and Electronic Engineering Department at the University of Hong Kong.

Ms Diana Mak Ping See has postgraduate qualifications in both social work and education, specializing in evaluation. She has worked as Planning and Evaluation Officer at the Hong Kong Council of Social Service and then as Head of the Department of Social Work at Hong Kong Polytechnic, where she has been closely involved in quality assurance procedures.

Dr Austin Reid is Associate Director (Academic) at Hong Kong Polytechnic. He has extensive experience of external validation as a Registrar with the UK Council for National Academic Awards and as a member of the Hong Kong Council for Academic Accreditation. Since 1986 he has been responsible for internal validation of all courses at the Polytechnic.

Allan Sensicle is the Executive Director of the Hong Kong Council for Academic Accreditation (HKCAA). He was formerly Education Director of the UK Institution of Electrical Engineers, and Chief Executive of a UK trade association. He has worked in universities, polytechnics and with the UK Overseas Development Administration.

Dr Shen Chun Ming is a lecturer in the Department of Electrical Engineering at the University of Hong Kong, and is responsible for examination matters in his department.

Professor André Staropoli is the General Secretary of the Comité National d'Evaluation in France. He has worked for the Prime Minister's Office and as Director for Research and Higher Education within the Ministry of Agriculture, in addition to a period as executive vice-president of a bank.

Dr Ton Vroeijenstijn was involved from 1973 to 1985 in research and development in Dutch universities, and in the European Association for Research and Development in Higher Education. He is now senior policy adviser of the Association of Dutch Universities (VSNU), with particular reference to external quality assessment.

Peter Williams is the first Director of the new UK Academic Audit Unit. A graduate in English, he has been an administrator at the Universities of Surrey and Leicester. From 1984 to 1990 he was Deputy Secretary of the British Academy, with responsibility for a national scheme of postgraduate studentships in the humanities.

Index